# Praise for *Driven b*

"This gem of a book is one of the most important books to come out on American education in years. Paul Bambrick-Santoyo speaks from a platform of immense credibility given the tremendous results of low-income students under his leadership. Three cheers to a front-line educator for kicking off a new genre of non-fiction writing in education: a practical guide for dramatic school improvement that proves that children from every background can achieve at high levels when we as adults get our part right."

> – Jon Schnur, Chairman and Chief Executive Officer of America Achieves

"This book superbly describes the change process a leader can go through with faculty to make data driven instruction a reality in their school. Amazingly practical. There's nothing like it out there!! You'll also find the rationale and all the structures for data analysis, scripts of how to analyze student thinking and come up with appropriate re-teaching strategies for weak areas, and precise guidance on how to run effective data meetings. This is the whole package."

> – Jon Saphier, Founder and President of Research for Better Teaching and Chairman Emeritus of Teachers 21

"Paul Bambrick-Santoyo's book is a triple threat to the achievement gap: not only has he presided over dramatic achievement gains at the schools he leads in Newark, NJ, but he has helped scores of other schools make similar gains in New York City, Chicago, New Orleans, Oakland, and elsewhere around the country–and he has been able to distil the lessons learned into a brilliant, tightly organized, and highly practical book. Bravo to Paul for an amazing contribution to the field!"

> – Kim Marshall, Leadership consultant and author of the Marshall Memo

"*Driven by Data 2.0* is a stand-out among the million books principals have cluttering their shelves on leadership and student achievement. This one won't collect dust! Bambrick-Santoyo provides an unequivocal blueprint on implementing effective change that will bolster student achievement in an actionable way."

> – Nakia Haskins, Principal, Brooklyn Brownstone School

# DRIVEN BY DATA 2.0

A Practical Guide to Improve Instruction

Paul Bambrick-Santoyo

Uncommon Schools | Change History.

**JB JOSSEY-BASS™**
A Wiley Brand

Jossey-Bass

A Wiley Imprint

535 Mission St, 14th Floor; San Francisco CA 94105-3253—www.josseybass.com

**Uncommon Schools** | Change History.

Jossey-Bass books and products are available through most bookstores. To contact Jossey-Bass directly, call our Customer Care Department within the U.S. at 800–956–7739, outside the U.S. at +1 317 572 3986, or fax +1 317 572 4002.

Wiley also publishes its books in a variety of electronic formats and by print-on-demand. Some material included with standard print versions of this book may not be included in e-books or in print-on-demand. If this book refers to media such as a CD or DVD that is not included in the version you purchased, you may download this material at http://booksupport.wiley.com. For more information about Wiley products, visit www.wiley.com.

**Library of Congress Cataloging-in-Publication Data**

Names: Bambrick-Santoyo, Paul, 1972- author.

Title: Driven by data 2.0 : a practical guide to improve instruction / Paul Bambrick-Santoyo.

Other titles: Driven by data two point zero | Driven by data two point ott

Description: Second Edition. | San Francisco, California : Jossey-Bass, [2019] | Includes bibliographical references and index.

Identifiers: LCCN 2019000175 (print) | LCCN 2019002524 (ebook) | ISBN 9781119524779 (Adobe PDF) | ISBN 9781119524762 (ePub) | ISBN 9781119524755 | ISBN 9781119524755¬(paperback) | ISBN 9781119524779¬(eBook) | ISBN 9781119524762¬(eBook)

Subjects: LCSH: Education—United States—Data processing—Case studies. | Educational tests and measurements—United States—Case studies. | Educational evaluation—United States—Case studies. | School improvement programs—United States—Case studies. | School management and organization—United States—Case studies.

Classification: LCC LB1028.43 (ebook) | LCC LB1028.43 .B35 2019 (print) | DDC 370.285—dc23

LC record available at https://lccn.loc.gov/2019000175

Cover image: Courtesy of Uncommon Schools
Cover design: Wiley

Printed in the United States of America
second edition
*PB Printing*   V10011926_071819

# Contents

## Data-Driven Success Stories

# Contents of the DVD

Here is an overview of the video clips for your quick reference.

**Analysis—Where and Why We Left the Route (Chapter 2)**

| Clip | Technique | Description |
|------|-----------|-------------|
| 1 | **See It (Success)— Weekly Data Meeting** | **"I'd like to start with what I noticed is strong..."** Paul Bambrick-Santoyo praises a specific achievement in classrooms and connects the teacher action to the successes. |
| 2 | **See It (Standard)— Weekly Data Meeting** | **"What would a student need to know and be able to do to show mastery . . .?"** Mary Ann Stinson has her teachers begin their weekly data meeting by analyzing a Common Core State Standard for writing, a teacher exemplar, and a student exemplar. |
| 3 | **See It (Standard & Exemplar)— Weekly Data Meeting** | **"One of our favorite power standards . . ."** Na'Jee Carter works with teachers to unpack the standard, to analyze the teacher and student exemplar, and to create a robust know/show chart before analyzing the student work for the gap. |
| 4 | **See It, Name It (Gap)—Weekly Data Meeting** | **"Using the language of the standard . . ."** Juliana Worrell works with a team of teachers to utilize the language of the standard and the exemplar to determine the highest-leverage gap. |
| 5 | **See It, Name It. (Gap)—Weekly Data Meeting** | **"We want to ground ourselves in the language of the chart."** Na'Jee Carter leverages the know/show chart to identify the highest leverage conceptual and procedural gap in the student work. |

| Clip | Technique | Description |
|---|---|---|
| 6 | See It, Name It. (Gap)—Weekly Data Meeting | **". . . What are the key misconceptions demonstrated in this student work?"** Mary Ann Stinson and her teachers identify the highest leverage gap that needs to be re-taught using student work. |

## Action—Charting a Better Path (Chapter 3)

| Clip | Technique | Description |
|---|---|---|
| 7 | Re-Teach Modeling—Set the Task (Teaching Clip) | **"I want you to write down what I'm doing."** Art Worrell prepares his students to take notes during the think-aloud. |
| 8 | Re-Teach Modeling—Model the Thinking (Teaching Clip) | **"When I think about the Era of Good Feelings, right away I'm thinking about nationalism."** Art Worrell walks his students through the thought process he uses to read a history text effectively, modeling annotation skills and providing the rationale for them step-by-step. |
| 9 | Re-Teach Guided Discourse (Teaching Clip) | **". . . one-third black, one-third white, one-third gray . . ."** Andrew Shaefer shows students three different examples of how their classmates have solved a math problem, pushing them to determine through discourse which one is correct. |
| 10 | Aggressive Monitoring: Mark Up Student Work and Cue Students (Teaching Clip) | **"How did you know to use addition?"** Sari Fromson aggressively monitors as her students complete their independent practice in math, giving meaningful feedback to each student multiple times in one lesson. |
| 11 | Do It (Plan)—Weekly Data Meeting | **"Create the best re-teach plan possible."** Juliana Worrell works with a team of teachers to collaboratively plan a re-teaching script. |
| 12 | Do It (Plan)—Weekly Data Meeting | **"It's time to consider the re-teach plan . . . "** Denarius Frazier plans a re-teach alongside his teacher, and then they compare their plans to craft a final re-teach plan for a geometry class. |

| Clip | Technique | Description |
|------|-----------|-------------|
| 13 | Do It (Practice)—Weekly Data Meeting | **"We want to get through the model succinctly."** Mary Ann Stinson has her teachers practice the re-teach plan. |
| 14 | Do It (Practice)—Weekly Data Meeting | **"What is the conceptual understanding that [your students] would need?"** Laura Garza works with her teachers to determine the key understanding for a reteach lesson, planning side-by-side before they practice. |
| 15 | Do It (Practice)—Weekly Data Meeting | **"Now we are going to take this practice live."** Denarius Frazier gives specific feedback while his teacher practices the re-teach lesson. |
| 16 | Do It (Follow Up)—Weekly Data Meeting | **"I am going to come in on Friday at 9 a.m."** Mary Ann Stinson asks her teachers to list all the action items at the end of the weekly data meeting and to schedule the follow-up. |
| 17 | Do It (Follow Up)—Weekly Data Meeting | **"We can spiral this task . . ."** Denarius Frazier works with his teacher to identify multiple opportunities for assessing the identified re-teach skill, and they establish a comprehensive timeline for next steps. |

**Leading PD (Chapter 6)**

| Clip | Technique | Description |
|------|-----------|-------------|
| 18 | See It, Name It—Leading PD | **"Let's put all of these three comments together."** Paul Bambrick-Santoyo prompts participants to unpack a video of an effective weekly data meeting and stamps the key points and core idea. |
| 19 | Do It (Plan)—Leading PD | **"You've just walked through the beginning of a weekly data meeting."** Paul Bambrick-Santoyo asks participants to plan the know/show chart for the case study embedded in the weekly data meeting PD. |
| 20 | Do It (Practice)—Leading PD | **"What are the key actions they could take to improve?"** Paul asks the group of leaders in Dallas to practice the See It, Name It of the weekly data meeting they planned. |

| Clip | Technique | Description |
| --- | --- | --- |
| 21 | **Reflect—Leading PD** | **"Take two minutes in your school teams: what are the key actions we can take to improve our meeting?"**<br>Paul Bambrick-Santoyo prompts the group to reflect on their own gaps in implementation and name key takeaways. |

# DVD Additional Materials

Here is a quick overview of additional materials available on the DVD.

| **Description:** |
| --- |
| All the materials needed to lead a professional development session for instructional leaders on data-driven instruction:<br><br>• Session plan for Data-Driven Instruction 101<br>• PowerPoint Presentation for Data-Driven Instruction 101<br>• Logistics Memo—Order of DDI Materials |

| **Handouts:** |
| --- |
| 1. Introduction to DDI<br>   • DDI Reflection Template<br>   • Handout<br>2. Interim Assessment Case Study, 5th Grade Literacy<br>   • Literacy 5-3 Assessment<br>   • Literacy 5-3 Results<br>   • Analysis and Action Plan Template<br>3. Interim Assessment Case Study, 4th Grade Math<br>   • Math 4-2 Assessment<br>   • Math 4-2 Results<br>   • Analysis and Action Plan Template<br>4. Interim Assessment Case Study, 9th Grade Algebra<br>   • Algebra 1-2 Assessment<br>   • Algebra Results<br>   • Analysis and Action Plan Template |

**Handouts:**

5. Exemplar Analysis
   - Exemplar Math ES Analysis and Action Plan
   - Exemplar Literacy MS Analysis and Action Plan
   - Exemplar Math MS Analysis and Action Plan
   - Exemplar English HS Analysis and Action Plan

6. Leading Analysis Meetings
   - One-pager—Weekly Data Meetings
   - Cheatsheet—Weekly Data Meetings

7. Action
   - Re-teaching One-pager
   - Follow-up Accountability Measures
   - Student Assessment Reflection Template

8. Teacher Video-Date Case Study
   - Elem Case Study Assessment Results

9. Douglass Street Case Study
   - Douglass Street School Case Study

10. Calendars
    - MS Assessment Calendar
    - HS Assessment Calendar
    - ES Assessment Calendar
    - Monthly Map Blank Template
    - How to Create Monthly Map
    - Monthly Map—Data-Driven Instruction Sample

11. Rubrics
    - Implementation Rubric for Data-Driven Instruction
    - Implementation Rubric—What to do When You're a 2
    - Results Meeting Protocol

# About the Author

**Paul Bambrick-Santoyo** is the Chief Schools Officer for Uncommon Schools and the Founder and Dean of the Leverage Leadership Institute, creating proofpoints of excellence in urban schools worldwide. Author of multiple books, including *Driven by Data*, *Leverage Leadership 2.0*, *Get Better Faster*, *A Principal Manager's Guide to Leverage Leadership*, and *Great Habits, Great Readers*, Bambrick-Santoyo has trained over 20,000 school leaders worldwide in instructional leadership, including multiple schools that have gone on to become the highest-gaining or highest-achieving schools in their districts, states, and/or countries. Prior to these roles, Bambrick-Santoyo co-founded the Relay National Principals Academy Fellowship and spent 13 years leading North Star Academies in Newark, NJ, whose results are among the highest-achieving urban schools in the nation. He also taught for six years in a bilingual school in Mexico City.

# Acknowledgments

The ideas in *Driven by Data 2.0* were formed and shaped through the work with thousands of schools across the country. Each interaction with a school leader—and each opportunity to give a workshop—helped sharpen the focus of the model presented here and allowed it to be tested in a wide variety of environments. All of those who put it to the test and gave me feedback along the way had a profound influence on the end product. Along the way, Alyssa Ross was our writer extraordinaire who deftly managed the revisions of this book with a sharp mind and gift for the right words, and David Deatherage brought his clear vision to the creation of the videos that accompany the text. Thank you, Alyssa and David, for working alongside me on so many of these books! Thanks as well to Sam, Judy, Jacque, Angelica, Jesse, Christine, Brett and everyone who supported me along the way.

Uncommon Schools was the first laboratory where we honed data-driven instruction. From my early work with Jamey Verrilli, Mike Mann, and Julie Jackson to the nearly one hundred leaders who have put this work to the test every day in the last 20 years.

The real heroes of this book are all the school leaders who have launched this work successfully and are transforming urban education nationwide. Only 22 of those school leaders were able to be highlighted in this book's success stories, but there are so many more!

While the school leaders are the heroes of the book, the heroes of my heart are my wife and children. Ana, Maria, and Nicolas were all quite young when I started on this journey, and they have watched this work grow while I have seen them head to middle school, high school, and now college. All along, they endured many an afternoon of me writing on the computer or staring thoughtfully off into space! Gaby stood by me through it all, supporting me in my weakest moments and providing me daily inspiration of how to love and listen.

Thank you to each and every one of you who have had an impact in the field. With your help, we will improve and re-shape education worldwide.

# Foreword

If you've ever taught in an American public school, you know the drill. The principal alerts you to her upcoming annual trip to "observe" your class. You sweat the preparation of what you hope is your best lesson. She jots notes in the back of your room. Your kids muster their least disruptive behavior, perhaps on account of the rare presence of two additional humongous eyeballs on their necks.

A few weeks later (if all goes well, not a few months later), there's the post-observation conference. The principal slides a comprehensive teacher evaluation rubric in standard-issue form across her desk. She's rated you "satisfactory" in most of the boxes, "needs improvement" in a few. Should you dispute the recommendations in the space allotted on the bottom of the template or smile and pledge to do better? Best-case scenario: the principal supports you, knows her stuff, and shares helpful feedback on your craft—for example, how you can be more engaging in your delivery. More typically, she encourages you to pick up the pace so that you can "cover" the required curriculum by year's end or urges you to "integrate technology" per the district mandate to modernize. You sign your review, close your classroom door, and resume teaching, relieved you won't have to relive these rituals for another year. As both professional development and accountability, this has been our education system's losing playbook for as long as the oldest teachers you can remember can *themselves* remember.

Then came Paul Bambrick-Santoyo—a brilliant instructional leader and trainer of principals—charging onto the field like a middle linebacker with the game-changing volume you're holding in your hands, now updated and revised: *Driven by Data 2.0*. Mr. Bambrick—as he's known to students—has the instructional equivalent of linebacker eyes. His peripheral vision catches all the subtle teacher moves in any one lesson, and he's peripatetic, ranging widely across a school, weaving in and out of classrooms. Gone are the set-piece annual observations. But what's really significant here—in light of the broken observational paradigm—is that Bambrick has trained his eyes on *the students* as much as the teachers. The first question provoked by his work is ontological, the schooling equivalent of the fabled tree-forest conundrum:

*If there's teaching going on, but the students aren't learning, is it really teaching?*

I first met Bambrick in the late summer of 2002, when he arrived at North Star Academy. Five years earlier, I had co-founded and then co-led North Star with one of the greatest teachers and principals of our generation, James Verrilli. It was one of New Jersey's very first charter public schools, located in the city of Newark, a troubled district that had been taken over by the state. We'd begun with seventy-two fifth and sixth graders, picked from a random lottery, 90% of whom were eligible for a subsidized lunch, 99% of them black or Latino, and who scored—on average—worse than their Newark peers on the state test. North Star was immediately successful at generating huge demand from low-income families, creating an electric student culture that was celebrated in the media and copied by countless other schools, and posting initial test state results that were well above the district average.

Bambrick had been sent to us by an organization with which I'd been involved—New Leaders for New Schools—as the principalship equivalent of a medical resident. He was supposed to spend the year with us and learn how to be a school leader. Had he been born a century ago, my hunch is that Bambrick would have been a priest. Instead he's tethered his humble but deep commitment to social justice—most manifest in two years of Jesuit Community Service as a campus minister in Mobile, Alabama—to the work of closing the achievement gap, one of the most pressing issues of our day. At the same time, he generated a strong sense of academic rigor and the value of high educational expectations and standards during six years as an AP English teacher, basketball coach, and assistant principal at an International Baccalaureate high school in Mexico City, where his wife is from and where he started his family. A 1994 graduate of Duke University, Bambrick is a chronically curious student of how humans learn and a habitual problem solver. He found in North Star a school committed to innovation and excellence.

At North Star and literally hundreds of other schools, I'd watched teachers *covering* an ambitious geometry curriculum, the *Diary of Anne Frank,* an entire earth science textbook; observed teachers standing in front of the classroom *covering* World Wars I and II, or assigning students to write e-mails on laptops to pen pals in Australia. But what math, science, reading, writing, and history had the students really learned?

What portion of the intended skills and covered knowledge had lodged in their brains? Where did the lessons fail to meet their mark? Who wasn't getting what?

Many strong teachers know the answers to these questions because they constantly "check for understanding" throughout their classes, and the very best adjust their instruction to meet the learning objectives. But it's hard even for the best teachers, and nearly impossible for novices, to track student progress in an organized, effective way in real time. Novice teachers are, after all, learning to teach, but are they teaching to learn? It's a well-worn convention for teachers to give weekly quizzes or unit tests, which should ostensibly address our core problem, except when those assessments—as is so often the case in the vast majority of schools—lack alignment with the meaningful standards for which students are meant to gain mastery.

As a result, for decades, American public schools have given students passing marks, promoted them to the next grade, and then (in the summer) received state test scores showing an alarming number of those promoted students lack basic proficiency, much less mastery, of the concepts they were supposed to learn. Come the fall, even when enterprising teachers use those state test results to inform their instruction, it's already too late. Students have moved on to new teachers and teachers have moved on to new students. Such a vicious cycle tragically harms precisely those children who need the greatest attention: those who come into the lowest-performing public schools with the weakest skills and the most challenging social and economic circumstances. Without the ability to diagnose and support their progress toward meeting college-prep learning standards on a systematic basis, too many adults consign too many of our children to a destiny based on their demography.

About the same time Bambrick started at North Star, another young leader named Doug McCurry had begun to build data systems to track student learning at Amistad Academy, a high-performing charter school serving low-income students in New Haven, Connecticut. Every six weeks, Amistad administered "Curriculum-Based Measurements"—aligned with the state standards—to track student progress. One day I watched as McCurry's team, teacher by teacher, came to see him armed with data on which students had learned which state standards. They used the data to diagnose, for example, which individual students were struggling with multiplying fractions.

To me, it looked like McCurry had created the school equivalent of what data-driven leaders had done to revolutionize public service, business, politics, and sports. In the mid-1990s, for instance, Oakland A's General Manager Billy Beane armed his scouts with new metrics to find productive, undervalued baseball players. *Money Ball* was born, and it launched a new era of data analytics that has revolutionized every sport from basketball to swimming to tennis.

Not long after, I encouraged my colleagues to spend time watching McCurry's data meetings in New Haven. Bambrick did that—and he also went to school on the whole subject. He looked at how the public schools across the country had been quietly doing similar work over the preceding decade. He led a team of teachers in writing a set of interim assessments aligned with the New Jersey state standards; used the assessments to push our program toward increasing levels of college-ready rigor and expectation for all students; designed an effective spreadsheet system for tracking student progress; and, along with co-leader and co-founder James Verrilli, changed the culture of the school so that our leaders and teachers gathered around data to drive student learning. Our teachers began to engage and own responsibility for upping the rigor of student learning, re-teaching failed lessons, analyzing errors in understanding, and creating better assessment tools. Their meetings moved from the sad convention of post-observation conferences to data meetings in which they fought as tenaciously for student achievement gains in their classrooms as the A's did to land the best player.

Fast forward to today, and the idea of data-driven instruction has caught on in a larger educational universe. Bambrick has become a pathfinder on the entire subject, having trained more than twenty thousand school leaders serving millions of children in cities all over the country and across the globe. The results can be seen not only in the twenty-two case studies in this book but in schools and classrooms worldwide.

Legendary principals like Nikki Bridges at Leadership Prep Ocean Hill, a USDOE Blue Ribbon School, pioneered *weekly* data meetings, in which they met with each teacher once a week to look carefully at student work and the details of student learning patterns. Dallas Independent Schools Principal Laura Garza (featured in this book) followed suit, with weekly data meetings held in her "data room" that helped them visualize student progress against the standard. They paved the way for other leaders to follow.

As it happens, leaders and teachers often arrive at his sessions highly skeptical about an over-tested culture. They imagine that data-driven instruction is an elaborate stratagem for promoting "test prep." They often show up because under the accountability pressure generated by federal law, they are desperate to find a magic formula to improve their state test results and avoid public censure. At the highest conceptual level, this accountability—despite all its faults—has indeed focused educators' minds on accountability for student achievement in low-income communities. If accountability gets them through the door, Bambrick is waiting for them on the other side with meaning-ful strategies and ideas that are at the heart of this wonderfully accessible and practical book. What's most remarkable about his training—and it's captured in this book—is that Bambrick gets the adults to "live the learning." Instead of lecturing or hectoring his audience, he creates a highly energetic learning environment where his audience does the heavy intellectual work. (His subsequent books have shared all the details of that success!)

We are very fortunate that Bambrick has codified his work in *Driven by Data 2.0*. Data-driven instruction is not a panacea. But—developed and used in the way that Bambrick describes—we have here one of the more important tools to ensure that America's classrooms are not simply filled with teaching but are assuredly alive with learning, growth, and meaningful achievement for all students.

*October 2018*                                                                                                 Norman Atkins

---

**Norman Atkins** *is the CEO of Together Education. He is the Founder and Board Chair of Uncommon Schools, Co-Founder and former President of Relay Graduate School of Education, and Co-Founder of Zearn.*

# Introduction

In fall 2013, Lincoln Elementary School in Ogden, Utah, was struggling. Fewer than 20% of the students were proficient in math and only marginally more were proficient in reading. Ross Lunceford, the new principal who arrived mid-year, could sense how unhappy the staff was, resigned to accept low performance. When he first shared the vision with them that Lincoln could be the highest achieving school in the state, they scoffed.

Flash forward just four years: Lincoln Elementary School had doubled their proficiency rates, making 30 point gains in math achievement and nearly the same in reading. The results earned Ross the distinction of Utah Distinguished Principal of the Year and the school a National Distinguished Title I School award. The work Ross and his colleagues were doing had changed the game.

How did they do it? Ross sums it up in five words: implementing data-driven instruction without fail. "We started making some clear goals," says Ross, "and really just getting everybody focused on the student work."

Over the past decade, "data-driven instruction" (DDI) has become one of the most widely discussed concepts in education—and among the most misunderstood.

For some, a data-driven school is simply one that conforms to the dictates of federal or state education legislation. For others, it is any school which uses assessments. At worst, calling a school "data-driven" conjures up images of educators sacrificing genuine learning in a single-minded focus on "teaching to the test."

But the experiences of Lincoln Elementary School's students—and thousands like them across the globe—tell a very different story. Since *Driven by Data* was originally published in 2010, more and more educators have adopted the practices behind data-driven instruction. Their results reveal that this shift has been extraordinarily powerful. When leveraged properly, data-driven instruction is an incredibly effective pathway to academic achievement.

## Data-Driven Success Story

## Lincoln Elementary School, Ogden, Utah

The Results

**Figure I.1** Utah State SAGE Assessment: Lincoln Elementary School, Percentage at or Above Proficiency

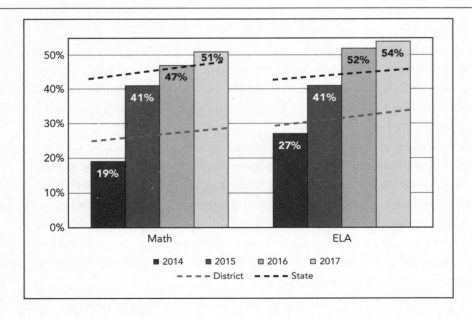

## The Story

Ross Lunceford is the kind of principal who stands out as a superstar to the families at Lincoln Elementary School in Ogden, Utah: he knows his students' names, communicates fluently with families who primarily speak Spanish, and even picks up trash outside the school building in the morning. But Ross didn't just know his students' names: he knew exactly what they were learning—and what they weren't.

He describes Lincoln as "chaotic" at the time when he took on leadership of the school. "There was a lot of unhappiness with the way things were going," Ross recalls. "So we started making some clear goals and really just getting everybody focused on the student work." From the very beginning, Ross recalls pinpointing the results of specific students and classes and making immediate action plans for them. "We told teachers," says Ross, "that this is the percentage of your kids who were proficient last year on state assessment, so we need to grow to this percent now," Ross says.

Ross also created explicit time for his teachers to focus on data, reframing pre-existing professional learning community meetings as opportunities to review student work. Ross didn't run these weekly data meetings, but he attended nearly every one of them. He allowed the teachers to drive the meeting, but he jumped in whenever they could go deeper in identifying the student gaps.

After teachers got better at analyzing student work, Ross says the next step was to plan how to act on it. "We would formulate a group of topics for re-teaching that teachers would work on for the next week," he recalls. "Then we would look at the next week's standard to be taught, and how it would be assessed. Then we would plan our week."

This cycle continued, week after week. Just in the first 18 months, Lincoln's results took off, with gains so significant that Ross was named Utah's National Distinguished Principal in 2015. But the success didn't end there—results continued to climb and Lincoln was named a National Distinguished Title I School in 2017. Today, his staff are in awe of their own collective growth. "Teachers would say, 'Wow! When we set our goals, I didn't really believe that we could do it,'" recalls Ross. They turned aspirations into reality.

---

## Key Drivers from the Implementation Rubric

- *Implementation calendar:* begin school year with a detailed calendar that includes time for assessment creation/adaptation, interim assessment analysis, weekly data meetings, and re-teaching (flexible enough to accommodate district mandates/changes).

- *Teacher-owned:* teacher analyzes own student work supported by instructional leaders.

- *Test and student work in hand:* start from the exemplar and identify the gaps.

- *Re-teach:* use guided discourse or modeling strategies to re-teach difficult standards.

---

These numbers in Figure I.1 represent hundreds of additional students reaching proficiency, greatly increasing the likelihood that they will go on to succeed in college and life beyond.

How did these schools facilitate such tremendous student achievement? They focused on the core drivers that affect student learning, separating themselves from schools that didn't. At the heart of it all is data-driven instruction.

## THE FRAMEWORK: WHAT IS THIS ALL ABOUT?

Data-driven instruction is a philosophy for schools that focuses on two simple questions:

- How do we know if our students are learning?
- And if they're not, what do we do about it?

> ### Core Idea
>
> The key questions that drive effective data-based instruction are:
> - How do we know if our students are learning?
> - And if they're not, what do we do about it?

By making these two questions the center of their work, successful schools made a fundamental break from traditional education. What matters is not whether the teacher taught it, but whether the students learned it. By following this premise, successful schools create a powerful paradigm to drive academic excellence.

But how do these methods diverge from those of the thousands of other schools across the nation that assess student learning—something nearly every school does in some way or another? Let's consider what separates schools like the ones in Ogden from schools that assess data without seeing comparable gains in achievement.

### The Road to Rigor: What Sets the Success Stories Apart?

There are so many resources about data that it can be difficult to know what is effective and what is not. *Driven by Data 2.0* takes the guesswork out of deciding which drivers to prioritize, basing its entire framework on the actions of schools where leaders have succeeded on the ground.

These schools are home to students who have an overwhelming tendency to struggle within the US educational system: those who qualify for free or reduced lunch, belong to groups that are considered racial minorities, or speak English as a second language. In too many cases, schools fail to meet the needs of students like these, starting at an incredibly early age: by fourth grade, black public school students in the United States already receive lower academic scores than their white peers by 27 points in reading and 26 points in math; for Hispanic students, the gap is 25 points in reading and 21 in math.[1] Overwhelmingly, these disparities only grow as students continue through primary and secondary school.

But at the schools featured in this book, leaders used data-driven instruction to make their students some of the highest-achieving in their respective districts or states. It is from this small subset of outstanding schools that the guidelines in this book were built—schools like Yinghua Academy, a Chinese immersion language school in Minnesota that has become a superlative school by any metric; and Denver Green School, that rose to being 8th of 203 schools in their district; and Northeast Elementary School, that transformed education for students in New Mexico.

What are the core action steps that these incredibly successful schools have taken to guarantee student achievement? Which action steps are consistent across multiple schools in different cities, suggesting far-reaching applicability? The answers to these questions are the core drivers for data-driven instruction presented in this book.

To get a sense of how this plays out on the ground, imagine planning a long road trip. Unless you're following in the path of Jack Kerouac, your road trip will include a clear destination, be it a major city, a national park, or a family member's front door. Chances are you wouldn't hit the road without a clear destination—and the pace you'd need to set to reach your destination by the desired time. In fact, for a longer road trip you'd probably set out with multiple destinations to keep you on the right path. You'd have a few major landmarks to hit: nightly places to sleep, tourist attractions to visit, and so on. And between those stops, you'd check exit signs and mile markers along the highway to make sure you stuck to your route, knowing that a wrong turn would take you further away from your goal.

Education is no different. To teach our students what they need to be successful, we need to clearly define what they must learn and be able to do; set clear progress points they'll need to meet along the way; and keep an eye on other signs that show whether they're learning so we can course-correct sooner rather than later if they aren't. That's the heart of data-driven instruction and the ultimate roadmap to rigor.

## THE SEVEN MISTAKES THAT MATTER

The actions described in this book will get you and your students on the road to rigor. Before we turn to those, however, it's worth considering a few key actions that *won't*, so as to be able to avoid them. Here are the seven mistakes that matter most when you set out to implement data-driven instruction in your school.

1. **Inferior Interim Assessments:** Interim assessment of students is the lifeblood of data-driven instruction. Without well-thought-out and carefully written tests, effective analysis of student strengths and weaknesses is impossible. Unfortunately, many schools employ inferior interim assessments that suffer from serious shortcomings, including setting bars that are too low, failing to align to end-goal tests, and neglecting the art of writing. Effective data-driven instruction is impossible unless schools invest in creating/acquiring excellent interim assessments. Particularly since the introduction of the Common Core State Standards, schools have scrambled to meet the raised bar on their own state tests—whether adopting Common Core or not—and begun using assessments that meet new levels of rigor. This is a step in the right direction—but it's only effective when those assessments are college-ready. Too often, educators roll out assessments that aren't sufficiently rigorous only to be shocked and dismayed when their students don't do well on state tests, AP exams, or SATs. Those results only change when we are vigilant about avoiding inferior assessments.

2. **Secretive Interim Assessments:** As we shall posit later in the text, if interim assessments drive rigor, then teachers and schools must know the end goal in order to work toward it. Unfortunately, most schools and districts prefer to be secretive. There are many reasons for this. For one, it costs money to develop new assessments, so if you believe (questionably) that you cannot re-use an interim assessment, then it's economically unviable to release interim assessments. The result is that educators hit the road without a clear destination.

3. **Too-frequent Assessments:** A huge misconception is that data-driven instruction means more assessment. Yet more assessments do not equal better teaching. Test students too frequently—and with too many different assessments—and you won't be able to see the forest that is student learning for the trees. You also won't have enough time to focus on better teaching.

4. **Curriculum/Assessment Disconnect:** One of the more common mistakes made in implementing data-driven instruction is to view curriculum design as separate from interim assessment creation—an extremely dangerous move. If curriculum scope and sequences do not precisely match the standards on the interim assessments, then teachers will be teaching one thing and assessing something else altogether. Then any assessment results gathered have no bearing on what actually happens in the classroom. Furthermore, if curriculum and assessment are disconnected, then teachers will (rightly) complain that the tests are unfair and that they should not be accountable for student performance, which will make the implementation of data-driven instruction all the more difficult.

5. **Delayed Results:** Even the most nuanced assessments lose their value quickly. The prompt scoring of results may seem to be a menial housekeeping task, but without it, schools can't make meaningful adjustments during the year. Every day that passes between the assessment and analysis of results is another day in which we teach new material without correcting errors.

6. **Separation of Analysis and Re-Teaching Follow-up:** What happens after teachers have analyzed their results? In all too many schools, the answer is a vague and nebulous commitment to take action that is generally ignored. Yet if we don't teach it any differently, how do we expect outcomes to change? Districts and schools that do not create a clear, simple system to implement specific plans at a specific time won't be able to make real change at the level of the classroom.

7. **Not Making Time for Data:** School years are busy, and if data-driven instruction is not explicitly embedded within the calendar, it will be overlooked, ignored, and ineffective. The same is true for school leaders. Data-driven instruction will not be implemented effectively if the leader does not embrace the process and make it a priority in his/her own scheduling.

## Data-Driven Success Story

### Blanton Elementary School, Dallas, Texas

The Results

**Figure I.2** Texas State Assessment (STAAR): Blanton Elementary School, Reading and Math Percentage at or Above Proficiency

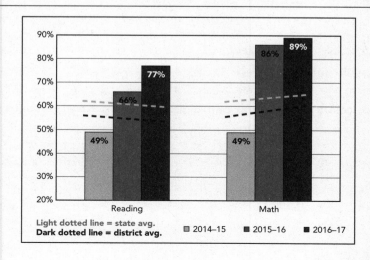

The Story

Annie Webb Blanton Elementary School was struggling: 84% of the students qualified for a free or reduced lunch, 80% were Latino and 58% were English Language Learners. More to the point, when Laura Garza took leadership of Blanton in 2015, these children weren't learning what they needed to prepare for middle school, let alone high school and ultimately college: less than half of them were achieving at grade level for math and literacy.

Laura made it no secret that she was setting out to change those results—quickly. And she got pushback. "Some were so used to the way things were that they didn't see the need for change," she recalls. "Others saw the need, but didn't think it could be done."

Just like Jody Jones at North Star Clinton Hill Middle School (see her success story in Chapter 2), Laura's turnaround effort narrowed to two areas of focus: fixing student culture and implementing data-driven instruction. "The teachers weren't paying attention to whether students learned," Laura recalls. "They thought that if they taught it, it was up to the students to learn it." That changed quickly as Laura implemented interim assessments and immediately launched data meetings with her teachers. She transformed the faculty room into a "Data Room," where they tracked all the students' performances on their leveled reading and math interim assessments. The leadership team distributed the observation of all the grade-level data meetings, and each Monday they would meet to discuss what next. "Those Monday leadership team meetings were critical," shares Laura. "Based on what happened in last week's data meetings, we would determine which teachers we should observe, what growth in student learning we should be looking for when observing, and the focus of our next round of data meetings. It created a continuous cycle of improvement."

Flash forward a few years later: The results were in, and student learning at Blanton had skyrocketed. The results were so impressive that Laura was named Dallas Principal of the Year and now manages a group of schools herself as she drives them to higher achievement.

---

## Key Drivers from Implementation Rubric

- *Active leadership team:* facilitate teacher-leader meetings looking at student work (interim assessment analysis and weekly data) and monitor the follow-up.

- *Immediate:* turnaround of assessment results (ideally 48 hrs).

- *Simple:* user-friendly, succinct data reports include: <u>item-level</u> analysis, <u>standards-level</u> analysis and <u>bottom line</u> results.

- *Teacher-owned:* teacher analyzes own student work supported by instructional leaders.

## Roadside Distractions: False Drivers

Fortunately, although these mistakes can pose serious problems, none of them are insurmountable. By vigilantly guarding against these particular dangers, savvy school leaders can go a long way toward achieving success. Beyond these seven, however, there is another, subtler, source of error in data-driven schools: focusing on *false drivers*.

As their name suggests, false drivers are factors that appear to be causes of school success but are, in fact, surface changes that don't influence results. Though they may appear as pathways to excellence, they are instead more like roadside distractions. By mistaking these symptoms of success for root causes, school leaders waste tremendous resources on factors that have little to do with actually improving their school. Many well-intentioned data-driven school leaders have failed because they have emphasized false drivers while overlooking other, more necessary changes. Of these false paths, three are the most commonly traveled:

1. **The Pursuit of Total Buy-in:** Any leader who thinks that an initiative requires complete buy-in before beginning will fail. Initiatives mean change, and teachers and school leaders are wary of change until it demonstrates results. Time and effort invested in making people love an unproven idea are almost always wasted. Indeed, one of data-driven instruction's greatest strengths is that it does not require faculty buy-in; it creates it. Buy-in is generated through tangible achievements. As long as faculty members are at least willing to try the methods outlined in this book, they will eventually come to believe in them. Focus on the fundamentals, achieve results, and faith in the program will follow. (We'll cover this in more detail in Chapter 4.)

2. **Reliance on Poorly Implemented "Professional Learning Communities":** A second false driver is inappropriate faith in unstructured "professional learning communities" (PLCs). The original concept behind PLCs was to design meetings to ensure that teachers collaborate and share experiences with one another. By the time Rick DuFour championed them in 1998, his definition of PLCs was completely data-driven: maintain an unrelenting focus on results.[2] What DuFour made clear was that while it is critical that teachers share strategies and knowledge, collaboration for collaboration's sake is not inherently valuable. In implementing data-driven instruction, what matters most is not how much time is used for faculty collaboration but rather how meaningfully such time is employed. Professional

learning communities can offer significant benefits if they return to DuFour's original intention: be explicitly focused on analyzing student learning and identifying key action steps based on that analysis. If not, too many schools get off track.

3. **Year-end Assessment Analysis:** Many schools invest a great deal of time in creating elaborate analyses of the end-of-year assessment. Such reports are often exhaustively detailed, breaking down student results by every conceivable demographic or academic attribute. Yet while they compile a great deal of data, analysis of these tests is of little use to the students who took them. Indeed, they may show what went wrong, but they come too late to make a difference. Rather than pouring time into figuring out what students failed to learn at year's end, it is much more effective to focus on interim assessments and avoid failures altogether.

---

### *Year-end Assessment Analysis—Performing an Autopsy*

*In many different sources, educators have referred to year-end assessment analysis as equivalent to performing an autopsy. If you had a sick child, what would you do? You would seek medical help to heal her. No one would recommend waiting until death to determine what made her sick—they would hold you liable for that child's life! Yet schools do just that with student achievement. Rather than identifying what's making a child's learning "sick" during the school year and finding the right medicine to attack the disease (i.e., learning more effectively), schools wait to analyze year-end assessment results after some of the students have already failed to learn. Rick DuFour stated it succinctly in 2004:*

> *The difference between a formative and summative assessment has also been described as the difference between a physical and an autopsy. [We] prefer physicals to autopsies.*

---

These false drivers are not, by themselves, undesirable. All schools want teacher buy-in, all want professional collaboration, all want year-end tests to be carefully examined and all want detailed analyses. With scarce time and resources, however, schools cannot afford to invest in initiatives that will not lead directly to student excellence.

## THE KEY PRINCIPLES OF DATA-DRIVEN INSTRUCTION

How do we know that these errors and false drivers don't support game-changing data-driven instruction? Because we've also seen the actions that do. This book was not created in a theoretical laboratory; it comes from the experience of working with more than 20,000 schools across the globe. These stories range from district schools to charter schools, from urban schools to rural, from large schools to small. Some schools before implementation had only 7% of students proficient on state exams while others moved from decent results to the top of their cities and states. They each journeyed upward on the ladder of student achievement. More than anything, they show that when one makes student learning the ultimate test of teaching, teaching improves to produce better learning.

What did all of these schools have in common? Although each of the schools is unique, they achieved remarkable results by setting just a few fundamental building blocks in place. These four foundational elements are the *core principles of school success*. They are:

---

### The Four Key Principles

**Assessment:** Creating rigorous interim assessments that provide meaningful data.

**Analysis:** Examining the results of assessments to correctly identify the causes of both strengths and shortcomings.

**Action:** Teaching more effectively what students most need to learn.

**Culture:** Creating an environment in which data-driven instruction can survive and thrive.

---

Each of these four principles is fundamental to effective data-driven instruction. In the chapters that make up this book, we'll break them down one-by-one.

## HOW TO USE THIS BOOK

This book is intended to be your instruction manual and field guide as you implement the principles of successful data-driven instruction in your own classroom, school, or district. Regardless of your role as an educator, the actions outlined in each chapter will be of value to you and the children you serve—and we'll name specific steps for both teachers and school leaders throughout the book.

Part I of this book—The Roadmap to Results— tackles each one of these critical drivers of school success in detail. Particularly noteworthy is the Implementation section at the end of each chapter. This section offers concrete actionable first steps targeted at three audiences: teachers, school-based leaders (principals, coaches, instructional leaders, etc.), and multi-campus/district-level leaders. By following these, you should be able to apply the keys to data-driven instruction directly to your role in your school community.

Part II—Where the Rubber Hits the Road—focuses on overcoming obstacles and leading effective professional development around data-driven instruction. A school's ability to turn data-driven instruction from educational theory to concrete reality is fundamentally driven by effective leadership and teacher training. If school leaders and teachers are not taught how to use data in their schools and classrooms, then they, like too many before them, will fail. After establishing these basic guidelines, the Appendix (located on the DVD) contains extensive workshop materials for teaching data-driven instruction to leaders and/or teachers in a variety of contexts. The Appendix also includes the highest leverage support materials that are mentioned throughout the book and have already been tested in schools worldwide.

I strongly recommend that you do not jump to Part II without first reading Part I. Part I explains many of the pedagogical choices made in Part II and can help you avoid the common pitfalls of schools that have struggled to implement data-driven instruction effectively.

If you're not yet sure if this framework will work for your school, consider starting by reading some of the success stories dispersed throughout the book (use the Contents to identify the location of each one!). The variety of contexts in which these case studies take place shows the flexibility that makes this approach to data-driven instruction effective at any school—and in each one, the key drivers successful leaders have used are highlighted to reveal the connection between theory and practice.

## CONCLUSION

Assessment, analysis, action, and culture. These are the principles of data-driven instruction that have set tens of thousands of schools on the road to rigor. The framework, training methods, and school success stories outlined in this book make up an instruction manual that can live in your glove compartment as you turn your eyes toward the destination that is unprecedented student achievement. Read on, and let's hit the road!

## Reflection and Planning

Take this opportunity to reflect upon data-driven instruction at your own school or district. Answer the following questions:

- What are the most common mistakes/false drivers that are a struggle at your school?

  _____

- What are the first action steps that you could take to address these pitfalls?

  _____

- Who are the key people in your school with whom you need to communicate these steps and have on board? How are you going to get them on board?

  _____

# PART ONE

# The Roadmap to Results

## Chapter 1

# Assessment: Set Your Landmarks (and Your Mile Markers)

## An Opening Story

In one of the first years of implementation of data-driven instruction in our school, we had a principal intern who was supervising one of our sixth grade math teachers. One morning, he came to my office and put a sheet of paper in front of me: it was the Do Now worksheet that he had just seen used in the sixth grade math classroom.

"What do you notice?" he asked me. I reviewed the worksheet and saw 10 problems on basic addition of fractions.

"This looks like a basic review of fractions," I answered.

"Exactly," the intern replied. "But the interim assessment we just reviewed asks students to solve word problems with fractions, and even the fractions themselves in those word problems are more complex than these ones. Yet the teacher is confident that she's preparing her students to master adding fractions."

These might seem like common-sense conclusions to many of you, but for us, the principal intern's insight was a watershed moment in identifying the common disconnect between what the teacher was teaching and what the interim assessment was measuring. What ensued was a deeper look at assessment at all levels of teaching.

# Data-Driven Success Story

## North Star Washington Park High School, Newark, New Jersey

The Results

**Figure 1.1** Advanced Placement (AP) Exam: North Star Washington Park High School, AP Index—Percentage of All Students with Scores of 3+[1]

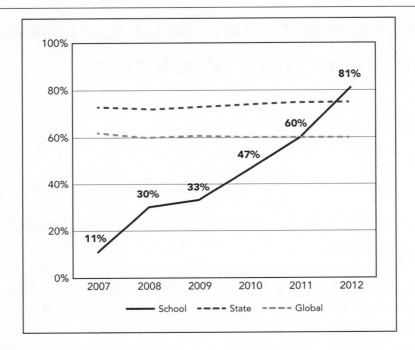

## The Story

Walk around North Star Washington Park High School with Mike Mann, and you'll observe someone who is passionate about results. Serving students in Newark, New Jersey, of whom 90% qualify for a free/reduced lunch, Mike does not hesitate to say how much he believes in them. "I know that my students are capable of competing with students anywhere in the country. The only thing holding them back is the quality of education that we can provide them."

When Mike first took on the role of principal, the teachers were working hard to develop a strong culture and wanted all their students to graduate and enter college, but the academic results did not match those desires: only 11% of students were able to pass Advanced Placement (AP) exams and their SAT scores were far below the national average.

"We needed to change the teachers' expectations, not the students," Mike shares. "That started with raising the bar on the rigor of assessments, and designing curriculum to match." To start, Mike pushed the school to abandon its focus on the New Jersey State Test and shift its sights to the AP and SAT exams. "We knew the data," Mike recalls. "If our students could master the SAT and AP exams, the doors of college would open wider for them." So they planned assessments backwards from the rigor of the AP assessments, all the way down to ninth grade. Then they determined exactly what sort of score on the interim assessments would predict a passing score on the AP exams. That number drove teachers to work with every child to get over the bar. "Our teachers were already working hard," Mike recalls, "we just had to get them working 'smarter.'" Teachers began utilizing regular exit tickets at the end of each class, and adjusting their opening Do Now to spiral content they had learned before. Rather than impose SAT/AP test prep classes, they embedded the rigor of the SAT/AP into daily lessons.

The results are nothing short of remarkable: their students made dramatic gains on both the AP and SAT exams, and in recognition Mike went on to win the Ryan Principal of the Year national award, recognizing the top principal to eradicate the achievement gap. The results don't stop there: Mike's students are persisting in college at rates not seen before in Newark. And these results have sustained themselves in the years since. "Data-driven instruction isn't just a set of tools," Mike says, "it is a mindset. It communicates to students that I care about you, and I won't stop until you learn it."

---

## Key Drivers from Implementation Rubric

- *Common Interim Assessments: 4–6 times/year.*
- *Aligned to state tests and college readiness.*
- *Aligned to instructional sequence of clearly defined grade level and content expectations.*

---

## Core Idea

Effective instruction isn't about whether we taught it.
It's about whether students learned it.

---

# TOWARD MEANINGFUL RIGOR: CREATING THE ROADMAP

Ask a teacher to define what the students should be learning, and chances are the teacher will talk about conforming to school, district, or state standards (or to the standards embedded in a mandated textbook/curriculum). Yet while meeting such standards is necessary, it is nearly impossible to measure a teacher's success simply based on a list of standards. To illustrate this, consider a basic standard taken from middle school math:

> Use ratio and rate reasoning to solve real-world and mathematical problems.
> (Common Core State Standards for Mathematics, 6.RP.A.3)

To understand why a standard like this one creates difficulties, consider the following premise. Six different teachers could define the following six questions as each of their attempts to assess one of the ration concepts: percent of a number. Each could argue that their assessment question is "aligned" to the standard and is an adequate measure of student mastery. As you review them, try to answer the following two questions:

- What are the differences between what students have to know and be able to do in each question?
- If these assessment items were used by six different teachers to drive instruction, what conclusions do you have about the importance of assessment?

## Six Assessment Questions "Aligned" to the Same Standard

1. Identify 50% of 20.
2. Identify 67% of 81.
3. Shawn got 7 correct answers out of 10 possible answers on his science test. What percent of questions did he get correct?
4. Steph Curry was one of the best free-throw shooters in the NBA in 2018. When playing at home, he made 110 of 116 free throw attempts. What percentage of free throws did he make?
5. Steph Curry was one of the best free-throw shooters in the NBA in 2018. Prior to the playoffs, he made 110 of 116 free throw attempts when playing at home. In the first playoff game, Curry missed his first five free throws. How far did his percentage drop from before the tournament game to right after missing those free throws?
6. Steph Curry and Kevin Durant were competing for the best free-throw shooting percentage. Curry made 94% of his first 103 shots, while Durant made 47 out of 51 shots.

   a. Which one had a better shooting percentage?
   b. If in the next game, Curry made only 2 of 10 shots and Durant made 7 of 10 shots, what would be their new overall shooting percentages?
   c. Who has the better shooting percentage?
   d. Jason argued that if Curry and Durant each made the next ten shots, their shooting percentages would go up the same amount. Is this true? Why or why not?

As you answer the questions above, you probably would make the following observations. For starters, these questions vary wildly in their degree of difficulty. The first few questions require straightforward calculations—yet question 3 is still what some people call a "real-world problem," even if it is simple. As you progress, however, the questions require deeper conceptual understanding of percents and percent change. The sub-question (6b) goes to the furthest depth: you have to know that if two people have different starting percentages, they will change differently with the same number of made shots (in other words, if you are a horrible free-throw shooter making ten in a row will increase your percentage much more significantly than it will for a shooter like Curry).

Though these six questions vary this notably, all of them are still "aligned" to the standard. Indeed, even if the standard was made more specific and called for "high-level problem-solving skills," choices 4, 5 and 6 would still all be plausible options. Thus, if teachers were only given this standard, one could not fault them for only teaching and assessing the skills needed for the question that they chose, even if the end-of-year state test demands the skills needed to answer a question like number 6.

This exercise reveals something crucial: standards are meaningless until you define how to assess them. You haven't set the bar for rigor until you've identified what students will have to do to demonstrate what they have learned.

---

## Core Idea

Standards are meaningless until you define how to assess them.

---

Think about the implications of this. Traditionally, a week of teaching goes something like this: on Sunday night, you finalize your lesson plans for the week. After a few days of teaching, on Wednesday or Thursday you design a quiz to see if they've learned. In doing so, you might pull up an item bank with the six question options above and easily decide to remove questions 5 and 6 because you know you didn't teach to that level of rigor so they'll be too difficult for your students. And that decision makes sense: why test what you already know you didn't teach?

What happens if we turn the conventional planning and teaching process on its head? What if instead of starting with lesson planning, first you design your *quiz* on Sunday night? Then before planning, you can ask yourself, "What do I have to teach them to be able to master questions like #6 by the end of the week?" You've just changed how you think about teaching.

Assessments, then, are the starting point for instruction, not the end. They are the roadmap for rigor.

> ### Core Idea
> Assessments are the starting point for instruction, not the end.

By following this core idea, effective teachers and schools first create a rigorous test and then teach to meet the level of skill it demands, as opposed to teaching first and then writing an assessment to match. That makes all the difference.

As we consider all the different ways we could assess a single standard, the clear next question is: what separates an effective, rigorous assessment from one that won't get our students where we need them to be?

## Data-Driven Success Story

### Yinghua Academy, Minneapolis, Minnesota

**The Results**

**Figure 1.2** Minnesota Comprehensive Assessment (MCA): Yinghua Academy, Reading Grades 3-8 Learner Percentage at or Above Proficiency

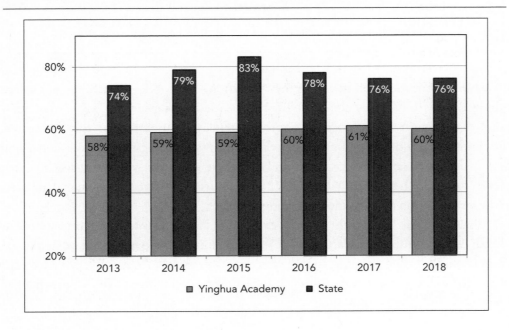

### The Story

Yinghua Academy is a one-of-a-kind school: the first K–8 Chinese immersion school of any type to be founded in the Midwest and only the second Chinese immersion public school to be founded in the United States. Students take core academic classes entirely in Chinese until they reach second grade, at which point English instruction is integrated into the curriculum. But despite being taught almost entirely in Chinese, Yinghua's students are required to take state tests in English, just as they would at any other public school. "No matter what language we're using in our classrooms," says Sue Berg, the CEO of Yinghua, "we need to show results."

Dr. Luyi Lien, Yinghua's Academic Director, shares that data-driven instruction has been the key to getting those results. In 2013, she trained Yinghua's instructors in the principles of data-driven instruction, and they rolled out the whole cycle of assessment over the course of the year. Now, data is a way of life at Yinghua. "We check our assessment questions to make sure they're rigorous enough," says Luyi. "We analyze results after the assessment, and we have teachers write action plans to decide which questions we still need to focus on."

Luyi recalls that one of the greatest challenges early in the process of implementing data-driven instruction was getting teachers to recognize whether a question was sufficiently rigorous. She worked with them directly to review the assessment questions they planned to ask students. "We spend a lot of time discussing each question," Luyi explains. "And then we link every item to the standard and say, 'What can we do better?'"

Sue adds that assessment on a lesson-by-lesson level, as well as interim assessment, has been a game-changer at Yinghua. "We break down every lesson into three points: teach, practice, and check for understanding," she says. "If teachers check every student's understanding, any surprises come during the lesson, not after the interim assessment. That means the teacher is always on the same page as the kids." Sue urges her teachers to modify lesson plans in-the-moment as needed. "Don't be so tied to the lesson plan that you can't modify it when you need to," she cautions. "It's not a great lesson unless the kids are learning."

Yinghua Academy's hard work has paid off in results for their students—and recognition on a national level. In 2015, Yinghua became a National Blue Ribbon School and their results have maintained excellence ever since. "Because we're data-driven," says Sue, "we can be a Chinese immersion school and still get that distinction." Their work is a testament to the effectiveness of great assessment in any context: when learning is the bottom line, success is guaranteed.

## Key Drivers from Implementation Rubric

- *Transparent starting point:* teachers see the assessments at the beginning of each cycle; assessments define the roadmap for teaching.
- *Aligned to state tests and college readiness.*
- *Aligned to instructional sequence* of clearly defined grade level and content expectations.

## Common Characteristics of Effective Assessments

If standards are meaningless until you define how to assess them, and assessments are the starting point rather than the end, then we need to start by developing quality assessments. A few basic building blocks emerge for writing quality assessments. Whether you're gathering interim or in-the-moment data, effective assessments are:

- **Common.** Think back to the six different levels of mastery demonstrated in the "Percent of a Number" questions: if every teacher uses a different assessment, all students are being assessed—and likely taught—to a different level of rigor. You can't tell whether every student is meeting the desired destination for rigor or not. Different assessments administered by individual teachers also make it nearly impossible to meaningfully track test-to-test progress or to coordinate fully shared standards across the entire student body. By committing to the process of establishing a common assessment, faculty has a valuable opportunity to share ideas and collaborate to create the best curriculum possible for all students.

- **Transparent.** If standards are meaningless until we know how to assess them, we don't know how to teach until we've seen how our students will be assessed. As a result, teachers, students, and parents should all know exactly what skill level the class will reach and what steps they will take to get there. Of course, this does not mean giving out copies of test answers to students on the first day of class, but it does mean publicly posting the exact sorts of questions students will be given so that every member of the school community knows what to expect—and ensuring teachers see the test before they begin teaching. By making assessment expectations transparent and clear, schools can take control of their curriculum and guide learning based on their vision. *Since this is the area where districts fail more than any other, we devote a whole section in Chapter 5 (Overcoming Obstacles) to "coping mechanisms" when schools are forced to use secretive district-mandated assessments*.

- **Aligned.** What end goal will you set for your students? Defining the bar for your assessments sets the bar for your expectations. Remember: it is not enough to say that we want them to be capable of "critical thinking" or "problem-solving." Too many schools have fallen into the trap of thinking they're making progress simply by espousing these words. Your assessment will define what you mean by those words—and if it's not carefully aligned to the end goals you set, it won't prepare your students to meet those goals. Here are a few different levels of alignment to consider when you set your assessment:

  o **State test-aligned:** State tests are a necessary but insufficient stepping stone to rigor: there are scarcely any students who can fail their state tests and be ready for college, but there are many who pass their state tests and are *still* not ready to attend or succeed at college. Aligning part or most of your interim assessment to the preliminary rigor of the state test is a prerequisite for making that assessment effective—but there's more to come!

- o **College-ready-aligned:** When we look to the futures we desire for our children, we see college education. College readiness is our ultimate goal for our students—which makes it the cornerstone of effective assessment. We'll address the task of aligning assessments to college-ready rigor in more depth in the next section of this chapter! A point worth noting here, however, is one common pitfall of implementing data-driven instruction: if schools do not have a single "north star" assessment they can use to align their rigor to college-ready standards, they err on the side of administering too many different assessments, few of which reflect a college-ready level of rigor. Thus, an important step is to eliminate any assessments that *aren't* aligned to college-ready rigor, and to build all assessments and curriculum around a limited number that *are*.

- o **Curriculum sequence-aligned:** Once you have an assessment that establishes the appropriate level of rigor, the next step is to make sure that those assessments are aligned to your curriculum. In the lessons approaching each assessment, does your curriculum teach the standards that will appear on that assessment and to the appropriate level of difficulty? If not, teachers will rightfully protest that you're not testing what they're teaching—defeating the whole purpose of interim assessments.

- **Interim.** If assessments aren't administered frequently enough, then weaknesses cannot be corrected until it is too late. If, on the other hand, assessments are administered *too* frequently, then teachers cannot do the depth of analysis described in Chapter 3 without burning out. The most effective schools we've observed administer at a minimum quarterly assessments,[2] and some of them complement those with biweekly formative assessments. What's certain is that educators need more than two assessments annually to track student learning in time to improve it before the year is out.

- **Re-Assess—Cumulative.** Think about your own education. Many of you took classes like calculus in high school or college. If you had to take a final exam in that subject today, you likely would not do nearly as well (unless you continue to use that math). Why? If you don't use it, you lose it. The same is true for our students: we need to build on and re-assess the material they learn over the course of the year, or we'll lose the learning.

> ## Core Idea
>
> If you don't use it, you lose it:
> Keep re-assessing student material yearlong to hold onto the learning.

You now have all the drivers you need to make quality assessments:

> ## Assessment: Five Core Drivers
>
> - **Common:** assessments are common across grade levels and subject areas.
> - **Transparent:** assessments are shared with instructors so they can teach to the level of rigor the assessment demands.
> - **Aligned:** assessments are aligned to the level of rigor demanded by state tests, college instruction, and the curriculum sequence.
> - **Interim:** assessments are administered more than twice annually.
> - **Re-Assess:** assessments continuously re-assess previously taught standards.

So how does this all look on the ground? Think back to our road trip analogy from the Introduction. You need to set a number of destinations along the route to rigor: your end-of-year goal, the major landmarks you'll have to hit along the way, and the smaller mile markers that will keep you on track between those larger landmarks. In the world of data-driven instruction, those major landmarks are interim assessments, and the mile markers are in-the-moment assessment (such as mid-lesson checks for understanding).

Let's break down how both interim and in-the-moment assessments look when implemented successfully.

## Interim Assessments: Your Landmarks

The major landmarks on the roadmap of effective data-driven instruction are **interim assessments**: formal written examinations taken at 6–8-week intervals during the school year. Interim assessments give standards a clear definition of the level of rigor needed to succeed. Rather than have each teacher choose his/her own level of rigor in response to vaguely written standards, the effective data-driven school leader/teacher works to create challenging interim assessments that set a high bar for student achievement.

As one of the better-known facets of data-driven instruction, interim assessments have been the focus of a great deal of academic research. Thus far, the evidence strongly suggests that, when properly applied, interim assessments are among the most powerful drivers of academic excellence.[3] Here are the advantages that come with interim assessment.

- **They provide a roadmap for instruction:** This point cannot be made more emphatically: rigorous interim assessments define the standards and provide a roadmap to rigorous teaching and learning. When educators know precisely what skill level their students must reach on each standard, they will have a clear roadmap toward creating a challenging and dynamic curriculum. Traditional curriculum scopes and sequences do not do this on their own.

- **They improve teaching:** Well-designed interim assessments serve to identify weaknesses during the course of the school year. Meticulous care regarding results and a constant feedback loop allow teachers to improve their craft, changing strategies in response to changing needs.

- **They establish accountability for cumulative learning:** By creating concrete benchmarks, interim assessments allow for classroom strengths and weaknesses to be clearly identified and systematically targeted. In providing a baseline standard for comparison, interim assessments offer a comprehensive checkpoint of where a class needs to go and what it will take to get them there. Moreover, their cumulative nature helps to hold teachers and principals accountable to student learning results over time throughout the year. Rather than only checking the learning in the moment or alternatively waiting for a year-end result, they can identify failed teaching strategies when there is still time to fix them.

- **They create visibility:** Interim assessments allow for performance to be charted graphically so that school leaders and staff may see visual evidence of improvement.

- **They check for independent understanding:** Many times during instruction teachers provide what is often called "scaffolded" support to their students: nudging them to consider alternative ideas, correcting minor mistakes, guiding them through the process of solving a problem, etc. Because of their nature as formal written assessments, interim assessments measure student understanding without any of that scaffolding, which can often reveal great differences between student output when supported by the teacher and when not!

- **They prepare students for high-stakes written assessment:** Be it law, social work, or fighting fires, most careers require us to demonstrate our knowledge via a written assessment. Not preparing our students for that is to deprive them of skills they'll need to pursue whatever dreams they choose. Unlike other types of assessments, written interim examinations can adopt the structure and content of end-goal tests to determine whether students have precisely the skills they need.

So how does one turn to the task of developing the tests themselves? The success stories represented in the book show that effective results can emerge either from schools creating their own rigorous interim assessments or selecting already available assessments. Either choice can lead to success so long as one follows the core principles listed here:

- **Start from the end-goal exam:** All public schools (and even most private schools) face the high stakes of end-goal tests by which student achievement is measured. At the primary school level, such assessment often includes statewide or district-wide exams; at the secondary level, it could include SAT/ACT tests or AP/IB assessments. In any case, when designing or selecting interim assessments, it is critical that decisions be made in reference to the specific demands of the end goal and not to vague, ill-defined academic standards, as discussed earlier in this chapter.

- **Align the interim assessments to the end-goal test:** Once the specific sorts of questions that are employed by the end-goal test are noted, schools should work to create/select interim assessments that are aligned to the specific demands of the end-goal examination. This alignment should not be limited to content but should also follow the format, length, and any other replicable characteristic of the end-goal test.

- **If acquiring assessments from a third party, be sure to see the test:** Test sales representatives have a very simple goal: to sell more tests. Because of this, they will do anything in their power to convince schools that their exam is aligned and will meet their needs. Don't take their word for it. Instead, school leaders and teachers should personally inspect actual copies of their product to ensure that it does line up with the end goals in question. Even then, no third-party test is perfect, so push to modify the examination in order to exactly align with your school's academic goal. *This is one of the most overlooked steps in schools and districts that do not have well-aligned interim assessments.*

- **Assess to college-ready standards:** At every level, it's important to realize that the skills needed to pass state tests are often insufficient to ensure success in college or other post-secondary environments. As such, a final goal of well-written interim assessments is that they prepare students not only for a state test but also for college and beyond. This is a challenge at every grade level, but there's also a growing bank of resources educators can draw on in order to succeed! Here are some strategies to implement college-ready rigor for every grade span:

o **Elementary School Reading—Assess for analytical skills, not just basic meaning:** At the elementary level, a key way to push for greater rigor is to evaluate students' ability to read analytically, not merely to demonstrate basic comprehension. Later in this chapter, we'll show an example of an assessment that accomplishes this. Moving to analytical questions when students are beginning their reading careers helps ensure that when the time comes to analyze much more challenging texts, they'll be ready. (See Myth 3 in the upcoming section for additional ideas on early elementary reading rigor.)

o **Elementary Math—Set higher grade-level expectations:** Most states in recent years have raised expectations in their K–4 math standards. If that is not the case, set a goal for each grade level to accomplish a certain percentage of the standards for the subsequent grade level. For example, second graders can accomplish all of the operations standards associated with third grade.

o **Middle School Math—Embed Algebra in every strand:** Most eighth grade state tests have a rudimentary inclusion of basic linear equations or expressions, but few measure all of the rigor of an HS Algebra I curriculum. Middle schools can quickly increase the college-ready rigor in their classrooms by exploring Algebraic applications for each mathematical strand that they teach. For example, a fifth grade teacher presenting addition of fractions could add a question like the following into his/her Do Nows or in-class activities.

## College-Ready Example—Algebra in Fifth Grade Math

Write an expression for the following:

> Mr. Smith has X books in his classroom. He gives three of them to students. Then he splits the rest of them evenly on his two bookshelves. How many books are on each shelf? Justify your answer.

- **Middle School Reading—Push for deeper reading and supports to more complex texts:** Adding college-ready rigor to reading can be challenging. Giving students harder texts to read is laudable but does not accomplish this task in itself: if the book is well above the students' reading level, vocabulary knowledge might limit their ability to comprehend the text. An exciting new strategy is being developed by organizations like Student Achievement Partners rooted in the work of Marilyn Jager Adams.[4] When reading a challenging text like *Beloved*, you create "expert packs" of informational texts around slavery that start from basic elementary reading level and progress to high school level so students build knowledge and vocabulary to access the novel. Building these sorts of knowledge-building texts into the teaching of complex texts can accelerate reading growth. Still, an overlooked strategy is choosing text with grade-level vocabulary but complex meaning. This allows the teacher to assess for more critical reading than is often possible with middle school novels. Here is an example of a poem that can be used that has very accessible language but requires deep, critical thinking:

---

## College-Ready Example: Rigor in MS Reading

### Chicago Poet
### by Carl Sandburg

I saluted a nobody.
I saw him in a looking-glass.
He smiled—so did I.
He crumpled the skin on his forehead, frowning—so did I.
Everything I did he did.
I said, "Hello, I know you."
And I was a liar to say so.

Ah, this looking-glass man!
Liar, fool, dreamer, play-actor,
Soldier, dusty drinker of dust—
Ah! He will go with me
Down the dark stairway
When nobody else is looking,
When everybody else is gone.

. . .
When everybody else is gone.

He locks his elbow in mine,
I lose all—but not him.

1. In stanza 1, Sandburg looks into the mirror and says, "Hello, I know you," but then calls himself a liar to say so. How is this possible when he is looking at himself? (Inference)
   A. He is still figuring out his identity.
   B. He is insulting himself because he is angry.
   C. He does not recognize his physical self.
   D. He is being playful and joking.

---

- **High School—Start with existing high-rigor materials:** At the high school level, an abundance of college preparatory materials is already available to set the bar for rigor. Beth Verrilli, a celebrated English teacher at North Star Academy Washington Park High School in Newark, New Jersey—Beth moved her students from only 11% passing AP English exams when she first arrived to over 80% passing[3]—shares: "It starts with taking every practice AP and SAT exam out there and looking at the types of passages they have: the lengths, whether fiction or non-fiction, if non-fiction, then what type of non-fiction?" Once she had identified the passages, Beth then looked at the type of questions being asked and their level of challenge: literal comprehension, main idea, tone, and perspective. Finally, based on the level of challenge identified in order to be "college-ready," Beth and the English Department adapted their curricula accordingly. "The early high school years serve as a bridge between the eighth grade state test level of challenge and the more rigorous demands of college-ready assessments," Beth explained. "Because we know where our end goal is in year four, it makes planning years one and two much easier."

- **Design the test to reassess earlier material:** Additionally, effective assessments revisit material from earlier in the year. In nearly every field this review is vital to retaining information and learning new concepts (e.g., in math you need to know fractions to do linear equations, and in history you need to retain basic knowledge of historical events to analyze a primary source or answer critical thinking questions). It also ensures that teachers have the opportunity to see if their re-teaching efforts were effective. One such method of review is to make tests longer as the year progresses; a second is to test all material from day one and then track student improvement as they actually learn the concepts being tested. No matter which method is chosen, however, it is important that review of past material is made a central part of interim assessments. *This is a common, critical mistake of schools and districts where assessments fail: they convert interim assessments into unit tests (just covering material in that time period) rather than cumulative assessments.*

- **Give teachers a stake in the assessment:** Finally, when assessments are created or selected, teachers should be able to have meaningful input. This is critical, because it ensures accountability; teachers who are included in the assessment writing/selecting process become invested in the assessments' effectiveness. Give teachers a stake in the assessment, and you'll give them a stake in the results too.

## In-the-Moment Assessment: Your Mile Markers

There is a body of research primarily championed by Paul Black and Dylan Wiliam stating the power of in-the-moment assessments—checking for student understanding in the very moment something is learned.[5] Done skillfully, real-time assessments have a powerful effect on improving teaching because teachers have immediate data on which students aren't learning and why. They're your mile markers: the signs along the road to rigor that alert you quickly if a student is taking a wrong turn.

What's necessary for in-the-moment assessments to be constructive is for them to be the connecting points between interim assessments, the starting point for rigor. Interim assessments have the ability to create what Kim Marshall coins the "ripple effect": they influence every component of the teaching process. Marshall's graphic (Figure 1.3) shows how interim assessments can drive unit planning, lesson planning, teaching, in-the-moment assessments follow-up, and, finally, improved year-end results:

**Figure 1.3** The ripple effect

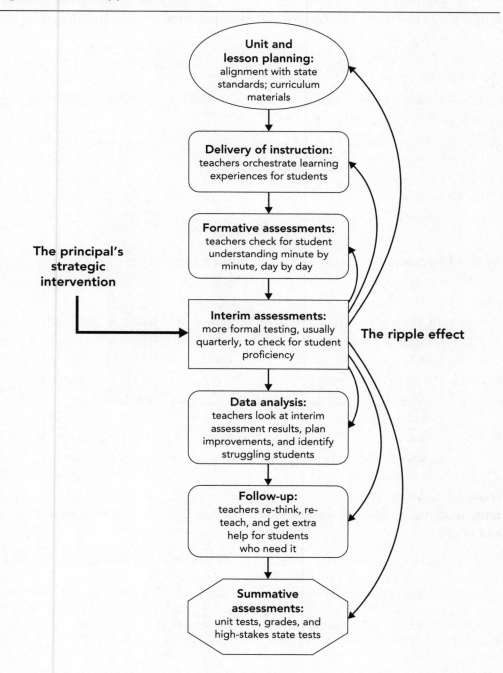

The principal's strategic intervention

The ripple effect

Unit and lesson planning: alignment with state standards; curriculum materials

Delivery of instruction: teachers orchestrate learning experiences for students

Formative assessments: teachers check for student understanding minute by minute, day by day

Interim assessments: more formal testing, usually quarterly, to check for student proficiency

Data analysis: teachers look at interim assessment results, plan improvements, and identify struggling students

Follow-up: teachers re-think, re-teach, and get extra help for students who need it

Summative assessments: unit tests, grades, and high-stakes state tests

## Data-Driven Success Story

## Nathaniel Hawthorne Elementary, Dallas, Texas

The Results

**Figure 1.4**  Texas State Assessment (STAAR): Nathaniel Hawthorne Elementary School, ELA Percentage at or Above Proficiency

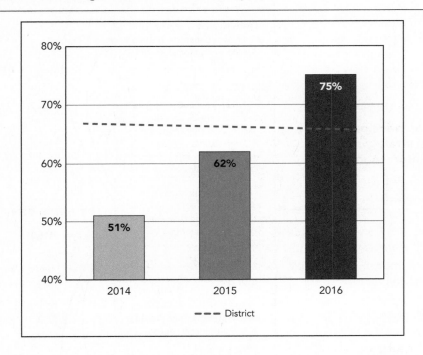

The Story

Nathaniel Hawthorne is a school of 500 students in Dallas in what principal Ana Fernandez describes as a very high-need community: 97% qualify for a free/reduced lunch and 65% are English Language Learners. Before Ana rolled out data-driven instruction, their results were "just okay"—which wasn't good enough. "We have to keep our babies from going back to the cycle of poverty," says Ana. "They finish elementary and they can't continue anywhere else. They don't go on to succeed in middle school or high school."

So Ana brought her staff together to issue a powerful call to action. She presented a PowerPoint that celebrated some recent gains in achievement at Nathaniel Hawthorne—but then showed another slide that compared their results to those at outstanding schools. Ana explained that what they were achieving at Nathaniel Hawthorne was the minimum level of success, but that the level of success that defines a master was within their reach. "Do you want to be the minimum, or do you want to be the masters?" Ana asked her team.

Ana quickly realized that if data was going to work for her teachers, analysis had to be intuitive. At first, this was a challenge. Teachers struggled to determine how to unpack knowledge and skills, and to understand how the information they gathered would impact practice in their classrooms. So Ana worked hard to make the processes that fueled data-driven instruction user-friendly.

That's when teachers' eyes really began to open. "I had one teacher who had been teaching third grade for six or seven years," Ana shared, "and she said, 'This is the first time I have had every answer. I was able to see where they were going to have misconceptions and I was able to see why they were having problems with some vocabulary words.'" Two years ago, that same teacher had been extremely resistant to the notion of data-driven instruction; the year she had this realization, she showed more growth than any other teacher for her grade level. "I'm proud of her because she tried something new and she did so well," says Ana.

Nathaniel Hawthorne is still working to harness data-driven instruction to do even more for students. "It is a process that never ends," acknowledges Ana. "Data is so big! I learn more every single day from my teachers, from everybody. Every day I learn something new, and I'm very grateful to be part of something as big as this."

---

### Key Drivers from Implementation Rubric

- *Build by borrowing:* Identify and implement best practices from high-achieving teachers and schools: visit schools/classrooms, share and disseminate resources/strategies.

- *Transparent starting point:* teachers see the assessments at the beginning of each cycle; assessments define the roadmap for teaching.

- *Simple—user-friendly,* succinct data reports include: <u>item-level</u> analysis, <u>standards-level</u> analysis and <u>bottom-line</u> results.

- *Deep:* move beyond *what* students got wrong and answer *why*: identify key procedural and conceptual misunderstandings.

---

## ASSESSMENT MYTHS DISPELLED

Given the widely conflicting attitudes and understandings of assessment, it is unsurprising that many myths and half-truths surround the assessment process. Before we move forward, let's take a moment to address a few myths that *won't* get you on the road to rigor.

### Myth 1: Multiple Choice Questions Just Aren't Rigorous

**Reality:** One of the most common criticisms of data-driven instruction is that assessment types like multiple choice questions are inherently low in rigor and lacking in value. By this logic, multiple choice assessment reduces instruction to rote learning, preventing students from engaging in "real" learning. What underlies that critique is a belief that the *type* of question matters more than the content. Let's evaluate that claim by taking a look at the following question about Shakespeare's *Macbeth*:

---

## College-Ready Example: Rigor in HS Reading

Directions: In this scene, Macbeth is discussing a prophecy he received from the witches. Read the passage, then answer the questions that follow:

> Macbeth: They hailed him [Banquo] father to a line of kings
> Upon my head they placed a fruitless crown,
> And put a barren sceptre in my grip,
> Thence to be wrench'd with an unlineal hand,
> No son of mine succeeding. If 't be so,
> For Banquo's issue have I fil'd my mind;
> For them the gracious Duncan have I murder'd.

1. The description of Macbeth's "barren sceptre" contributes to the unity of the passage in which of the following ways?
   A. As a parallel between Macbeth's possible children and Banquo's possible children.
   B. As a satirical comment on the challenges Macbeth will face with infertility.
   C. A comparison between Macbeth's strong formal authority and his lack of popular influence.
   D. As an ironic contrast between Macbeth's power and his inability to produce future kings.

---

Think of all the skills it takes to answer this question correctly. Students need to be able not only to understand complex vocabulary in context, but also to parse the larger connotative and figurative meanings of the phrases. Even if they correctly identify the meaning of "barren sceptre," they may still select option B, unless they can discern that this phrase is not a work of satire, which leads to the correct answer of D.

All of the skills required by this multiple-choice question demand a rigorous level of reading comprehension and analysis of students. If our goal is for students to be able to read complex texts deeply, it's hard to imagine a better way for them to exercise those skills. Moreover, this is the sort of question that appears on Advanced Placement exams: questions like these prepare students to thrive in college.

Now consider an alternative option—having students write an essay or short answer to the following prompts:

- Analyze the following passage of Shakespeare. How does it contribute to one of the central themes of Macbeth?

Without doubt, this is a quality prompt that could be used to assess students' analytical abilities. The difference is that here, students would have to generate their own argument and support it with evidence from the text, instead of analyzing evidence presented for them in a multiple-choice question. What will determine the rigor of this open-ended prompt is what you consider to be a sufficiently deep and convincing analysis, or an exemplar student response to this question. See the box below for more information about exemplar responses.

---

## A Word On . . . Developing Exemplar Responses for Open-Ended Response Questions

When it comes to data-driven instruction, open-ended response questions present a unique set of challenges—and opportunities. Steve Chiger, an acclaimed former HS English teacher and the Director of MS-HS Literacy for Uncommon Schools, shares that the beauty of analyzing student-generated responses is that it gives us the opportunity as educators to "geek out" together about the content we fell in love with.
   Let's take a look at this open-ended response prompt designed by Steve.

### Isaac, After Mount Moriah
### by Saeed Jones

Asleep on the roof when rain comes,
water collects in the dips of his collarbone.

Dirty haired boy, my rascal, my sacrifice. Never
an easy dream. I watch him wrestle my shadow, shut eyelids
trembling, one fist ready for me.

Leave him a blanket, leave him alone.
Night before, found him caked in dirt,
sleeping in a ditch, wet black stones for pillows.

What kind of father does he make me, this boy
I find tangled in the hair of willows, curled fetal
in the grove?

Once, I found him in a far field, the mountain's peak
like a blade above us both.

Prompt: How does Jones use language to characterize the relationship between Isaac and Abraham in "Isaac, After Mount Moriah"? Mention specific cases of figurative language the poem uses to make its point.

On paper, this looks like a very strong prompt. Yet we recall from earlier that the rigor will only be determined by how we will evaluate the responses. While a rubric will get us part of the way there, the best way to begin your analysis is with your own exemplar response. As I often state in PD on data-driven instruction, *you raise the bar when you spar with an exemplar.* Why? Because you don't limit yourself to what students were able to do but keep a clear focus on where you want them to go.

When you set out to script your own exemplar student responses to open-ended prompts, keep in mind the following tips:

- Write at the level the medium- to high-achieving students in your class are capable of. Ultimately, exemplar student responses come from your mid- to high-level students, so you'll set the right level of rigor by emulating them.

- Don't worry about the exact wording or precise thesis of your response. There could be many correct arguments to make about this poem, or any poem! The goal of an exemplar isn't to create a cookie-cutter answer that every student's response should match, but to write a high-quality piece of literary analysis that would earn your students a 4 or a 5 on the AP exam if they were to produce it themselves.

Crafting the exemplar changes the game for any subject—not only for open-ended literary analysis, but also for written response questions in science or history and for problems that require showing your work in math. With an exemplar in hand, you will find that the analysis of student work becomes so much easier: you look for the gaps (e.g., thesis statements, evidence, transitional phrases, inferences, structure, etc.). In doing so, you will push the quality of the writing faster and more effectively.

---

In the end, both multiple choice *and* open-ended response questions add value, and they complement each other in crucial ways. One (open-ended) requires you to generate your own thesis, and the other (multiple choice) asks you to choose between viable theses—with one being the best option. Ultimately, we need both of those skills: the ability to identify a strong argument and the ability to generate one of our own. We need those skills not only on formal assessments, but whenever we vote in an election, learn about a new scientific study, or go to work. To assess learning using either multiple choice or essay questions *exclusively* is to miss out on valuable opportunities to develop a student's intellect more fully.

The key, then, is to make sure that our assessments reflect multiple types of questions, and that each of those questions is rigorous. For multiple-choice questions, the options and the text difficulty determine the rigor.[5] For open-ended questions, it's not the prompt but the exemplar that determines the rigor. Keep those principles in mind, and you can create effective, balanced assessments that prepare children to demonstrate mastery now and in the future.

---

### Core Idea

In a multiple-choice question, the **options and text** define the rigor.
In an open-ended question, the **exemplar** defines the rigor.
Any good assessment will combine multiple forms to achieve the best measure of mastery.

---

## Myth 2: Tests Such as the SAT Don't Really Measure Student Learning

**Reality**: A second common misconception is standardized assessments like the SAT are simply tricky tests that don't really show student mastery. While this is sometimes true, it is not categorically correct. Consider the two questions below:

---

### Two Questions on Quadratic Equations

1. Solve the following quadratic equation:

$$x^2 - x - 6 = 0$$

2. Given the following rectangle with the lengths shown below, find the value of x:

$x$ | Area = 6

$x - 1$

---

If you solve question 2 algebraically, you arrive at the same quadratic question that is listed for question 1. However, you needed mastery of many additional mathematical concepts to set up the equation: properties of a square, area, distributive property, and more. Question 1 also has two possible answers: –2 and 3. In Question 2, however, the student must eliminate −2 as a possible answer, because a square would not have a negative side!

Question 1 is taken straight from an Algebra textbook; question 2 is a SAT question. The issue with the SAT question is not that it's trying to trick the student; it's that it requires a deeper, more conceptual understanding of quadratic equations, as well as the ability to apply it in the context of geometric properties. So when a student struggles with the SAT but does well in Algebra, the first thing a teacher/leader must consider is whether the rigor of class instruction matched the rigor of the SAT. Defining the rigor of the questions on our assessments to the highest bars that students are expected to reach makes sure that students will master any sort of test put in front of them.

---

### SAT Rigor: The Experience of a HS Math Teacher

*In our first round of implementation of data-driven instruction at our high school (North Star Academy Charter High School), we designed interim assessments that were aligned both to the New Jersey state test and the SAT. After we implemented the first round of interim assessments, one of the math teachers complained that there were too many SAT prep questions that weren't really connected to teaching HS math. As a school leader, I had a choice to make about how to respond. I could explain to the teacher why I thought the assessment was a valuable tool with rigorous SAT questions embedded, or I could try to get her to reach the conclusion herself. I decided for the latter. I said that I appreciated her concern and invited her to look at the assessment together to identify the questions that were problematic. We then identified the questions that were aligned to the rigor of the SAT, and with each one I asked her, "Are these skills that your students should know in your class?" After each question, she acknowledged that the question did indeed measure standards she was teaching. We repeated this exercise throughout the entire test, and the teacher slowly realized that her concern was not about SAT prep, but the high level of rigor of the questions. Without her feeling challenged directly, our whole conversation had shifted from test prep critique to how much additional work it would take students to reach a higher level of standards mastery. The rest of our time was focused on new strategies and schoolwide systems to support student learning.*

*Too often our critiques of tests are done from the 20,000-foot aerial view. However, when you get up close and examine actual test items, you start to discover the real issues of rigor (or the lack thereof).*

---

## Myth 3: Doing Well on the DIBELS, DRA or a Running Record in Early Elementary School Will Guarantee Reading Proficiency in the Upper Elementary Grades and Beyond

**Reality:** Although it might seem counter-intuitive, schools assess more in early elementary school than at any other grade level: there are individual reading assessments, observation checklists, sight word checks, etc. This is justifiable because the ability to read is one of the critical foundations of elementary education. The issue at hand, however, is whether they are using the right assessments to prepare critical readers.

Consider four different early literacy assessments all testing students at Level C on the Fountas-Pinnell scale (a K–1 reading passage). Each test claims to be an accurate, adequate predictor of future reading performance. They all monitor how quickly a student reads and how many mistakes she/he makes (and each has unique additional components focused on decoding, spelling, and other areas). However, note how they vary significantly in how they assess for comprehension:

---
●
---

### Four Early Literacy Assessments

**Story text** (assume that every line is a separate page and accompanied by a picture):

> *When I grow up, I want to put out fires.*
> *I want to play ball.*
> *I want to go to the moon.*
> *I want to teach school.*
> *I want to fix cars.*
> *But now, I am happy to be a kid.*

Here are the comprehension questions required by four major early childhood assessments:

### DRA (Diagnostic Reading Assessment):

Students need to:

* re-tell the story
* make a personal connection

### DIBELS (Dynamic Indicators of Basic Early Literacy Skills):

* No test for comprehension given: fluency in reading combined with proper de-coding via "nonsense" words is considered an adequate predictor of comprehension

**Running Record** *(this is a sample; there are many different versions)*:

Students need to:
- tell what happened in the story
- answer "right there" basic comprehension questions

**STEP (Strategic Teaching and Evaluation of Progress) Assessment:**
Students need to answer the following questions:
- What is the first job the girl thinks about doing?
- What job would make her leave Earth?
- What does she think she will do as a teacher?
- Why does the girl say that for now she is happy being a kid?

---

Considering that most elementary educators consider these assessments to be interchangeable, it is striking how each one requires a radically different level of mastery of reading comprehension. As is true in later grades, the assessment selected goes a long way in determining just what will be learned and therefore, what will be taught. While every elementary teacher that I know strives for deep understanding with their students, passing an assessment that doesn't require critical comprehension can lull him/her into a false sense of security about the student's progress. Particularly in urban schools, ignoring the importance of selecting rigorous assessments for the early years of education will leave students at a tremendous disadvantage as they move toward later grades. Countless schools have shared their experience of having students with excellent mastery on DRA or DIBELS who then struggle with state assessments. It is not that the state assessments are unfair measures of student learning at the early grades; it is that the state assessments ask for critical reading comprehension that the other assessments did not. Choosing an effective quality early assessment that measures not only fluency, decoding, and basic comprehension but also inferential thinking will push schools and teachers to introduce more rigor and better prepare young students for the challenges ahead.

# Data-Driven Success Story

## Whittier Education Campus, Washington, DC

The Results

**Figure 1.5**   Washington, DC, PARCC Assessment: Whittier Education Campus, ELA Percentage at or Above Proficiency

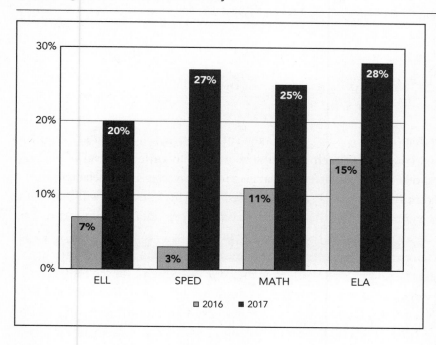

The Story

With Tenia Pritchard at the helm of Whittier Education Campus in Washington, DC, all of her Pre-K through eighth grade students benefited from data-driven instruction. But Tenia is especially proud of the impact on two groups of students in particular: special education students and English language learners, who make up about 25% of the student population. Tenia could not understand how some educators could miss the value of improving the learning for them as well. Rather than submit to hopelessness, she put data into action.

"We would give a diagnostic assessment at the beginning and the end of each learning cycle to see where our kids were," Tenia says. "Then, our upcoming learning cycle was based on re-teaching the standards that students did not master. We examined the rigor of instruction that aligned to the standard, and we used that to determine whether students were completing tasks that were aligned to the rigor of our assessment."

From there, Tenia and her staff went even deeper, creating individual learning plans for students and individual professional development plans for teachers. That included after-school "power hours" where teachers and students could accelerate the learning in certain content areas. "A lot of our PD was devoted to looking at student work and assessment. We defined what was exemplary work and then pushed to get every student to reach it."

The results were evident—they had closed the achievement gap in special education in math and nearly closed it in ELA as well.

"As a school, we eat, sleep, live by data," says Tenia. "All the decisions that we make are based on data. I know all my children's data. I know if that book they're walking around with isn't challenging enough or that math problem a teacher just assigned them isn't rigorous enough." The result is a school that meets children where they are and gives them what they need every step of the way.

---

### Key Drivers from Implementation Rubric

- *Common interim assessments:* 4–6 times/year.
- *Re-assess:* previously taught standards.
- *Six-week action plans:* execute plans that include whole-class instruction, small groups, tutorials, and before/after-school supports.
- *Ongoing professional development:* the PD calendar is aligned with data-driven instructional plan: includes student work analysis, action planning, and learning how to teach content.

---

## IMPLEMENTATION: FIRST STEPS FOR TEACHERS AND LEADERS

A summary of the keys to effective assessment is listed here as part of the overall implementation rubric:

---

### Implementation Rubric

### Assessment

The rubric is intended to be used to assess the present state assessment in your school. The rubric specifically targets interim assessments and the key drivers leading to increased student achievement.

4 = Exemplary implementation  3 = Proficient implementation
2 = Beginning implementation  1 = No implementation

---

| Assessments | Lit. | Math |
|---|---|---|
| **1. Common interim assessments:** 4–6 times/year | __/4 | __/4 |
| **2. Transparent starting point:** teachers see the assessments at the beginning of each cycle; assessments define the roadmap for teaching | __/4 | __/4 |
| **3. Aligned to state tests and college readiness** | __/4 | __/4 |
| **4. Aligned to instructional sequence** of clearly defined grade level and content expectations | __/4 | __/4 |
| **5. Re-assess** previously taught standards | __/4 | __/4 |
| | **TOTAL:** | _____/40 |

So what is the most effective way to implement these principles of assessment as a classroom teacher, school leader, or multi-campus/district office leader? What follows are the first steps that could be taken to put this into action.

## Level 1—Teachers

In some schools, teachers will have a fundamental role in the creation of interim assessments. If that is the case, please view the steps discussed at the district/multi-campus level. If, however, you work in a school where you do not have input into the interim assessments, the following steps can help you develop in-class assessment tools that will set up the end bar for driving change in your classroom:

- **Analyze the interim assessment or end-goal test:** Acquire the closest version that you can find of your state test, interim assessment or other year-end assessment by which your students' learning will be measured. (Note: this will vary from state to state: some states have actual prior-year state tests available, others have one practice test, some just have sample questions. You can also try to acquire the interim assessments from a high-achieving school in your state that have been proven to work and be aligned to the state test.) Jon Saphier, author of *The Skillful Teacher*, offered me the following precise question to use when analyzing the end-goal assessment: "What are the skills and knowledge needed to master each assessment question?" In the case of a multi-step word problem or analytical essay, this list could be quite extensive. This serves as the starting point for determining what to teach to your students. "Which of these skills/ knowledge do the students already know and which ones will I need to teach them?"

- **Build your in-class assessments *prior* to teaching the unit:** Before teaching your next unit, design your unit-ending assessment as well as your exit tickets. As you make each question, create questions that mirror the format of the end-goal test that you acquired in the first step. Make sure you have questions that match the rigor, format, and question-type. At the same time, include "building block" questions: questions that are below the rigor of the end assessment but are necessary steps toward proficiency. In math, this could include basic computation skills even as you are pushing for word problem application. In literacy, this could include using a lower-level text at first, even as you push for them to eventually demonstrate comprehension on grade-level passages.

- **Plan lessons to meet the rigor of that assessment:** Now that you've designed your in-class assessment, start planning your lessons. With the end assessment clearly defined, you have a roadmap to all of the skills/knowledge—and to what degree of rigor—that you will need to teach to ensure that your students are proficient on the unit-ending assessment. Keep referring back to the actual assessment questions while you plan to make sure that every activity sets up the students to succeed at that level of rigor.

- **Where applicable, set your college-ready goal:** As stated earlier, proficiency on state assessments is a necessary but insufficient bar for preparing our students for success in college and life beyond. If your students are currently well below grade level, state test proficiency goals could be an appropriate step for the moment. Once you start to achieve that, higher goals can continue to drive needed student college readiness.

## Level 2—School-based Leaders

Coaches, assistant principals, principals, and other school-based leaders all have different levels of authority and interaction with teachers. The degree to which each of following steps is implemented will depend on your role. Here are the critical first steps you can do in the area of assessment.

### Make Sure Your Interim Assessments Are Aligned *and* Rigorous

- **Analyze the quality of the interim assessment vis-à-vis your state test:** Acquire the closest version that you can find of your state test (see creative means of doing so in Level 1 Teacher section above). Line up actual test items from both assessments that are assessing the same standard, and determine if the interim assessment is meeting or exceeding the rigor of the state assessment. Table 1.1 is a guiding worksheet that could help with doing that analysis. If interim assessments are not aligned or rigorous, see Chapter 5—Overcoming Obstacles—for creative "workaround" solutions.

**Table 1.1**   Assessment Evaluation Worksheet

| INTERIM ASSESSMENT ITEM | STATE TEST ITEM | THE RIGHT CONTENT • Addresses the same standards • Addresses the standards as rigorously as the state test | THE RIGHT FORMAT • Reflects format of and type of questions from state exam • Reflects format of and type of questions from college-ready exam • Rubrics are used, if applicable • Wrong answers illuminate misunderstanding | THE RIGHT COLLEGE-READY EXPECTATIONS • Rigor and content seem appropriate for developing college-bound students • Content is "State test plus" in areas where state test is not college-preparatory: ○ more complex than state tests (require additional critical thinking/application) ○ more standards covered within the test and within the same question | COMMENTS Comments and suggestions to improve question |
|---|---|---|---|---|---|
| 1 | | Yes/no | Yes/no | Yes/no | |
| 2 | | Yes/no | Yes/no | Yes/no | |
| 3 | | Yes/no | Yes/no | Yes/no | |
| 4 | | Yes/no | Yes/no | Yes/no | |
| 5 | | Yes/no | Yes/no | Yes/no | |
| 6 | | Yes/no | Yes/no | Yes/no | |
| 7 | | Yes/no | Yes/no | Yes/no | |
| 8 | | Yes/no | Yes/no | Yes/no | |
| 9 | | Yes/no | Yes/no | Yes/no | |

- **Revise the interim assessments to close the identified gaps:** With this analysis completed, you can revise your interim assessment to align more completely with your state test and college-ready rigor. Simply revise, add or eliminate questions to meet your needs. (If you don't have that flexibility, check out Chapter 5 for overcoming this obstacle!)

## Manage and Support Teachers to Use Effective Assessments

- **Look at teacher materials and in-class assessments when observing:** One overlooked observational tool for a principal can be observing the quality of the rigor of the actual activities and assignments going on in the classroom. Do the in-class assessments or exit tickets meet or exceed the rigor of the interim assessments and year-end assessments (use the criteria listed in the worksheet above)? Do the teacher's activities and plans match the rigor of these assessments? Where are there gaps?

- **Facilitate teachers creating high-quality in-class assessments and planning backwards from them:** Teachers can always use more planning time to focus on doing the activities listed in Level 1. Use individual meetings with teachers, grade-level meetings, and professional development time to give teachers the opportunities to do this sort of planning. Once the unit assessment has been properly aligned to the interim assessment, the planning process can mirror the work highlighted in the Planning chapter of *Leverage Leadership 2.0.*[6] What makes the process so beneficial is that the interim assessment has already clearly defined the bar for rigor, so the planning is double the value!

## Level 3—District-Level or Multi-Campus Leaders

The biggest impact that district-level leadership can have is in the creation or selection of rigorous, high-quality interim assessments. One of the single most limiting factors in schools' achievement growth is poor interim assessments mandated by their districts. The five core drivers of assessment are listed here. Using the implementation rubric listed above, does your district/network have quality interim assessments?

If they don't meet all the criteria listed below for each subject, then your critical task is to re-design your interim assessments. Here are some key points that are worth reiterating:

- **Interim assessments are instructional tools first, validity tools second:** Many companies that are selling interim assessments do not allow schools to see the interim assessments—neither before or after administration—because they want to keep the results "valid." It cannot be put more strongly: *if standards are meaningless until you define how to assess them, then curriculum scope and sequences lack a roadmap for rigor without a transparent assessment.* Transparent assessments allow teachers to plan more effectively and increase rigor across schools. The goal is not to compare schools (that's the purpose of summative state tests!); it is to guide instruction at the classroom level. This is not possible without transparent assessments.

- **Don't take their word for it—check out the test itself:** Since assessments define standards, then it is insufficient to align an interim assessment to a scope and sequence alone. You must compare it with the end-assessment to make sure it assesses standards at a similar or higher bar of rigor (see Level 2 for more details). You'd be surprised at how few test creators actually do this carefully. Ask the assessment creator to prove alignment by showing actual tests in comparison to your state tests.

- **Involve teachers and leaders in the interim assessment selection/creation process:** Don't underestimate the talent of your highest-achieving teachers and leaders: they can be an invaluable resource in building a quality interim assessment program. They have as much expertise as anyone!

# Reflection and Planning

Take this opportunity to reflect upon assessment at your own school or district. Answer the following questions:

- After reading this chapter, what are the key action steps around assessment that you are going to implement in your school (which can you realistically do)?

  _____

  _____

  _____

  _____

- Who are the key people in your school with whom you need to communicate this plan and have on board? How are you going to get them on board? What are you going to do when someone says no? (What's Plan B?)

  _____

  _____

  _____

  _____

- Set the key dates for each action step, write them here, and then put them in your personal agenda/calendar to hold yourself accountable for implementing these steps.

  _____

  _____

  _____

  _____

## Chapter 2

# Analysis: Where and Why We Left the Route

## A CASE STUDY

Let's return to the opening sixth grade math case study from Chapter 1. Imagine you've just gotten back the results on the latest assessment. Here is how the students did on ratios and proportions.

### Sixth Grade Math Results—A Sample

| Assessment Results | Multiple Choice: | Open-Ended: | Overall: |
|---|---|---|---|
| Class Average | 69% | 47% | 63% |

| Ratio-Proportion Results Overall: | 70% |
|---|---|
| Ratio-Proportion—General: | 82% |
| Ratio/Proportion—Rates: | 58% |

You are tasked with analyzing the results to determine what to focus on. On the surface, the answer is easy: students need to get better at rates. What happens next, however, is what separates teachers and leaders who get results from those that don't. To drive home this point, let's consider a competitive swimmer.

Imagine a swimmer who is a hard worker in practice, but when she goes to her first competition, she finishes in third place. If the coach skips the meet and only reads the results in the newspaper, his advice will probably be that his student should focus on swimming faster. That is a coach, however, who would fail.

Had the coach actually gone to the pool, he would have seen that his swimmer was actually the fastest in the pool, and that her slow time was the result of her being the last one off the starting blocks. This simple story, taken from the 2004 film, *Man on Fire*, reflects a powerful truth: schools that take a superficial approach and "read the newspaper" will not draw the right conclusions about how to lead their students' success. Only once we enjoy a "view from the pool" can we begin to see what must be done.

---

### Core Idea

To transform your school, get the view from the pool.

---

This is the insight from which we all must draw guidance when we start to put data-driven instruction into practice. How can we get the "view from the pool" in our classrooms? Of course, we cannot watch our students take the SATs or state exams (without facing serious legal consequences), but we can do the next best thing by employing effective, rigorous analysis on the results of interim assessments and in-class student work.

If assessments define the roadmap to our ultimate goals, analysis helps us figure out where and why we left the path to allow us to determine how to get back on track. By effectively examining raw assessment data, teachers and school leaders can systematically identify their students' strengths and weaknesses and determine what specific steps they must take to achieve their goals.

# Data-Driven Success Story

## Nations Ford Elementary School, Charlotte, North Carolina

### The Results

**Figure 2.1**   North Carolina End of Course Test: Nations Ford Elementary School, Percentage at or Above Proficiency

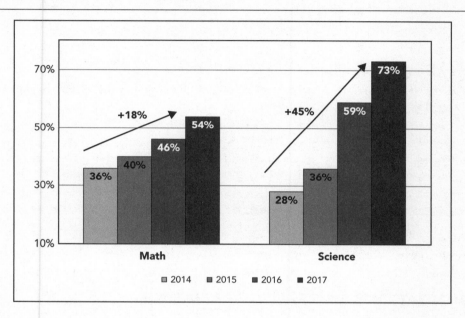

### The Story

When Alejandra Garcia became the principal of Nations Ford Elementary School, she knew she had her work cut out for her. Her state had gathered ten low-performing schools with the intent of turning them around, and Nations Ford was one of them. Alejandra was intimidated, but she was sure of one thing: that data would make a difference.

"Coming into this huge task, I started by meeting one-on-one with teachers," Alejandra says. "I'd say, talk to me about data. How do you track it? What does it do?" With this information in hand, Alejandra implemented the key systems she believed would make a difference at Nations Ford: basic data trackers and a six-week assessment cycle.

The calendar was critical: she made sure interim assessments were locked in, but what was truly transformative was when Alejandra built in specific weeks set aside for re-teaching. Teachers finally felt like they had time to revisit difficult standards and teach them to mastery. Alejandra rolled out six-week action plans, where a key component of this was planning re-teaching in team meetings. "Every week we look at the lesson plan tracker and create an action plan," says

Alejandra, "and then we coach our teachers." Looking at specific data points and developing concrete re-teaching plans to address them was instrumental at Nations Ford.

As the data-driven assessment cycle became habit, teachers became more invested in improving their teaching skills. Alejandra's leadership team gave feedback to lesson plans and during observations, and they built an instructional framework with personalized growth plans for each teacher. "Every week we met as a leadership team," shares Alejandra. "We looked at the data and our lesson plan tracker and we would make a plan to coach and support each teacher."

The results speak for themselves: Nations Ford has steadily improved for three years, and Alejandra was named principal of the year in her cluster of schools. "If you follow this cycle," says Alejandra, "I promise you it's going to work."

---

### Key Drivers from Implementation Rubric

- *Simple*—user-friendly, succinct data reports include: <u>item-level</u> analysis, <u>standards-level</u> analysis and <u>bottom-line</u> results.
- *Six-week action plans*: execute plans that include whole-class instruction, small groups, tutorials, and before/after-school supports.
- *Follow-up/accountability*: instructional leaders review lesson and unit plans and give observation feedback driven by the action plan and student learning needs.

---

How do we make this happen? With speed, simplicity and depth. Read on.

## FOUNDATIONS OF EFFECTIVE ANALYSIS

Effective analysis—and resulting action—need to be built upon a solid foundation. Here are the keys to that foundation.

### Immediate—Find the Error Before You're Too Far Down the Wrong Path

If you take a wrong turn on your journey and wait an hour to figure out what happened, you will be well on your way to being seriously lost. As soon as you know you've left the path, it's time to stop and figure out why! This highlights the first key point: for analysis to be useful, it must be timely.

Yet many schools don't approach learning in this way. Assessment results are not returned and analyzed in a timely manner, and thus precious learning time is wasted. Because of this, it's important to put systems in place to ensure that the insights of data-driven instruction are quickly put to use. Ideally, schools should design their calendar to ensure that interim assessments are analyzed within 48 hours of being scored. One example of this can be seen at North Star Clinton Hill Middle School (see Fast Turnaround Example), where the calendar includes several half-days following each round of interim assessment to allow for analysis, resulting in a three-day turnaround from results to action plans. By keeping the analysis process under a week, schools can ensure that information gained from data-driven analysis is quickly applied to the classroom and that re-teaching targets weaknesses while material is still fresh in students' minds.

● 

## Fast Turnaround Example

### North Star Clinton Hill Middle School
### Interim Assessment Schedule

| WEEK OF ASSESSMENT | | | | | |
|---|---|---|---|---|---|
| | **MON** | **TUES** | **WED** | **THURS** | **FRI** |
| Morning | Literacy interim assts (during class) | Math assts (during class) | Science & history assts (during class) | Regular classes | Regular classes |
| Afternoon | Literacy teachers grade assts | Literacy and math teachers grade assts | Everyone grades assts | Faculty meeting: Cancel—give time to fill out analysis templates and action plans | ½ day PD (or 2nd week): EITHER: Results Meetings by grade level/department OR: Ind. creation of action plans |

| WEEK FOLLOWING ASSESSMENT | | | | | |
|---|---|---|---|---|---|
| Morning | Re-teach | Re-teach | Re-teach | Re-teach | Re-teach |
| Afternoon | 1-on-1 Analysis Meetings: Literacy | 1-on-1 Analysis Meetings: Math/ Science | Regular classes | Regular classes | ½ day PD (or 1st week): See above |

## Data-Driven Success Story

## Northeast Elementary, Farmington, New Mexico

**The Results**

**Figure 2.2** New Mexico PARRC Assessment: Northeast Elementary School, ELA Percentage at or Above Proficiency

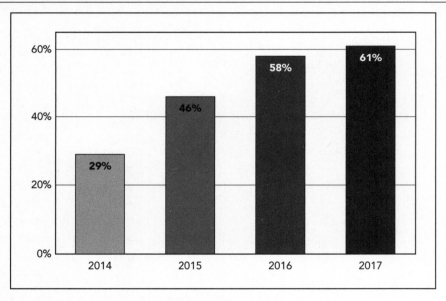

**The Story**

Northeast Elementary School's student population is a vulnerable one: many students come from the nearby Navajo reservation, and many others are transient. "Language is challenging for our kids," Candace Young explains. "They don't speak Navajo, but they also don't have the academic language necessary for English instruction either."

Candace Young had only expected to be reassigned to Northeast for a short time. The school, where Candace had served as principal six years previously, was now receiving a failing grade and was being threatened with takeover.[1] "We didn't have another principal to take that school," says Candace, "so I went back to Northeast thinking it would be temporary." Candace remembers returning to Northeast and feeling unsurprised it had earned an F: the school was an unsafe place to learn then, with rocks being thrown in the hallway.

Dedicated to transforming Northeast into a school where students could thrive, Candace quickly trained her staff in the art of holding weekly data meetings. "First, as a leadership team, we sat down at the table and I modeled leading the data meeting for them," Candace says. "We practiced that, and then we rolled it out with our teachers. We made sure we always had someone at each table who already knew how to discuss data."

It was slow going at first, with meetings requiring continuation over multiple days as Candace coached her leaders to analyze individual student data. Little by little, though, instructional leaders and then teachers mastered the art of analyzing data—and using it to inform their teaching. Candace recalls that a big piece of the puzzle was working with teachers to increase their own understanding of the curriculum they were teaching. They had to recognize, for example, that when they taught comparison problems, they were teaching subtraction problems.

Making data analysis a consistent part of instruction at Northeast may not have been easy, but it's paid off in spades. The school went from failing to receiving a National Title I Distinguished School award for high achievement in the state.[2] Her students aren't just doing well for disadvantaged students—they're outperforming the most advantaged students in the state. And Candace's "temporary" placement at Northeast? So far, it's continued for six years.

Like many educators, Candace remembers one student in particular who inspires her to keep doing the work she's doing at Northeast. "I had a hundred first graders my first year," she says. "There were ninety-nine who know all their letter sounds by the end of the year. When teachers told me we were at 99%, I said, 'Wow, that's great.' But they said, 'No, it's not great. Our goal was 100% proficiency.'" Candace's teachers took the final student under their wings and dove in. Each of them worked individually with the student for a few minutes a day and in the process, they uncovered the root learning challenges that were preventing him from learning to read. By the end of the year, he was on track.

"I asked, 'How did you figure out what he needed?'" says Candace, "and his teachers said, 'Because he's not just that last 1% to us.' Data changes kids' futures."

## Key Drivers from Implementation Rubric

- *Active leadership team*: facilitate teacher-leader meetings looking at student work (interim assessment analysis and weekly data) and monitor the follow-up.

- *Teacher-owned*: teacher analyzes own student work supported by instructional leaders.

- *Test and student work in hand*: start from the exemplar and identify the gaps.

- *Six-week action plans*: execute plans that include whole-class instruction, small groups, tutorials, and before/after-school supports.

- *Engaged students* know the end goal, how they did, and what actions to improve.

## Simple—Data Reports that Chart a Course to Success

The biggest challenge in education is not the lack of available data but drowning in too much of it. Effective schools sharpen their analysis by narrowing their focus. What might some effective analysis templates look like? One good example is the data template (Table 2.1) from North Star Clinton Hill Middle School in Newark, New Jersey (see Success Story).

What is powerful about this template is that everything essential for this group of students fits on one page. From this page you can see the analysis at the following levels:

- question level (the most overlooked level of analysis)
- standard level (all questions measuring the same standard)
- individual student
- whole class

Not only does this template do this level of analysis—it does so on a single page.

> ## Core Idea
>
> Less is more:
> the best data reports collect data at four levels on a single page.

Look at how the template does so. Every blank space represents a question that the student answered correctly. Every letter represents the wrong answer they chose on a multiple-choice question. A number shows the number of points they received on an open-ended response. The results are color-coded: above 75% is green font, between 60% and 75% is yellow, and less than 60% correct is red. You can look at the class performance by question, by standard, and overall. As added value, the scores are sorted from strongest to weakest, allowing you to look for questions that separate proficient from non-proficient students (e.g., #11 above). The shading also makes it easier on the eye, and even if printed in black-and-white (the reality at most of schools), you can clearly distinguish between the different results.

What also makes this report template effective is that it also has a *teacher-friendly learning curve*. Templates need not be overly simplistic, but they must be designed so that most teachers can, with reasonable effort, master their complexities. Templates that are too difficult to be useful will lead to frustration, not to results.

**Table 2.1** North Star Interim Assessment Results Analysis Template

Column key (standards assessed):
1. (1) Computation: add/subtract decimals/money
2. (NSA) Fractions in Context: +/−
3. (2) Computation: 3 × 2 multiplication
4. (3) Computation: division by 1–2 digits
5. (4) Fractions: add/subtract mixed numbers
6. (5) Computation in Context: multiplication
7. (6) Computation with money: subtraction
8. (5) Computation in Context: division
9. (5) Computation in Context: division
10. (7) Estimation/rounding: division
11. (8) Estimation/rounding; addition of decimals

| JUSTICE Student: | MULT. CHOICE: % CORRECT | OPEN-ENDED: % CORRECT | COMBINED PROFICIENCY SCORE: | 1 | 2 | 3 | 4 | 5 | 6 | 7 | 8 | 9 | 10 | 11 |
|---|---|---|---|---|---|---|---|---|---|---|---|---|---|---|
| Moet | 82% | 81% | 81% | | | | | | | | | | | |
| Jaleel | 82% | 62% | 76% | | | | | | | | | | | |
| Terrell | 79% | 42% | 69% | | | | | C | | | | C | B | |
| Aniya | 79% | 38% | 68% | | | | | C | | | | | | |
| Juwan | 68% | 58% | 66% | | | | | A | | | | | | B |
| Aziz | 74% | 42% | 65% | | | | | A | | E | | D | B | D |
| Juan | 63% | 58% | 62% | | | | | D | | | | | D | B |
| Shannon | 71% | 31% | 60% | | C | | | | | | | | | B |
| Maniyah | 71% | 31% | 60% | | | | | | | | | | | D |
| Kabrina | 63% | 38% | 56% | | C | | | A | | C | | | B | B |
| Keshawn | 55% | 54% | 55% | | B | | B | A | | | | D | | B |
| **PERCENTAGE CORRECT:** | 95% | 85% | 95% | 95% | 85% | 100% | 95% | 40% | 90% | 90% | 90% | 80% | 60% | 45% |

**TOTAL: 85%**

**Repeated 6–1 Standards:**

| | |
|---|---|
| Comp: +/− decimals/money (1): | 95% |
| Comp: 2 x 2 multiplication (3): | 100% |
| Comp: divide by 1–2 digits (4): | 95% |
| Multiply/divide in context (6,8,9): | 87% |
| Estimation/Rounding (10,11): | 53% |
| Charts: missing element (23): | 75% |
| Add/subtract with money (7): | 90% |

| | Multiple-Choice | Open-Ended | COMBINED |
|---|---|---|---|
| JUSTICE | 69% | 47% | 63% |

Note: This particular template is reprinted in blank form in the Appendix on the DVD, but here is a sample section of it.

Creating a data report template that meets these criteria (question level, standard level, individual student, and whole class data—in one brief report) keeps the ultimate users—teachers and school leaders—in mind.

To see how these core principles can be applied effectively in different styles of data reports, multiple templates have been included in the Appendix on the DVD. Pick one that meets your technical needs- as long as it meets the requirements above!

### Beware the False Driver of Over-Reporting

If test-in-hand analysis between principals and teachers is the real driver of student achievement, then schools don't need all the fancy data reports to drive change. This is especially important in the current landscape where companies and districts are marketing the fact that they have 40+ data reports, as if volume is more important than quality. Incredible amounts of time are wasted looking at reports that analyze the same data in multiple ways or are a few steps removed from the classroom-level analysis. Moreover, *the more pages an assessment report has, the less likely the teacher will use it*. Keep it simple: a one-page (maximum two) data report per classroom—you don't need more!

### A Note on Commercial Products

As of this writing, many commercial companies offer analysis sheets of their own (Illuminate is one example of a product that is aligned with the principles outlined in this book and may aid educators in implementing them). As was true for commercial versions of interim assessments, it is essential that school leaders *personally examine these sheets* to make sure that they contain all relevant information mentioned above. *If you cannot have the test in hand when using these analysis reports, they will be of little value*, no matter what information they contain (see next section for more details on this point).

## Teacher-Owned, Test and Student Work in Hand

Think back to the swim meet we imagined at the beginning of this chapter. What if after the swim meet, the head of the athletic department (rather than the coach) compiled the swimmers' results and presented them to the coach (who hadn't attended the meet) in a written report?

However elaborate this report was, it wouldn't be useful if not owned by the coach—the person responsible for working with the swimmers directly. The same is true of analyzing classroom data: effective instructors do it by ensuring the staff who work directly with students analyze student work directly.

# Data-Driven Success Story

## North Star Clinton Hill Middle School, Newark, New Jersey

The Results

**Figure 2.3**  New Jersey PARRC Assessment: North Star Clinton Hill Middle School, 2017 ELA and Math Percentage at or Above Proficiency

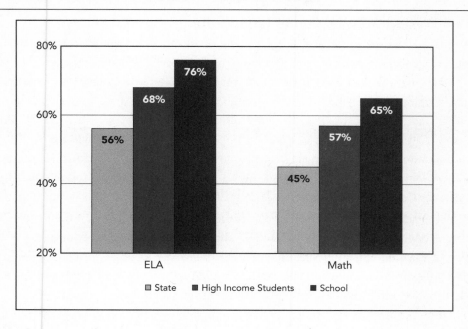

The Story

Jody Jones was a home-grown talent at North Star Clinton Hill Middle School in Newark, New Jersey: she began her teaching career there and after ten years she accepted the invitation to be the principal. Despite all her preparation, the competing demands of the principal role left her feeling overwhelmed. "There was so much to do, I wasn't sure where to focus."

Fast forward five years later, and Jody is one of the highest-achieving principals in the country, winner of the 2018 Ryan Principal of the Year national award for eradicating the achievement gap. The secret to her transformation? "I had to be relentless about pushing the data," she recalls. "I placed student achievement at the center of our school culture."

While her school always had data-driven instruction systems in place, Jody quickly realized that if she did not immerse herself in the work alongside her teachers and instructional leaders, she would not drive the strongest results. So she started leading weekly data meetings herself with her teachers. She would collect the student work, analyze it before the meeting, and then guide teachers to identifying the gap and making an action plan. "If I didn't look at student work myself, I couldn't tell if the teacher had a good analysis or was focused on the wrong thing. I couldn't drive better learning without preparing."

Walk into Jody's school today, and you'll see weekly data meetings and consistent follow-ups happening across all teachers in all subjects. Instructional leaders dig into data during observations and make sure that individual students are getting the proper strategic supports. The results show: Clinton Hill is one of the highest-achieving schools in the state of New Jersey. "It's all about the students," Jody shares. "If you look at the data and see that this represents the minds of your students, learning can fly."

---

### Key Drivers from Implementation Rubric

- *Teacher-owned*: teacher analyzes own student work supported by instructional leaders.
- *Test and student work in hand*: start from the exemplar and identify the gaps.
- *Deep*: move beyond *what* students got wrong and answer *why*: identify key procedural and conceptual misunderstandings.

---

One of the quickest ways that I can identify whether analysis is deep enough to be effective is to observe a group of teachers/leaders in the midst of analysis. If they don't have the test in their hand, I know their analysis will be superficial. Why? Because you cannot possibly identify the student error without looking at the question—and the student work—itself. Without doing so, you run the risk of the "Percent of a number" example in Chapter 1: you'll decide to re-teach percents without any idea of where the breakdown occurred, and at what level of rigor.

Without owning test-in-hand analysis, the teacher either would have re-taught percents generally, or just as ineffectively would have re-taught percent change. Both of these efforts would have led to little change in student achievement. Imagine the implications of this type of analysis on all of the standards on a given interim assessments: proper test-in-hand analysis saves countless hours of valuable re-teach time and energy.

---

### Core Idea

**Test-in-hand** analysis is not one possible way to analyze student error:

it is the **only** way by which to figure out what students need.

---

How can you do this? We've highlighted a process below:

## Look for the Patterns

With a solid data report, the most basic strategy for results analysis is to visually scan the template and identify the questions and standards on which students generally performed poorly. This strategy allows educators to quickly identify weaknesses and act on them. Teachers should constantly ask *why* students bombed given questions: did students all choose the same wrong answer? Why or why not? By comparing similar standards to one another or by examining trends within given standards, teachers can find the trends in student errors. Do results in fractions influence division of mixed numbers? Do systemic failures in sequence have any relation to the ability to summarize? By understanding the linkages between disparate standards, educators can better understand *why* a given question posed problems. At the level of the individual standard, consider if students performed similarly on all questions or if they found some harder than others. If so, why?

## Search for Separators

Another important technique is to seek out questions on which the generally stronger academic students outperform their weaker peers. Such questions are relevant because they reveal areas where smaller group focus and/or pullout groups would be highly effective at targeted instruction. Looking closely at the North Star Interim Assessment Results Analysis Template (Table 2.1), the three lowest achieving students answered #2 incorrectly. Those results clearly indicate that a targeted re-teaching/support for those three students on that particular standard could help them catch up to their peers. On the other end of the spectrum, the top 1/3 of the class answered question #11 correctly, suggesting that they could be given a stretch assignment while the teacher focuses on re-teaching that standard to the rest of the class—either learning a more challenging application/standard or serving as tutors to their peers during that re-teaching session.

## Scan by Student

Additionally, it's important to review performance not just between questions but also within students. Consider the case of Kenyatta, shown in the box below.

## Student-by-Student Analysis Sample

| Question: | 1 | 2 | 3 | 4 | 5 | 6 | 7 | 8 | 9 | 10 | 11 | 12 | 13 | 14 | 15 | 16 | 17 | 18 | 19 | 20 | 21 | 22 | 23 |
|---|---|---|---|---|---|---|---|---|---|---|---|---|---|---|---|---|---|---|---|---|---|---|---|
| Kenyatta | | | | | A | | | | D | | | | | C | D | A | B | D | D | D | C | D | A |

Following the guidelines listed with Table 2.1 (every blank space is a correct answer, and every letter represents the wrong choice on a multiple choice question), the teacher can quickly conclude that something happened starting on question #14 that completely changed Kenyatta's achievement up to this point. When this analysis is done in comparison to her peers (as can be accomplished in a spreadsheet like the one demonstrated in Table 2.1), Kenyatta outperformed her peers in the first half of the assessment, yet she finished with the lowest score in the class due to her performance on the second half.

If one only "read the newspaper" and looked at the girl's overall score, it would be easy to conclude that Kenyatta was one of the weakest in the class. The fact that she performed as she did after this question could mean many things: perhaps she fell asleep, perhaps she's a slow test-taker who rushed and filled in answers at the end; or perhaps she got bored. What these results do *not* indicate, however, is a lack of academic ability. As this example demonstrates, it is critically important to carefully examine anomalies in individual student performance before reaching any conclusion. Without it, Kenyatta could have been placed in endless re-teaching sessions, while she might have needed only a strong breakfast and a good sleep the day before an assessment.

The follow guide lists all the questions that teachers can ask themselves when looking for patterns in their assessment results.

## Looking for Patterns: Key Questions to Ask

### Global Questions

- How well did the class do as a whole?
- What are the strengths and weaknesses in the standards: where do we need to work the most?
- How did the class do on old vs. new standards? Are they forgetting or improving on old material?

- How were the results in the different question types (multiple choice vs. open-ended, reading vs. writing)?
- Who are the strong/weak students?

## "Dig In" Questions

- Bombed questions—did students all choose the same wrong answer? Why or why not?
- Compare similar standards: do results in one influence the other?
- Break down each standard: did they do similarly on every question within the standard or were some questions harder? Why?
- Sort data by students' scores: are there questions that separate proficient and non-proficient students?
- Look horizontally by student: are there any anomalies occurring with certain students?

### See the Gap

Let's take our opening case study and see what happens when you take a view from the pool.

## Standard-level Analysis of Student Performance: Sixth Grade Math Sample

| Ratio-Proportion Results Overall: | 70% |
|---|---|
| Ratio-Proportion—General (Questions #12, 21): | 82% |
| Ratio/Proportion—Rates (Questions #22, 30): | 58% |

If one looked only at performance on all Ratio-Proportion questions, the teacher would assume that most students are doing well and 1/3 of the students need overall remediation. Looking at the first breakdown of the standard, however, it would appear that this teacher should re-teach rates. Upon looking at the individual question results, however, one finds the following information.

## Question-level Analysis of Student Performance: Sixth Grade Math Sample

| Student Performance on Rates Questions: | |
|---|---:|
| Question #22: | **35%** |
| Question #30: | **80%** |

At this point, the only way for the teacher to determine what occurred is to look at the actual test items themselves. Here are the two questions and the most commonly chosen wrong answer for question #22:

22. Jennifer drove 36 miles in an hour. At this rate, how far would she travel in 2¼ hours?
    A) 72 miles (most commonly chosen wrong answer)
    B) 80 miles
    C) 81 miles
    D) 90 miles

30. If a machine can fill 4 bottles in 6 seconds, how many bottles can it fill in 18 seconds?
    A) 24
    B) 12
    C) 8
    D) 7

It appears that students knew how to calculate a rate in question #22, but they were unfamiliar with multiplying by a mixed number (and decided, in contrast, to simply multiply 36 by 2). Could operations with mixed numbers be the problem? A look back to the test and performance on related standards reveals that, sure enough, students performed dismally on mixed number operations:

## Related Standards Analysis: Sixth Grade Math Sample

| Student Performance on Mixed Numbers Questions: | |
|---|---|
| Multiply and Divide Mixed Numbers (Question #5): | **40%** |

In one simple question analysis, the power of "the view from pool" comes alive. If standards are meaningless until we define how to assess them, then analysis is meaningless without the assessment to guide us.

---

### Core Idea

If standards are meaningless until we define how to assess them, then analysis is meaningless without the assessment to guide us.

---

## Data-Driven Success Story

### IDEA Brownsville Academy, Brownsville, Texas

The Results

**Figure 2.4** Texas State Assessment (STAAR): IDEA Brownsville Academy, 2017 Math & ELA Percentage at or Above Proficiency

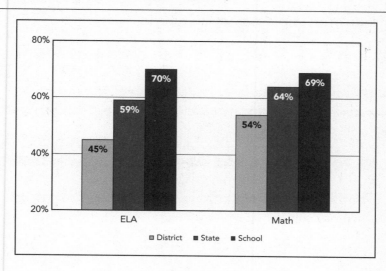

## The Story

When Erica Matamoros rolled out data-driven instruction at IDEA Academy Brownsville, she had a clear goal. "I didn't want my teachers to simply say, 'Students weren't successful because they don't comprehend the vocabulary'," says Erica. "I wanted my teachers to make choices that were more purposeful and specific."

One of the first things Erica observed was that if she modeled for her teachers, they caught on quickly. If she presented data in a meeting and modeled how to identify the most relevant gaps in teaching, they were able to replicate it. As Erica's instructional teams continued breaking down interim assessments and analyzing data, Erica stopped hearing "my students just didn't understand what they read" and began hearing "75% of my students missed the question on imprinting because they misunderstood foundational knowledge about that topic." Teachers began to understand the impact of their instruction on students and focused on the ways they could reshape what students absorbed.

Deep analysis like this led to more effective action, which Erica differentiated depending on whether she was responding to an immediate observation or a more long-term challenge. The data-driven foundation she'd already set in place allowed her and her leadership team to be strategic about the highest-leverage skills for students to learn, the information the data was telling them, and the actions that would offer the most support to high-need students (such as special education students and English Language Learners). "We could differentiate instruction and meet each student's needs," says Erica.

The action plans developed by Erica's instructional team got to a level of specificity as to include individual children's names and plans to support them. "Each teacher told us who was passing assessments and who was improving," Erica says. "From there they had to identify the top few missing skills and identify the gaps to student mastery of this particular standard. That would help us see what was behind the gap, and we'd develop either a short-term plan or one that would be ongoing."

It is no wonder, then, that IDEA Brownsville sits near the head of the class in achievement.

---

## Key Drivers from Implementation Rubric

- *Ongoing professional development*: the PD calendar is aligned with data-driven instructional plan: includes student work analysis, action planning and learning how to teach content.

- *Immediate turnaround* of assessment results (ideally 48 hrs).

- *Six-week action plans*: execute plans that include whole-class instruction, small groups, tutorials, and before/after-school supports.

---

# A Word On . . . Special Needs Students and DDI

In giving workshops across the globe, one of the most frequent questions/concerns that is raised is whether or not this type of data analysis actually works for special needs students.

I've had the chance to interact with and learn from the highest-achieving special education teachers, and to a person they tell me: data-driven instruction is at the heart of what they do. When you serve children with specific learning needs, you are identifying their personal gaps and designing teaching strategies to match. There is no other choice: without being data-driven, your children won't learn!

Natascha de la Torre, an incredibly successful SPED instructor at Vailsburg Elementary School in Newark, New Jersey, says data-driven instruction is one of the most important tools she uses to help special needs students meet learning goals. "You have to know where you want every student in your class to be, but also to understand each individual student's learning profile," Natascha says. "That means you need to identify a realistic place you might get that student to first. Being data-driven lets you build a trajectory that will get them to that larger goal eventually. It might take some of my students longer to meet those goals, but we're not going to lower the bar."

Here are some of the tips special educators like Natascha have shared with me to pass on to you and your special education teachers.

First Line of Action: Grab the Low-Hanging Fruit First

Often the challenge of analyzing interim assessment data for a student with special needs can be that there are too many questions "in the red"—that is, where they were not proficient. When that happens, start with the low-hanging fruit:

- Sort classroom data by students' scores: look for the questions that only the struggling students are getting wrong. These are likely the easiest access point, and other questions will likely be addressed by the general education teacher in the large group setting. Natascha points out that this helps students of all learning abilities, because it underscores standards that need to be re-taught to *everyone*, not just special needs students.

- From there follow the same steps of analysis as for any other student:
  - What are all the steps the students need to take to answer these questions correctly?
  - Which of these steps need to be made more explicit to the students?
  - What sort of practice do the students need to master this standard—heavy repetition of computational skills? Following a multi-step protocol?

Second Line of Action: Provide In-Class Support During Re-Teaching

For special needs students who take classes with their general education peers, the best thing to do is support the general teacher during re-teaching:

- What are the standards that will be reviewed or re-taught for the whole class?
- Are the struggling students' misunderstandings different than those of the rest of the students on these standards?
- What additional support or steps will the struggling students need when these standards are being reviewed?

In short, as Natascha's colleague Michelle Rolfert puts it, "The only difference between the general education setting and the special education setting is the need to reassess more frequently and with differentiated assignments. The process—re-teaching differently to meet student needs—is the same."

---

What the above shows is that teacher-owned, test-in-hand analysis paves the way for *deep* analysis. All of the foundations for analysis listed above can be synthesized into five core drivers.

---

### Analysis: Five Core Drivers

- **Immediate:** Aim for turnaround of assessment results, ideally within 48 hrs.
- **Simple:** User-friendly, succinct data reports that include: *item-level* analysis, *standards-level* analysis, and *bottom-line* results.
- **Teacher-owned:** Teacher analyzes own student work supported by instructional leaders.
- **Test-in-hand:** Have test and student work in hand to start from the exemplar and identify the gaps.
- **Deep:** Look for the patterns to see the gap—move beyond *what* students got wrong and answer *why*: procedural and conceptual misunderstandings.

---

When you put all of these ideas into action with teachers and instructional leaders, analysis starts to become transformative. But how do you make that happen? These can be hard to implement in isolation.

The most effective leaders don't leave this analysis to chance: they build structures for consistent, high-quality data meetings where instructional leaders can work with teachers to make these principles come alive.

Here is what the first half of those data meetings can look like.

## DATA MEETINGS, PART I: LOCKING IN DEEP ANALYSIS

The steps that follow will ensure you go as deep in analysis during data meetings as you do when looking at data on your own. That's how successful leaders lock in quality analysis.

### Rationale

As their name suggests, data meetings are conferences between teachers and instructional leaders in which results gathered from the last interim assessment—or weekly student work—are analyzed and discussed. They are a common best practice for the leaders in the success stories highlighted in this book. Here's why.

Unlike traditional post-observation conferences, which are based on a relatively small portion of teaching, interim assessment data span the entire test period and, as a result, analysis meetings offer insight into months of student learning. Additionally, analysis meetings allow for more specific and nuanced advice than traditional observations since year-long trends can be systematically assessed and analyzed. Analysis meetings also work to increase accountability by providing school leaders with a concrete record of class achievement.

Finally, and most importantly, such meetings are integral to changing from a culture focused on what students were taught to a culture focused on what students actually learned, which is the crux of data-driven instruction. Of course, this is not to say that traditional observations do not play an important role: they do. But interim assessment analysis meetings greatly enhance the effectiveness of observations to make them a more powerful tool to target and improve student achievement.

To see why, imagine a school leader who devoutly observes class instructions as often as possible. Observing every teacher in their school for fifteen minutes a week would make this leader among the most diligent in the country. But how much instruction would she actually see? Here's how it looks when we do the math:

- Typical teaching load: 5 classes/day, 50 minutes each.
- Total minutes of instruction per week: 5 classes/day × 50 minutes × 5 days/week = 1,250 minutes.

- One classroom observation per week: 15 minutes.
- 15 minutes/1,200 minutes total instruction = 1.2% observation of instruction.

For all her dedication, through observation alone, this leader would see only 1% of the week's learning:

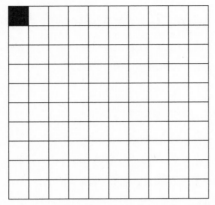

This breakdown reveals that as critical as on-the-ground observations are, they are insufficient in and of themselves to show a leader whether her students are succeeding. Even if a leader identified the most important 1% of instruction during observations, they would need to make broad, vague conjectures about what students learned the other 99% of the time.

Now picture a leader who has rolled out data-driven instruction. Through interim assessment analysis alone, that leader can gauge *six to eight full weeks of teaching*. No assessment can capture 100% of the learning that takes place in a class, but a good one can certainly capture 80% of it. Thus, in one data analysis meeting, that leader can change the percentage of instruction she observes from 1% to a groundbreaking 80%:

**Observation Alone**

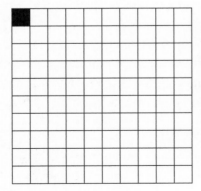

**Interim Assessment Analysis Meeting**

> ## Core Idea
>
> Data analysis meetings shift the focus from observing 1% of student learning to 80%.
> That makes all the difference.

Ideally, the school principal should conduct data analysis meetings, since this allows her to directly supervise the implementation of data-driven instruction. That said, most schools are simply too large for regular face-to-face meetings with all teachers. In these situations, meetings should be distributed among the principal and other school instructional leaders who have a formal supervisory role: assistant principals, coaches, team leaders, head teachers, etc.

## Common Errors in Leading Data Meetings—Responding to Resistance

Many schools have seen the value of having teachers and leaders come together to look at assessment results. Yet an often overlooked and equally critical component is the leadership training needed to lead these data meetings effectively. Too often schools assume that simply sitting down with the data is sufficient to ensure quality analysis. That assumption is fundamentally flawed.

Initially, it is likely that at least some teachers will be resistant to the very idea of the analysis meeting, especially when data-driven instruction is first introduced. We'll address how to build a culture where this presents less of a challenge in Chapter 4, but it bears some discussion now as well.

Tell-tale signs of resistance might include phrases like:

> This is just test prep.
> The students just make silly mistakes.
> I taught it and they knew it in class but just didn't perform on the test.
> I don't know why.

Such responses are unproductive and can quickly derail the analysis meeting. How, then, should one respond? What follows are the most common errors that school leaders make when dealing with such assertions.

# Three Common Errors in Dealing with Resistance

Ineffective Approach #1: The Concession

TEACHER    The students just make silly mistakes.
LEADER     Why do you think they made those silly mistakes?

**Error:** This sort of response is dangerous because it legitimizes the belief that the reason students failed to learn had nothing to do with teaching and everything to do with students' failure to learn. In effective data-driven education, however, the emphasis must shift from what was taught to what was actually learned, a process that will not happen if responses like these are accepted.

Ineffective Approach #2: The Fighter

TEACHER    The students just make silly mistakes.
LEADER     That's an unacceptable answer; we believe in accountability, and your attitude needs to change.

**Error:** If the instructional leader is too strident and overbearing, then the teacher will likely shut down, become defensive, and ignore the data. The benefit of using data-driven analysis is that it need not be personally charged; by making an aggressive gesture, the leader has forfeited this advantage.

Ineffective Approach #3: The Pedant

TEACHER    The students just make silly mistakes.
LEADER     If you look to question 18, you'll see that based on the results in the lower column, this error stemmed entirely from misunderstanding mixed numbers.

**Error:** Spoonfeeding one's own complete interpretation of the data takes away teacher ownership of the analysis, causing them to feel disconnected from the actual process of analysis and making it less likely that the teacher will own making the change. Additionally, because the teacher observes her students on a daily basis, it is likely that the conclusion she would reach on her own would be as useful—if not more—as the one the school leader has made.

Proper leadership and teacher training is a crucial component to guarantee quality analysis. What follows are the rationale for such meetings and the tools that school leaders should learn in preparing to lead such meetings.

## Prepare to Go Deep—Look for Patterns

To quote Muhammad Ali, "The championship is decided before you enter the ring." Most errors in analysis meetings come from a lack of effective precursors. Consider the following errors:

---

### Poor Preparation = Ineffective Data Meetings: Sample Failures and Their Root Causes

Note: Teacher responses are based on rates questions (#22 and #30) presented earlier in this chapter.

Failure #1

TEACHER     I have to teach rates better, so I have selected some new approaches to teaching rates more effectively . . .

LEADER     Ok. What new approaches are you going to use?

**Root Cause:** Analysis of questions #22 and #30 revealed that students were struggling not with rates but with multiplying mixed numbers! This teacher is about to embark on a misdirected action plan. Without proper analysis, action plans are meaningless.

Failure #2

TEACHER     I'm frustrated by this test because it has a number of standards that I didn't even know I had to cover, and the questions were much harder than what is in the curriculum!

**Root Cause:** The lack of transparency of the assessment—not letting teachers see the tests in advance—sets a teacher up to fail: the teacher cannot clearly lead his/her students to mastery if he/she does not know the end goal!

Failure #3

LEADER/TEACHER     So what we need to do is plan some effective lessons around multiplying mixed numbers. [After effective analysis, nothing is written down or recorded at the meeting.]

**Root Cause:** Few people are adept at following through on a plan without writing something down. In the context of an analysis meeting, the "writing" needs to occur on something that the teachers will reference when designing their lesson plans. By allowing a great analysis conversation to end without nailing down what will be done and when, it is highly unlikely that all actions will be implemented as effectively as they could.

The following precursors can make sure that all of these failures are avoided and thus double the impact of the meeting.

---

### Core Idea: Precursors for Effective Data Meetings

#### Before Giving Interim Assessment

1. **Six Weeks Prior:** Teachers review assessment and plan towards the rigor of those assessments.
2. **Professional Development (timing flexible):** Teachers receive model of how to do assessment analysis and complete action plan, and they see model of effective and ineffective analysis meetings.

#### Immediately Following Interim Assessment Administration

3. **Teacher Analysis:** Teachers do analysis of results prior to meeting, trying to answer the fundamental question: why did the students not learn it?
4. **Teacher Action Plan:** Teachers complete action plan explicitly linked to analysis.
5. **Leader Analysis:** Leader analyzes teachers' results and action plan in preparation for the meeting: looking closely at assessment items and student work to identify the root cause.
6. **Content Expertise:** If the subject in the assessment is beyond the expertise of the instructional leader, s/he identifies expert within or outside of school to call on for extra support.

---

In addition to solving the failures mentioned above, these precursors have some additional benefits. The single most effective way to ensure a quality analysis meeting is to model both effective and ineffective meetings with the faculty and school leaders in a non-judgmental way. The leadership training modules presented in Part II of this book provide excellent resources that motivate teachers to see the benefits of these meetings while also implicitly setting the expectation for what is effective and ineffective analysis. Moreover, by asking teachers to fill out an action plan prior to the analysis meeting, a leader creates a means for him/her to see in advance if the teacher has done a thorough analysis.

## A Word On . . . Content Expertise

One of the most challenging aspects of preparing for data meetings—and participating in them—is having a level of content expertise that allows you to dive into the assessments to determine the errors. This can be a daunting task for third grade math, but it definitely rears its head as you get into higher-level content. For a high school instructional leader, it is next to impossible to have enough content expertise to deeply analyze AP-level Chemistry, English, History, Calculus, Spanish, and more!

So what do leaders do when they have to coach outside of their own content expertise? They find other experts to help them.

Eric Diamon, principal of Vailsburg Middle School in Newark, New Jersey (highlighted in *Leverage Leadership 2.0*), has found this especially helpful when coaching his eighth grade algebra teacher. Eric's background is in the humanities, and his knowledge of the content she teaches is limited. "I find that my work with her is where it's most challenging for me to be a value add to her work," Eric confesses. To support this teacher, Eric takes two steps: (1) developing his own content expertise in math; and (2) seeking out help from other educators. "I attend any math PDs I can, which has definitely been helpful," Eric says. Eric's onto something: to become a content expert, participate in as many data analysis meetings, planning meetings and PD sessions as you can! Each time you engage in the content by looking at student work or planning a unit, by nature you gain more understanding. Little by little, you'll be on your way to supporting your teachers across all content areas.

Eric's other strategy is to work with another instructor who accompanies him on walkthroughs of STEM classrooms across his middle school campus. "That helps me develop my eyes for math," notes Eric. Support of this nature may come from a coach, department chair, strong teacher, or someone outside the school. Beyond this, you'll build your own content expertise simply by engaging in deep data analysis with your content experts again and again!

## Prepare to Go Deep—Script Your Meeting

All of the above work has allowed you to identify the key gap. Now it's time to prepare your meeting. Great leaders don't just hope for effective meetings—they prepare for them. Here are three key steps to take:

- **Room and materials ready:** One of the most frequently-asked questions about effective data meetings is how to make time for such deep analysis. One key is to set up materials before the meeting in order to have more time to dive deeper during the meeting. Here is a quick go-to list that highly successful leaders use to set up their meetings:

o Timer

o Copy of the standard and an exemplar response

o Chart paper and/or whiteboard to take notes

o Upcoming lesson plans and any materials needed to plan a re-teach lesson

o A sample of high/medium/low student work—typical errors that are representative of the majority of the students (this will save hours of sorting student work during the meeting and let teachers focus on the analysis itself!)

- **Prime the pump—Analyze the data and plan the re-teach *before* the meeting:** Effective leaders don't simply hope for good analysis—they set the stage for it. Once they've identified the key standard and assessment questions of focus, they prepare their meeting by doing the following:

o Review or write the ideal interpretation of the standard/exemplar being addressed.

o Identify the gap in student understanding.

o Plan the key part of an effective re-teach plan to address that gap (see this in more detail in Chapter 3).

What does this look like? Take a look at a preparation script from Juliana Worrell, principal manager in Newark and Brooklyn (highlighted in *A Principal Manager's Guide to Leverage Leadership 2.0*). What do you notice about her preparation?

---

## Prime the Pump: Sample Prep for Data Meeting

### Keys to Standard and Exemplar

3.NBT.A.2: Fluently add and subtract within 1000, using strategies and algorithms based on place value, properties of operations and/or the relationship between addition and subtraction.

| Know | Show |
|---|---|
| • Addition and subtraction are inverse operations, so you can find a missing addend by subtracting the sum from the known addend<br><br>• Moving to the left in place value represents ten times the value<br><br>• The commutative property of addition is<br><br>$$a + b = b + a$$<br><br>• You can use the commutative property of addition to determine what number is missing in the equation, because order does not matter when you add.<br><br>• Find a missing addend by subtracting the sum from the known addend | • Check your work by doing the inverse operation<br><br>• Use a traditional algorithm or a model to solve the problem<br><br>• Modeling: decompose numbers into their place values to add/subtract them for question<br><br>• When subtracting numbers where the place value of the number to be subtracted is higher than the first number, borrow a unit from the higher place value, convert to 10 units and regroup to be able to subtract |

Key Gaps to Close

• When subtracting two numbers where the place value of the subtrahend (number that is to be subtracted) is higher than the minuend (the first number), you need to borrow a unit from the higher place value and regroup.

Juliana has done the analysis herself, allowing her to be ready to step in to support the teachers whenever their analysis isn't deep enough or their action plan won't close the gap.

• **Preview protocol with teachers:** For a data meeting to run smoothly, teachers as well as leaders need to know the protocol the meeting will follow and the role they will play. This is simple enough to accomplish when a leader is meeting with an individual teacher, but it becomes more essential when leaders and teachers are meeting as a group. In that case, it is valuable to assign roles (note-taker, charter, timer) and to set norms (novice teachers speak first and veteran teachers add on and clarify, and preview the need for concision).

The importance of this preparation cannot be overstated. What Juliana just did will super-charge the meeting and strip away time that would otherwise have been lost for non-essential actions. In this way, you have 30 minutes of deep conversation, rather than just 10–15: that doubles the time you have to focus on learning.

## Facilitate—See It and Name It

With meeting preparation complete, it's time to lead the first few segments of an impactful data meeting. In this video, watch how we launch a weekly data meeting at Washington Park High School (see Success Story) with a HS English teacher.

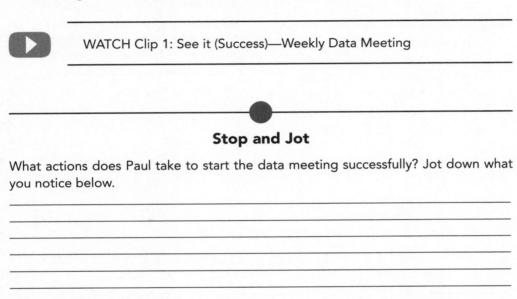

WATCH Clip 1: See it (Success)—Weekly Data Meeting

### Stop and Jot

What actions does Paul take to start the data meeting successfully? Jot down what you notice below.

_____

_____

_____

_____

_____

_____

_____

### See the Success

Sit down to a data meeting, and it's tempting to begin with the problem. Yet this meeting starts with their success on a previous standard. This is more than just praise: it shows teachers that you see their effort, and that their effort bears fruit. When teachers reflect on the actions that made them effective with a different standard, they will be more likely to reflect on areas where they were less effective, and they often can apply previous strategies to address the problem. See the success first, and seeing the gap is so much easier.

Once you've launched this way, you can dive into the task. Watch as Mary Ann Stinson (highlighted in *Leverage Leadership 2.0*) launches her weekly data meeting:

 WATCH Clip 2: See it (Standard)—Weekly Data Meeting

## See the Exemplar

After seeing the success, you might assume that Mary Ann would jump to the gaps in student work. Not yet! Instead, she pre-selects a key question to focus on, and her team gets started by reviewing the standard and the exemplar response. Why? Looking at incorrect student answers first would be like trying to figure out where you made a wrong turn on a road trip before determining where you are headed. Turn to the exemplar response first, and it will reveal your pathway.

---

### Core Idea

You don't know where to go if you haven't determined the destination.
Use the exemplar to start with the end in mind.

---

Reviewing the standard and exemplar side-by-side is especially illuminating, because the standard can give you academic language to describe the student thinking needed to answer the question. Given the pace at which Mary Ann moves and the precision with which her team identifies what students need, it would be easy to conclude that Mary Ann is simply a master of on-the-spot thinking. Break it down, though, and you'll see that she used a set of prompts that are pretty applicable to nearly any assessment item at any grade level:

- What does a student need to know and be able to do to master this standard?

- What were the keys to an ideal/exemplar answer?

- How does the exemplar response connect to the standard?

- How does your student exemplar compare to the teacher exemplar? What is the gap or does it offer something yours does not?

- Do students have different paths/evidence to demonstrate mastery of the standard?

For more evidence of the power of this way of kicking off a data meeting, we see Na'Jee Carter, current principal of Alexander Street Elementary School (see Success story—Juliana Worrell's successor) use this same strategy:

 WATCH Clip 3: See it (Standard & Exemplar)—Weekly Data Meeting

Starting with the exemplar gives Na'Jee and his team of teachers clarity on what students have to be able to do to master the standard.

---

### Core Idea

When you start from the exemplar, your analysis becomes exemplary.

---

### See the Gap

With an unpacked exemplar in hand, leaders and teachers are now more equipped to get to the heart of the matter: what are the gaps between the exemplar student response and the student responses that don't reflect mastery? Watch how all three leaders—Juliana, Na'Jee, and Mary Ann manage this.

 WATCH Clip 4: See It, Name It. (Gap)—Weekly Data Meeting

 WATCH Clip 5: See It, Name it. (Gap)—Weekly Data Meeting

 WATCH Clip 6: See It, Name it. (Gap)—Weekly Data Meeting

## Stop and Jot

What actions do Juliana, Na'Jee, and Mary Ann take to get their teachers to see the gap in student learning? Jot down what you notice below.

_____
_____
_____
_____
_____
_____
_____

Here we see the power of unpacking the exemplar: now, the teachers can use it as a reference to identify the gaps in the rest of the student work. Seeing and naming the gap in this way make the data meeting powerful. The teachers know what to target, and they've determined what that is in a collaborative environment that cultivates trust. They see what students need with shared clarity, and they can reach solutions together.

Naming the exemplar and the gap seals the deal. By having their teams write down the student error and the conceptual misunderstanding evident in the error, these leaders lock in *what* went wrong, allowing their teachers to pivot to *how* to fix it from a solid starting point.

---

### Core Idea

You don't lock in the learning until you stamp it.
Naming *what* went wrong makes it easier to plan *how* to fix it.

---

Think about the impact of data meetings like these. In just a few minutes, you've gone from a surface understanding of student performance to a targeted identification of the key gap that will change student achievement. In Chapter 3, we'll address what to do once you've identified the gap: taking action.

# Data Meetings, Part 1

## Leading Teacher Teams to do Deep Analysis

| See It<br>13–18 min. | See Past Success, See the Exemplar, and See and Analyze the Gap |
|---|---|
| | **See Past Success (1 min.):**<br><br>• "Last week we planned to re-teach XXX and we went from X% proficient to XX%. Nice job!"<br><br>• "What actions did you take to reach this goal?"<br><br>**See the Exemplar (8 min.):**<br><br>• Narrow the focus: "Today, I want to dive into [specific standard] and the following assessment item."<br><br>• Interpret the standard(s):<br>   o "Take 1 min. in your own words, what should a student know or be able to do to show mastery?"<br><br>• Unpack the teachers' written exemplar:<br>   o "Take 1–2 min. to review the exemplar: What were the keys to an ideal answer?"<br>   o "How does this [part of the exemplar] align with the standard?"<br>   o "Is there anything you would add to our chart of the unpacked standard?"<br><br>• Analyze the student exemplar:<br>   o "Take 1 min.: How does your student exemplar compare to the teacher exemplar? Is there a gap?"<br>   o "Do students have different paths/evidence to demonstrate mastery of the standard?"<br>   o "Does the student exemplar offer something that your exemplar does not?"<br><br>**See the Gap (5 min.):**<br><br>• Move to the sample of un-mastered student work (look only at a representative sample):<br>   o "Take 2 min. What are the gaps between the rest of our student work and the exemplar?"<br>   o "Look back at our chart of the standard and exemplar: What are key misconceptions?" |

| Name It<br>2 min. | State the Error and Conceptual Misunderstanding |
|---|---|
| | **Punch It—Stamp the Error and Conceptual Understanding:**<br>• "So our key area to re-teach is:<br>  ○ Describe the conceptual understanding<br>  ○ (if needed) Describe the procedural gap (e.g., memorize multiplication tables) and/or missing habits (e.g. annotating text, showing work)<br>• Write down and/or chart the highest leverage action students will take to close the gap |

## A Word On . . . Scripting Your Meetings

Using a list of sentence starters like those listed above can feel artificial and forced for many school leaders. Yet over and over again, in the course of delivering workshops to school leaders, I have seen the power of individuals practicing these phrases—forcing themselves to use them at first until it becomes more natural. There are a few key reasons for this power.

If we school leaders are honest with ourselves, we often talk too much. We can waste time adding extra language than what is necessary. (If you don't believe me, film yourself leading a meeting! Video is unforgiving, and you'll likely see your use of unnecessary language.) Using scripted questions—and sticking to them—can dramatically reduce the amount of time you speak, which increases the amount of time teachers speak and makes meetings so much more efficient.

Yet there is a second reason that is even more impactful. When we have standard questions that we use at every meeting, we build the habit of following a script, and that frees our mind to listen—deeply. When we are no longer thinking about what to say next, we can pay attention to teacher responses and monitor them for quality. We then shift from simple facilitation to monitoring our meetings for quality.

Scripting your meeting frees you to listen. Your teachers will be the better for it.

## IMPLEMENTATION: FIRST STEPS FOR TEACHERS AND LEADERS

A summary of the keys to effective analysis is listed here as part of the overall implementation rubric.

## Implementation Rubric

### Analysis

The rubric is intended to be used to assess the present state of data-driven analysis in your school. The rubric specifically targets interim assessments and the key drivers leading to increased student achievement.

4 = Exemplary implementation 3 = Proficient implementation 2 = Beginning implementation 1 = No implementation

| Analysis | |
|---|---|
| **1. Immediate:** Aim for fast turnaround of assessment results (ideally 48 hrs) | _____/4 |
| **2. Simple:** User-friendly, succinct data reports include: <u>item-level</u> analysis, <u>standards-level</u> analysis and <u>bottom-line</u> results | _____/4 |
| **3. Teacher-owned:** Teacher analyzes own student work supported by instructional leaders | _____/4 |
| **4. Test and student work in hand:** Start from the exemplar and identify the gap | _____/4 |
| **5. Deep:** Move beyond *what* students got wrong and answer *why*: identify key procedural and conceptual misunderstandings | _____/4 |
| | TOTAL: _____/20 |

What follows are the first steps that could be taken to put this into action for classroom teachers, school leaders, or multi-campus/district office leaders:

## Level 1—Teachers

If your school has effective analysis templates and data meetings, your work is perfectly focused: analyze the results as demonstrated above (that detail does not need repeating here!). You can turn to your instructional leader and colleagues for support in this analysis.

If your school lacks adequate analysis templates or data meetings, you can still take the lead yourself. Take one of the Excel templates provided in the DVD of this book, and adapt it to meet the needs of your class and your assessment. It is a worthy substitute for a lack of quality analysis template. As a last resort, turn to a pencil and paper! You don't need an Excel spreadsheet to do excellent results analysis. Afterwards, follow the steps for leading a data meeting. When you get stuck, find the best teacher/leader in your school (or in a school close by) to help you along the way.

## Level 2—School-Based Leaders

You play a critical role in ensuring that all teachers in your building analyze their assessments results effectively. The three fundamental steps to accomplishing this quality analysis are as follows:

- **Lead data meetings:** Follow the guidelines above and work side-by-side with your teachers.

- **Train all instructional leaders in your school to lead effective data meetings:** Part II of this book provides high-quality professional development activities to develop leaders in this area. This training allows you to distribute instructional leadership more effectively and guarantee that analysis is done consistently across the school.

- **(if needed) Select/change/adjust analysis templates to meet criteria listed above:** Some principals have the authority to design/select their own assessment analysis tools. See Level 3 for details on proper criteria for making/selecting an effective template.

## Level 3—District-Level or Multi-Campus Leaders

District-level leadership has a significant impact on school's performance in three critical areas: (1) the selection/creation of effective analysis templates; (2) ensuring a quick turnaround of assessment results; and (3) training all leaders to lead effective data meetings. Here's how to address each one:

- **Simplify—Data reports that are one page per classroom:** The first question for your district is the choice of whether to have a district-wide analysis tool or let schools design their own. Districts have been successful with both approaches. Either way, the key criteria for selection are one or two well-packed pages with item-level, standards-level and student-level analysis—that is all a teacher needs. Do not sacrifice item-level analysis for all the other analysis that can be done—all power of change in teaching practice will be lost without item-level analysis!

- **Immediate results—Turnaround that is 48 hours to one week maximum**: The fastest way to accelerate turnaround is to establish the district calendar with time built in for teachers to do analysis. This can be accomplished by building in PD days and also removing other requirements that get in the way. We'll address this further in Chapter 4—A Data-Driven Culture.

- **Train—Train all instructional leaders (including teacher team leaders) in leading effective data meetings that are deep.** Utilize the PD materials and resources to train your leaders across all schools in effective data-driven instruction.

# Reflection and Planning

Take this opportunity to reflect upon Analysis at your own school or district. Answer the following questions.

- After reading this chapter, what are the key steps around Analysis that you are going to implement in your school (which can you realistically do)?

  _____

  _____

  _____

  _____

- Who are the key people in your school with whom you need to communicate this plan and have on board? How are you going to get them on board? What are you going to do when someone says no? (What's Plan B?)

  _____

  _____

  _____

  _____

- Set the key dates for each action step, write them here, and then put them in your personal agenda/calendar to hold yourself accountable for implementing these steps.

  _____

  _____

  _____

  _____

## Chapter 3

# Action: Charting a Better Path

Many educators would argue that the number one challenge we face is a lack of time: we need more time with our students to teach them. Yet the deep analysis presented in the previous chapter offers us a creative opportunity to get more instructional time without lengthening the school day: spend less time on what students already know and more on what they need.

---

### Core Idea

How do we make more time for learning?
Spend less time on what students already know and more on what they *need*.

---

I have had the opportunity to work with and/or observe many of the highest-achieving teachers all across the country. When people ask me to describe what separates them from less effective teachers, the answer is not clear from observation of teacher craft alone. Many teachers have classrooms where students are highly engaged and show signs of loving learning. Many teachers are also expert facilitators of discourse. Yet these signs alone don't guarantee higher achievement.

The one factor that consistently separates the highest-achieving teachers from the rest is that they are relentless about student learning. How does that manifest itself? They are constantly re-teaching and spiraling based on analysis. As one of them said to me, "If you don't teach differently, they won't learn differently."

---

### Core Idea

If you don't teach differently, they won't learn differently.

---

## Data-Driven Success Story

## Whitewater Middle School, Charlotte, North Carolina

**The Results**

**Figure 3.1** North Carolina End of Course Test: Whitewater Middle School, Math and Science Percentage at or Above Proficiency

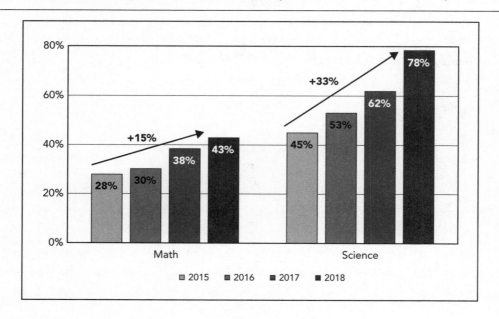

### The Story

When Beth Thompson began her journey as principal of Whitewater Middle School, the school was third from the bottom of all elementary and middle schools in Charlotte, North Carolina. Moreover, they had not even met state growth standards in any content area the previous year.

So Beth knew that this endeavor would be very hard work. She built her leadership team and dove in. "We committed to what I called running the program—implementing data-driven instruction," shared Beth. "Even if it felt like whack-a-mole at the beginning, we would run the cycle of assessment, analysis, and action, no matter what. This was the heart of it: we didn't quit the right foundation even when other things were still falling apart."

In year one the gains began. "The teaching wasn't very good yet," recalls Beth, "but because at least we were teaching to the right level of rigor based on the interim assessment, growth still occurred." Get the level of rigor of your assessments right, and results follow.

In her second year and beyond, Beth built more systems of accountability: the leadership team observed the re-teaching in action and the quality of data meetings. They also developed teachers to plan lessons backwards from assessment, and soon the teachers were able to lead their own data meetings without Beth's supervision. "In the beginning, we had to walk people through every step of the process," Beth remembers. "Now, teachers are coming to the table already having gathered their student work and are eager to dive into it. We've moved from pushing teachers to teachers pushing us to implement data-driven instruction effectively."

The result of all this hard work? Students are achieving at higher levels than before. Teachers love looking at their student data, and everyone shares the ownership of the results.

---

### Key Drivers from Implementation Rubric

- *Six-week action plans:* execute plans that include whole-class instruction, small groups, tutorials, and before-/after-school supports.

- *Follow-up/Accountability:* instructional leaders review lesson and unit plans and give observation feedback driven by the action plan and student learning needs.

- *Build by borrowing:* identify and implement best practices from high-achieving teachers and schools: visit schools/classrooms, share and disseminate resources/strategies.

---

In the end, all of the best assessments and analysis mean nothing if we don't improve the teaching—and thus the learning. Action gets right to the heart of the impact data-driven instruction can have. When action is carried out effectively, students see themselves succeed. This chapter will show how.

## ACTION PLANS: ALIGNING THE "WHY" TO THE "HOW"

To understand how analysis can translate to action, we've collected action plans from three high-achieving teachers from North Star in Newark, NJ—they are templates imitated in varying degrees by schools across the country. Take a look at these samples from each one: what are the keys to an effective action plan?

---

## Sample Action Plan, Part 1—Overall Analysis

### Seventh Grade Literacy

**Uncommon Schools** | Change History.

**INTERIM ASSESSMENT #7–1 TEACHER DATA ANALYSIS**

| What? | Deep Dive Analysis—Why? |
|---|---|
| **Standard/Questions not Mastered** | **Which incorrect answer did students choose? Why did students not master this standard?** |
| **Central Idea & Evidence:** Determine a theme or central idea of a text and analyze its development over the course of the text; provide an objective summary of the text. <br><br> **Multiple Choice:** Question #7 (evidence)—17% correct Question #18 (claim)—42% Question #19 (evidence)—20% <br><br> **Open-Ended:** Essay: Claim—71% Essay: Evidence—52% | **What misunderstandings are revealed in the responses compared with the exemplar?** Across the IA, students struggled to identify the best claim and matching evidence to establish the claim of the text, both in their writing and on the multiple choice section of the test: <br><br> • **Question 7 & 19** – Most students could find the main idea (questions #6 and 18) but that number dropped when needing to find evidence to support the claim. They often chose the answer that was general evidence but not the best answer that was more narrowly connected to the claim. <br><br> • **Writing** <br> ○ **Essay – Claim (71%)** – Students often gave the approximate claim in response to the prompt and addressed the viewpoints in a general sense – but struggled to articulate the distinct techniques (the how) that the authors' use to establish their viewpoints. This also led to an even lower evidence score. <br><br> ○ **Essay – Evidence (52%)** – Students chose evidence that was not completely without merit, but evidence chosen often was not the strongest possible to support the prompt – then students did not explain the "so what" behind their evidence, just restating the quote or simply explaining it without using it to build on the central idea. Students also struggled to limit their evidence ("chunk it") to the most critical part. |

| What? | Deep Dive Analysis—Why? |
|---|---|
| **Standard/Questions not Mastered** | **Which incorrect answer did students choose?** <br> **Why did students not master this standard?** |
| **Central Idea & Evidence (con't.)** | **What gaps in the instruction contributed to these misunderstandings?** <br><br> As I compared student work to the exemplar response, I noticed that my students did not annotate the text in any way. I realized that I had focused so much of my instruction on getting the general gist of the passage but I had not taught them to focus on key evidence and to annotate while reading. I also did not teach the students how to pre-write for the essay. Thesis statements, in some cases, were unclear or vague – they didn't provide a clear, underlying argument for the essay. <br><br> **What will you do to help students achieve mastery? How will it be measured?** <br><br> • We'll conduct a lesson in week 10 on creating "just right" claim sentences – ones that aren't too broad or too narrowly tailored. In the lesson, students will evaluate a series of claims/arguments based on recent class prompts, labeling them as "just right," "too general," or "too specific." They will then develop their own topic sentences/arguments, using a graphic organizer, and complete peer revision to evaluate each other's work. <br><br> • We'll also conduct a lesson where I will model how to annotate for claim: how to select evidence that supports my claim and how to take simple margin notes while reading. That will setup a 2nd model lesson later in the unit on how to pre-write for an essay: organizing evidence to support each sub-claim to make a stronger essay. <br><br> • We'll spiral this expectation into the grading of student writing by adding "best evidence" to the writing rubric. <br><br>     ○ <u>Re-teach Lesson Objective</u>: 70% of SWBAT earn a "3" or higher on the writing rubric for argumentation by writing a "just right" claims supported by the best evidence. |

# Sample Action Plan, Part 2—Small Group Work

## Second Grade Math

| Small group instructional plan—what techniques will you use to address these standards? |
|---|

**Week 1:**

**#13 – (Reasoning) Four-sided shapes (92%)**—*Makyah, Ibn-Karriem*

- Snack time: solve four-sided shapes story problems. Students will review how to identify various types of four-sided shapes and model crossing out strategy to show students how to keep track of shapes already eliminated because they are not four-sided.

**#1 – (Numerical operations) Missing addend (88%)**—*Ty-Teonnah, Nyree, Alyssa*

- Snack time: solve problems with one unknown addend. Students will debrief counting up/back strategies and using tens facts. I will ensure students double-check their work for accuracy.

**#11 – (Problem solving) Money/change (68%)**—*Beatriz, Ke'Ajah, Alexis, Karina, Benjamin, Alyssa, Makyah*

- Lunch: extra story problems about making change from a dollar. I will model counting up/back strategies using actual coins to show how change is calculated. I will highlight importance of representing money in dollars and cents.

**#21 – (Problem solving) JRU (72%)**—*Martain, Ke'Ajah, Jaylin, Alexis, Benjamin, Elijah, Ibn-Karriem*

- Snack time: solve story problems with extra information. I will emphasize returning to question to see what is being asked. I will have students retell story problem in own words. I will have students go back to text to identify relevant and non-relevant information.

# Sample Action Plan, Part 3—Six-Week Plan

## Seventh Grade Math

| WEEK 1 |
| --- |
| **Standards for Review (objectives and activities aimed to re-teach)** |
| Fluency Practice—area/perimeter of polygons<br>Homework and Do Nows—integers<br>Spiraled through Do Nows and Review—number sense and geometry<br>Mini-lesson: solve irregular polygon |
| **New Standards (objectives/standards to teach based on upcoming assessment content)** |
| Composite Figures; Inscribed Figures |

| WEEK 2 |
| --- |
| **Standards for Review (objectives and activities aimed to re-teach)** |
| Fluency Practice—two versions of integers<br>Homework and Do Nows—integers and percents<br>Spiraled through Do Nows and Review—symmetry (w/mirrors)<br>Mini-lesson: using a table to keep work organized |
| **New Standards (objectives/standards to teach based on upcoming assessment content)** |
| Congruent and Similar Figures, Translations |

| WEEK 3 |
| --- |
| **Standards for Review (objectives and activities aimed to re-teach)** |
| Fluency Practice—multi-step percents<br>Homework and Do Nows—integers, percents, composite figures<br>Spiraled through Do Nows and Review—powers of 2 vs. perfect squares |
| **New Standards (objectives/standards to teach based on upcoming assessment content)** |
| Translations, Reflections, Rotations about a Vertex |

| WEEK 4 | | |
| --- | --- | --- |
| **Standards for Review (objectives and activities aimed to re-teach)** | | |
| Fluency Practice—integers, percents, powers of 2<br>Homework and Do Nows—composite figures, translations<br>Spiraled through Do Nows and Review—translations | | |
| **New Standards (objectives/standards to teach based on upcoming assessment content)** | | |
| Rotations about the Origin, Rectangular Prisms, Cylinders, Classifying Prisms, and Pyramids | | |

Although they can vary greatly, effective action plans all share a fundamental principle: they put analysis into action. Here are the key factors that make for effective action plans.

### New Strategies—Change Your Teaching

If you don't change your teaching, results will not change. (Of course, change is only valuable if it is aligned to what students need—that involves quality analysis that we addressed in Chapter 2 on Analysis.) If an action plan calls only for a continuation of the status quo, then it is a waste of time and resources since more of the same will not yield different results. Bottom line: action plans target student gaps with new teaching.

### Every Second Used—Whole-Class, Small Group and Individual

Action plans utilize every format of class: teaching to the whole class and targeted re-teaching to small groups and individuals. This allows us to teach students not what they already know but what they need. Any and all suggested changes should be clearly marked with a date and a time for implementation; if a plan is made without a specific and well-defined time for action, then it will probably be neglected due to the perpetual competing demands for a teacher's time.

### Spiraled Review

Most learning is not like riding a bike. As a case in point, think about a class that you took in high school or college that you no longer use (like AP Calculus for non-math teachers). If you took a final exam on that course, you likely wouldn't do very well. If you don't use it, you lose it.

## Core Idea

If you don't use it, you lose it.
Spiral the content to strengthen knowledge retention.

Thus, the most effective teachers and schools consistently spiral previous content within each week so that students maintain their mastery. They do so by including questions on previous standards in their Do Nows (opening class activities), content reviews, in-class assignments, and homework.

## Data-Driven Success Story

### Leonore Kirk Hall Elementary School, Dallas, TX

The Results

**Figure 3.2**   Texas State Assessment: Leonore Kirk Hall Elementary School, Math Percentage at or Above Proficiency

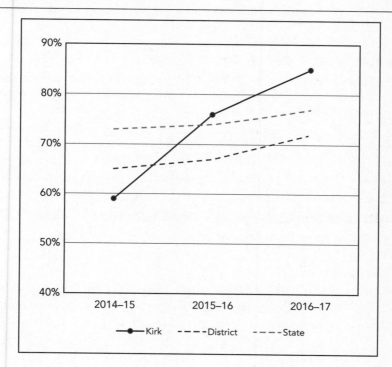

The Story

Adriana Gonzalez faced significant challenges when she took over as principal of struggling Lenore Kirk Hall Elementary School. Two-thirds of the staff had left, leaving her with nearly half of her staff being new to teaching altogether. It would take her years to develop this staff into accomplished teachers, but her students didn't have that kind of time.

At first, Adriana tried to implement what she had read in *Driven by Data*. "I had read the book and tried to create systems for data-driven instruction. But I didn't make much progress until I started to practice." Adriana found a cohort of fellow principals at the Teaching Trust, and she started rehearsing her conversations with teachers and her weekly data meetings. What was originally unnatural became a strength.

"When you are trying to change a culture, it is so important for your staff to feel like it's worth it. Those data meetings were a place where teachers realized that if they simply focus on one standard until students got it, the learning was better. That made the lightbulb turn on."

Adriana made sure that every teacher was using a "Demonstration of Learning" (what Doug Lemov calls an exit ticket) to measure whether or not students learned at the end of every lesson. She led PD for her staff on the two different types of re-teaching lessons: guided discourse or modeling. And every meeting ended with the teachers practicing one of those re-teach lessons. Slowly but surely the quality of teaching improved, and learning followed.

As the years went on, more of the teachers stepped into leadership roles on their teams. At first, Adriana led all the weekly data meetings at each grade level herself, but as her staff internalized the process, she turned them over to coaches and grade-level leaders. Data-driven instruction had become a culture that wasn't strange: it was just how you should teach.

Mutual support has become the norm, Adriana says. "We all work to help each other."

---

### Key Drivers from Implementation Rubric

- *Ongoing assessment:* check for understanding every day: aggressive monitoring of independent work, questioning, and in-class assessments to ensure student progress between interim assessments.

- *Active leadership team:* facilitate teacher-leader meetings looking at student work (interim assessment analysis and weekly data) and monitor the follow-up.

- *Build by borrowing:* Identify and implement best practices from high-achieving teachers and schools: visit schools/classrooms, share and disseminate resources/strategies.

---

### Make Every Second in School Count by Bringing All Hands on Deck

When designing the academic calendar, school leaders should take into account time needed for the re-teaching that action plans might require. All efforts should be made to use every minute of school time for learning and growth. Indeed, creative data-driven schools have not shied from utilizing breakfast, lunch, and even hallway time as opportunities to teach and review. To make these efforts possible, consider how staff members in the school beyond just the teachers can support the process. With the proper coordination and training, secretaries, parent volunteers, teacher aides, and other adults can provide many of these in-school supports.

## Align After-School Tutoring

Most schools have some sort of after-school tutoring program, but the tutors often do not have guidance on how to support the students other than helping them with their homework. The simple act of sharing assessment results with tutors and showing them the goals for each of their students can immediately double the impact of tutoring efforts.

Here is a template that summarizes the keys from each sample above:

## Action Plan Template
### Results Analysis

| RE-TEACH STANDARDS: What standards need to be re-taught to the whole class? | ANALYSIS: Why didn't the students learn it? | INSTRUCTIONAL PLAN: What techniques will you use to address these standards? |
|---|---|---|
|  |  |  |

### Six-Week Instructional Plan

| WEEK 1 Dates _____ | WEEK 2 Dates _____ | WEEK 3 Dates _____ |
|---|---|---|
| Standards for Review/ Re-teach | Standards for Review/ Re-teach | Standards for Review/ Re-teach |
|  |  |  |
| New Standards | New Standards | New Standards |
|  |  |  |

| WEEK 4 Dates _____ | WEEK 5 Dates _____ | WEEK 6 Dates _____ |
|---|---|---|
| Standards for Review/ Re-teach | Standards for Review/ Re-teach | Standards for Review/ Re-teach |
| | | |
| New Standards | New Standards | New Standards |
| | | |

### Individual/Small Group Work

| Which standards need targeted small group or individual re-teaching plans? | Students to be targeted: |
|---|---|
| | |
| | |
| | |

Effective action plans drive results. Yet a few questions remain to guarantee their impact:

- What does effective re-teaching look like?
- How do you develop teachers and leaders to sharpen their skills in making effective action plans?

Let's answer these questions one at a time.

## ACTION IN THE CLASSROOM: EFFECTIVE RE-TEACHING

Here, we'll address the two key components of successful classroom action: planning how to re-teach standards students still haven't mastered, and monitoring their progress on the ground.

# Data-Driven Success Story

## Cohen College Prep, New Orleans, Louisiana

The Results

**Figure 3.3** Louisiana End of Course (EOC) Test: Cohen College Prep High School, Percentage at or Above Proficiency

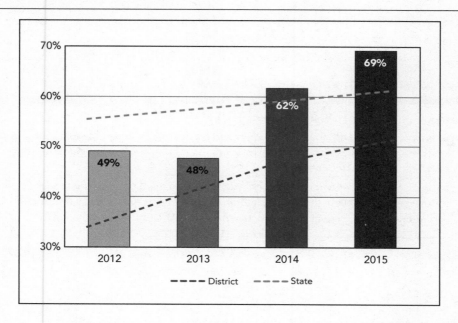

The Story

"We have enough to know there's a fire," Rahel Wondwossen thought after multiple years of unsatisfying results at Cohen College Prep in New Orleans. Growth at Cohen had already been stagnant for some time, and it faltered even more when students were tested to new, higher state standards. Rahel's solution? "My teachers just weren't getting enough time with the content," she says. So Rahel pulled out her calendar and got to work: time for data-driven instruction became a cornerstone.

At first, Rahel's staff was anxious about spending more time analyzing data, worrying: "Are we just going to start testing for the sake of testing?" But Rahel was sure frequent data analysis was right for their students, and she shared her conviction with her team. "We read a lot of research that showed that the way we'd been teaching—just teach all these units and they'll come together at the end—wasn't effective," says Rahel. She also remembers the consistency of belief she had to demonstrate to her staff, describing her approach as "a believe-it-until-it's-true" type of leadership.

Rahel's grit began paying off when her teachers administered their second interim assessment of that year. The improvement in student results between the first and second interim assessments—a period of time during which Rahel felt she never stopped holding her breath—built buy-in by demonstration. Teachers began taking the initiative to point out which students were struggling and with which standards, which led to the natural follow-up of teachers being invested in re-teaching what students hadn't mastered. "That was a defining moment for our school," Rahel says.

From there, Rahel's systemized the actions that were making her students successful. She maintained the data-driven instruction cycle relentlessly and issued biweekly assessments that set the groundwork for two-week action plans. Her teachers' mantra became: "What are we going to do, how will we know if it was successful, and how will we reassess?" That recipe for success continues to transform students' lives at Cohen.

## Key Drivers from Implementation Rubric

- *Six-week action plans:* execute plans that include whole-class instruction, small groups, tutorials, and before/after-school supports.

- *Ongoing assessment:* check for understanding every day: aggressive monitoring of independent work, questioning, and in-class assessments to ensure student progress between interim assessments.

- *Implementation calendar:* begin school year with a detailed calendar that includes time for assessment creation/adaptation, interim assessment analysis, weekly data meetings, and re-teaching (flexible enough to accommodate district mandates/changes).

## Re-Write Lesson Plans with Assessment Analysis in Mind

Often, an action plan is created in school (either individually or with a grade level team) and then stored in some sort of assessment binder. If teachers do their lesson planning at home (which is often the case), those action plans can often be vague memories at the time of planning. Effective schools make sure teachers have their analysis/assessment in hand when they are doing their planning! One example can be seen in this ninth grade English teacher's plans. She was focused on improving her student's ability to do characterization, so she planned a lesson for the novel they were reading, *The Color Purple*. Here is the assignment that reflects that objective:

## The Color Purple

### Reading Response Journal

For the *last* letter in this section, answer our four comprehension questions:

1. Whom is the letter from and to?
2. What happens in the letter?
3. What is the writer feeling?
4. What happened since the last letter?

Complete the characterization grid for any character in this section *except Celie*:

| Event | Inference about Character Explanation |
|---|---|
| | |
| | |

---

Whenever you design a new lesson, start by designing the in-class assessment (an exit ticket or assignment) that aligns to your end-goal assessment, and then plan the teaching that will get them there.

## Re-Teaching—Two Types

After traveling the country observing effective teachers, I began to realize that most re-teaching boils down to one of two strategies: modeling (teacher-driven) or guided discourse (teacher-facilitated)—with many variations within each.

Modeling, also called the "I Do," the "Think Aloud," or even the "Mini-lesson," is characterized by the teacher showing the students what to do. Guided discourse does the opposite. Often called "Inquiry," class discussion, or "Show-Call," guided discourse's goal is to guide student discussion to get the students to figure out the error themselves and coach each other to success.

Most instructors I've conferred with have a strong opinion as to which is more effective. The strongest teachers, however, use both methods, matching them to the needs of the students and the strengths of their teaching. Based on the guidance of teachers like these, here is a quick summary of some of the pros and cons for each approach that can help determine which method is the most appropriate with regard to specific student needs:

## Modeling vs. Guided Discourse

| Teaching method | Pros | Cons |
|---|---|---|
| Modeling | • Easier to plan<br>• If students don't have a model of success to refer to, they likely won't be able to replicate success<br>• Clarity: there are clear bright lines around what students must do | • Can be too procedural, as opposed to conceptual<br>• Dependent upon students learning passively at first |
| Guided discourse | • Stickier, since students learn more actively and do more of the thinking<br>• Easier to dig deeper on a conceptual level | • Harder to plan, as it's dependent on excellent questions and ability to manage the discourse<br>• Dependent on some students being close enough to push remaining students the rest of the way<br>• Can result in only the most advanced students understanding |

In sum, modeling is a better option for a newer teacher who is still working on classroom management and also for re-teaching when there's no exemplar answer in the classroom for students to turn to. If there is already an existing exemplar they can use to define what success looks like, guided discourse can often go deeper.

Let's take a closer look at how re-teaching functions on the ground, beginning with modeling.

### Re-Teaching—Modeling

On the surface, modeling is simple: show the students what to do. Effective modeling, however, takes that simple idea and adds much more depth—not only at younger grades, but for older students as well. In this video, Art Worrell from North Star Washington Park High School shows us what this looks like in his AP U.S. History class:

▶ WATCH Clip 7: Re-Teach Modeling. Set the Listening Task

▶ WATCH Clip 8: Re-Teach Modeling–Model the Thinking

●

## Stop and Jot

What does Art do to model the thinking for his students?

_____
_____
_____
_____
_____
_____
_____

In a few moments, Art took a complex skill—unpacking the previous knowledge that can be ascertained from the prompt—and made it simple. Moreover, he made sure the students were set up to maximally benefit from the model. Here are the key strategies Art used:

- **Clear listening/note-taking task:** Art gives students a clear listening or note-taking task that fosters active listening of the model. Then he debriefs the model, asking: "What did I do in my model?" and "What are the key things to remember when you are doing the same in your own work?"

- **Model the thinking, not just the procedure:** What makes Art's model different than many is that he models the thinking it takes to solve the problem, not just a rote procedure. Narrow the focus of the model to highlight the thinking students are struggling with, and then demonstrate replicable thinking steps that students can follow. Students will then learn how to think, not just act. That will enable them to take on a much broader set of future problems rather than becoming procedural.

- **End with You Do:** Of course, a model is only valuable if students then get the opportunity to apply it.

### Re-Teaching—Guided Discourse

As the alternative to modeling, guided discourse is often seen as the part of a lesson where the magic happens, with students engaging in rigorous dialogue and independently reaching deep, thoughtful conclusions. Yet it's all too easy for guided discourse to take place without that magic taking hold. As one teacher shared with me, discourse can be like a squirrel—you never know quite where it is headed, and it can run up the wrong tree really quickly! So how do you get that squirrel of discourse to run up the right tree?

Andrew Shaefer shows us an example of how to do this. Andrew worked with Juliana Worrell at Alexander Street Elementary School in Newark, NJ, where the most successful school turnaround in Newark took place: their results are truly groundbreaking (see Alexander Street success story below).

## Data-Driven Success Story

## Alexander Street Elementary School, Newark, New Jersey

### The Results

**Figure 3.4**   New Jersey PARRC Assessment: Alexander Street Elementary School, Math and ELA Percentage at or Above Proficiency

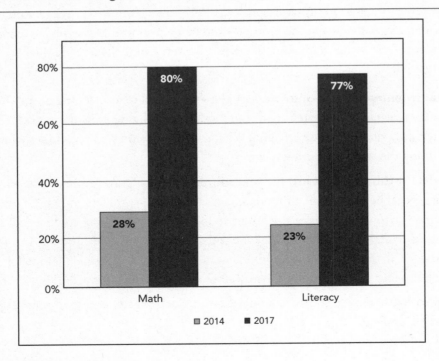

## The Story

Juliana Worrell was already a successful principal in Newark, New Jersey, when the call came. Would she be willing to leave her elementary school—which had some of the highest results in the state on the New Jersey state test—and take over Alexander Street Elementary School, which was one of the lowest-performing schools in New Jersey? Only a mile separated them geographically, but the two schools could not have been more different. "I remember our first conversations with the parents," Juliana recalls, "and they didn't really believe any change would happen. At first, they were more concerned about not losing the status quo."

Juliana accepted the challenge, and Alexander Street's transformation began. She immediately implemented not only six-week interim assessments but also weekly review of student performance in both reading and math. They utilized the data on leveled reading assessments to create targeted guided reading groups, and they relentlessly monitored student writing on every in-class task to see what the students were getting right and where they needed more support. The math teachers built a curriculum and embedded the standards from previous grade levels that the students had never mastered while still teaching that grade level's standards as well.

Above all else, Juliana maintained a relentless schedule of meeting with teachers about their student data and adjusting their lesson plans every week to close students' gaps. She was always observing class to support the teachers in implementation. She would not just watch the teacher but walk around the room, looking at student work and giving teachers a tip if she noticed an error in student work that they could address.

The results are one of the strongest turnaround success stories in the country. Visitors from all across the country have come to observe the transformation and learn from Juliana's actions. "It's all about how you use your time as a leader," states Juliana. "If you focus every day on whether or not students learned, you make an additional step, and after a year the results can be amazing."

## Key Drivers from Implementation Rubric

- *Re-teach:* use guided discourse or modeling strategies to re-teach difficult standards.

- *Ongoing assessment:* check for understanding every day: aggressive monitoring of independent work, questioning, and in-class assessments to ensure student progress between interim assessments.

- *Follow-up/accountability:* instructional leaders review lesson and unit plans and give observation feedback driven by the action plan and student learning needs.

In the video clip here, you'll see part of what made them so successful. As the clip begins, 50% of Andrew's class has gotten the wrong answer to a question on a fraction of a whole. Watch what Andrew does to drive discussion:

▶ WATCH Clip 9: Re-Teach Guided Discourse

● 

**Stop and Jot**

How does Andrew guide his students to generate the answer themselves?

_____
_____
_____
_____
_____
_____

- **Write first, talk second:** Before beginning the discourse, Andrew has students complete a task on their own. That allows him to monitor, collect data, and anticipate where the conversation will go. It will also give him the opportunity to determine which students have strong answers or which are struggling so he can call on them at key moments during the discussion. Let 100% of the class participate before you begin the discussion!

- **Show-Call:** Andrew starts the discourse with one simple move that changes everything. Instead of talking, he simply displays two samples of student work. Think about the power of this action: he reduced his language significantly, and he shifted all of the thinking back to the students. Doug Lemov, author of *Teach Like a Champion*, calls this Show-Call.[1] You can do this with exemplar student responses, incorrect responses, or, as Andrew does here, with both.

- **Turn and Talk, then poll the room:** Rather than begin with large-group discussion, Andrew starts with a Turn and Talk. Turn and Talk maximizes the number of students who are sharing during discussion, letting everyone work their thoughts out verbally with a peer before sharing in the large group. Andrew then takes it one step further by polling the room to see where the class stands before starting the discussion. In this way, he has an immediate idea of where students are—or, in other words, what tree that squirrel is rushing toward. This allows him to make an informed decision about how to manage the conversation.

- **Strategic questioning:** Once the class comes together for a large group discussion, Andrew uses the data he collected from the writing task and classroom poll to call on students based on their learning need. In this case, everyone agreed with the right answer after the Turn and Talk, so Andrew can call on a student who initially had the wrong answer to check for understanding to make sure they know why. If most of the class was still struggling, he could call on someone who had the right answer initially to justify their response. Strategic questioning allows Andrew to reduce the likelihood of haphazard conversation and get students grappling with the key learning challenge.

- **End with You Do:** Just as with modeling, guided discourse doesn't get solidified until students get the opportunity to try it again on their own.

## Ongoing Assessment—Monitor Student Work to Catch the Error in the Moment

Learning doesn't happen in a single moment—it happens over time. That's why active monitoring of student learning in the classroom is as important as the re-teaching itself. When you are learning to master something, like a piece of music on the piano, you start by learning the basic chords, and then you add intonation and complexity to create a beautiful sound. That doesn't happen overnight, and re-teaching doesn't either.

Denarius Frazier is a highly successful math teacher at Uncommon Collegiate High School in Brooklyn, New York. Denarius discovered quickly that a single successful re-teaching lesson didn't seal the deal for his students. "I needed to follow up for multiple days to see if they retained it," he recalls. "Only when they can utilize linear equations consistently in each upcoming unit do I know they have mastered it." Denarius stumbled on a crucial idea: re-teaching is a marathon, not a sprint.

---

### Core Idea

Re-teaching is a marathon, not a sprint.

---

Any re-teaching that ends after a single day won't lead to long-term success: you might have won that leg, but you haven't won the race. Monitoring means collecting data on an ongoing basis: paying attention to whether the students learned what the teacher taught, and doing that over and over again.

That's where aggressive monitoring during independent practice comes in. Bring up the subject of monitoring independent practice, and the image that typically comes to mind is of a teacher standing at the front of the classroom, scanning simply to make sure students are quiet and focused. But the limitation of this model is that it doesn't really show you whether students are doing quality work. Shift to aggressive monitoring, and independent practice becomes the rare opportunity to give students high quality feedback in a large group setting. Monitoring aggressively is about making independent practice the single most critical time for you as a teacher to change learning outcomes for your students. The keys are:

1. Create a monitoring pathway that enables you to get to as many students as possible during independent work (which means delivering feedback more swiftly).

2. Track student answers so that you can use them to inform your next teaching moves.

3. Give students immediate feedback.

---

### The Audible: Immediate Action in the Classroom

*Too often schools undervalue the importance of acting quickly on assessment analysis. No matter how well you plan your lesson and teach the standard, moments will come when students do not learn effectively. Football coaches know this well.*

*When a less experienced quarterback is at the helm of a football team, generally the coach plans a series of plays in advance of the game and calls all of the plays himself. Even if the quarterback notices something about the defense (e.g., they are planning on blitzing) that will cause the play to fail, they won't be able to make an adjustment on that play and will wait until the next down—or even half-time—to consider a more effective strategy. Great quarterbacks, however— from Peyton Manning to to Aaron Rodgers to the newest generation—are empowered to make "audibles:" on-the-spot changes to the play based on what they read in the defense. This adds incredible versatility to a football team and makes them much more difficult to defend.*

*Using the strategies listed above quickens the feedback loop and allows you to check for understanding consistently between each interim assessment. Teachers are essentially making more "audibles," which, if applied effectively, will lead to student learning in their classroom.*

---

Monitoring isn't a common practice while students are working independently—too often, an instructor's inclination is to take a back seat during independent work, or to spend all their time working with one or two struggling students. To show what it looks like to change the game, we've included a brief teaching clip of Sari Fromson monitoring student work during a lesson on area. Watch how she executes all of these key steps in just a few brief minutes:

  WATCH Teaching Clip 10: Aggressive Monitoring – Teaching Clip

On the surface, this looks similar to any class. Beneath the surface, however, a number of extraordinary things are happening. In the brief minutes of the clip, Sari has not only checked every student's work, she has marked it correct or incorrect, prompted students to fix areas of growth (without giving them the answer!), and she's even gotten back to some of the students for a second round of feedback! As importantly, the monitoring sends a great message to the students: I am watching your work, and I'm really happy to see your effort. That sends such a powerful message of valuing learning that makes students even more on task during independent practice. No wonder Sari's students ended up in the top 1% of New York State (and then she replicated that success when she moved to Boston)![2]

Here are the steps that the highest achieving teachers take to create a monitoring pathway this effective.

- **Choose the two or three students you will support first (hint: the fastest writers).** When monitoring independent work, most teachers go straight to the students who tend to have the most trouble with the content. But if the goal is to give *all* students powerful feedback, a better approach is to go first to the fastest writers, regardless of their learning level. Why? Because they'll have something for you to give them feedback on when you get to them. Then, by the time you get to the slower writers, they'll have something written down as well. Identifying those two or three first quick writers to coach, and going straight to them when independent work time begins, enables a teacher to get to far more students than he or she could otherwise do in the same amount of time. And giving as many students individual attention as possible maximizes both the instructional impact of a teacher's monitoring *and* the teacher's ability to keep everyone on task.

- **Create a seating chart that will make getting to all students as easy as possible.** By creating a data-driven seating chart that places the students in an order that mirrors the order in which you need to reach students when you monitor, you can save yourself valuable steps and time when you need them the most. Here's a sample image that reflects how you might cluster the students you need to reach first. The students are numbered according to their achievement (#1 is the highest achieving on the latest assessment; #30 is the lowest) (Figure 3.5).

**Figure 3.5**

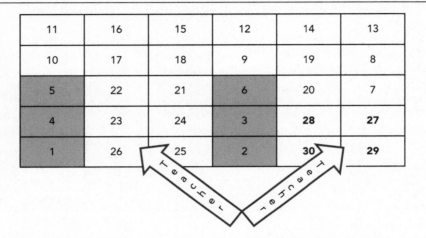

You could organize your students in any way you'd like. This particular arrangement pairs up the highest achievers with the most struggling students when they do pair work, and it puts those struggling students up front where the teacher can teach them most easily. Just as importantly, the teacher can quick scan the first and fourth rows and see how the highest students are doing and quickly scan the right corner to see how the lowest students are doing. This makes it easier to identify patterns in student responses.

- **Position yourself so you can still scan the remainder of the room for responsiveness.** From the right spot in the room, a teacher can tell whether all students are writing even at the same time as he or she gives in-depth feedback to an individual student. The keys are to position the teacher around the perimeter of the room as much as possible to make sure she or he is facing most of the students. This way, at any moment the teacher can poke his or her head up, see most of the students right away, and redirect any who aren't focused on the assignment.

In conjunction with aggressive monitoring, here are four core strategies instructors like Denarius and Sari use to monitor learning day-by-day:

- **Monitor independent practice.** By circulating when students do independent work and reading their responses, Sari can quickly see what they're able to do on their own.

- **Spiral content within lessons.** Denarius takes students back to previously-covered material when they struggle, working to discover where their knowledge is breaking down—and to make sure they're remembering what he's already taught.

- **Small-group work.** What do students say to each other in pairs or small groups as compared to in a whole-class discussion? Denarius finds that the answers are incredibly revealing.

- **Adjust Exit Tickets, Do Nows, or homework.** When necessary, Sari adjusts her assignments to her students both during and after class so that their work will show her what she needs to know about their learning.

## Student Engagement: Taking Action into Their Own Hands

The strategies mentioned up to this point guide leaders and teachers to making effective action. We would be remiss if we did not discuss the actions that should be taken by the most integral members of the data-driven process: the students themselves. In a truly effective data-driven school, students will be co-participants in improving their own learning.[3] Simply put, students need to know where they're headed and what it will take to get there.

> ### Core Idea
>
> Data-driven student engagement occurs when students know the end goal, how they did, and what actions they can take to improve.

Williamsburg Collegiate School in New York City has one of the most effective student engagement templates that I have seen. Consider the first and last page of their template shown below:

# Student Reflection Template

## Williamsburg Collegiate Charter School

| Questions | Standard/Skill: What skill was being tested? | Did you get the question right or wrong? | | Why did you get the question wrong? Be honest. | |
|---|---|---|---|---|---|
| | | Right | Wrong | Careless mistake | Didn't know how to solve |
| 1 | Algebra substitution: add | | | | |
| 2 | Algebra substitution: add 3 numbers | | | | |
| 3 | Algebra substitution: subtract | | | | |
| 4 | Translate word problems | | | | |
| 5 | Solve equations | | | | |
| 6 | Elapsed time—find end time | | | | |
| 7 | Elapsed time—find elapsed time | | | | |
| 8 | Elapsed time—word problem | | | | |
| 9 | Elapsed time—word problem | | | | |
| 10 | Elapsed time—word problem | | | | |

Using your test reflections, please fill out the following table:

| Type of Error | Careless Errors | Did Not Know How to Solve |
|---|---|---|
| Number of errors | | |

| If you have. . . | You are a. . . | In class you. . . | During class you should. . . | During assessments you should. . . |
|---|---|---|---|---|
| More careless errors than "don't know's". . . | RUSHING RABBIT | • are one of the first students to finish the independent practice<br>• want to say your answer before you write it<br>• often don't show work<br>• get assessments back and are frustrated | • SLOW DOWN!<br>• ask the teacher to check your work or check with a partner<br>• push yourself for perfection, don't just tell yourself "I get it."<br>• take time to slow down and explain your thinking to your classmates<br>• keep track of your mistakes, look to see if you keep making the same ones over and over | • SLOW DOWN. You know you tend to rush, make yourself slow down<br>• REALLY double-check your work (since you know you tend to make careless errors)<br>• use inverse operations when you have extra time |
| More "don't know's" than careless errors | BACK-SEAT BADGER | • not always sure that you understand how to do independent work<br>• are sometimes surprised by your quiz scores | • ask questions about the previous night's homework if you're not sure it's perfect<br>• do all of the problems with the class at the start of class<br>• use every opportunity to check in with classmates and teachers to see if you're doing problems correctly | • do the problems you're SURE about first<br>• take your time on the others and use everything you know<br>• ask questions right after the assessment while things are still fresh in your mind |

**Are you a Rushing Rabbit?** Then answer question #1:

1. In your classwork and homework, if you notice you keep making similar careless errors, what should you do?

**Are you a Backseat Badger?** Then answer question #2.

2. When you get a low score on a quiz, what should you do?

Clearly, this exercise allows students to share ownership in their improvement process. As a related activity, students can be asked to chart their performance throughout the year and to offer explanations as to why their results showed the trends they did. Doing so is not only a challenging and relevant math exercise, but it also allows schools to reinforce the central principle that academic achievement is everyone's responsibility. As a result, no effective action strategy is complete without including students in the mechanics of data-driven instruction.

## Data-Driven Success Story

## Northwest Middle School, Salt Lake City, Utah

The Results

**Figure 3.6** Utah State SAGE Assessment: Northwest Middle School, Math Percentage at or Above Proficiency

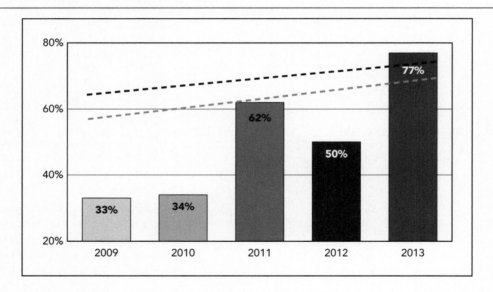

The Story
Northwest Middle School was Brian Conley's second school as a principal, but it was his first school after learning from *Driven by Data*. He saw need at Northwest—but more notably, he saw hope. "Northwest was a very low-achieving school," Brian remembers. "Between 90 and 95% of our students were on free or reduced lunch and 85% were students of color. There were twenty-eight

languages spoken in the different homes of our students. All I could think of was that reservoir of potential that was waiting to be tapped into. I saw right away a lot of character in kids, but it was character that wasn't being embraced, wasn't being cultivated." Brian's next step? Start with his staff to cultivate the potential in their students.

"I just went in with a lot of data about Northwest and tried to find anything positive I could tell them," Brian says. Despite Northwest's overall low performance, female students at Northwest were earning high math scores, and Pacific Islander students' scores had risen by a significant degree in the past three years. If they could succeed, argued Brian, other students could as well. Not all of Brian's team was convinced right away. "I had some teachers buy in," Brian recalls. "I had some look at me like I didn't know what I was talking about, but they weren't closed off to it. Then there were a few who were actively against the efforts I had planned. They'd say, 'Our kids can't do that. The test is written for white kids.'"

Brian stayed the course and started small. He recalls repeatedly telling staff: "We don't need to get it perfect right now, we just need to get *in* right now." Data-driven instruction was the key to getting in. Teachers started looking at student work and determining what NEEDED to be taught differently. "All of a sudden it wasn't about what we should teach, it was all focused on what students learned and how we knew. That was really powerful."

What also changed the culture of Northwest was celebrating the successes students were experiencing. Brian opened celebrations of Northwest's achievements to the wider community around the school, inviting families to an evening presentation that showed how Northwest's results were improving. And as achievement started rising, teachers started pushing further, analyzing their assessments even more closely and building tighter action plans to re-teach difficult standards.

That's when, as Brian puts it, people started to have a different story to tell about Northwest. "Our community started to view this school in a new way," says Brian. "Local store owners started to come in and say that shoplifting was down, and they thought it was because of what we were doing. They saw a difference. Northwest wasn't where kids went to drop out of school anymore; it was where they went to do more in their community."

Brian sums up the secret of Northwest's success in four words: "Student learning is boss." His students are living proof that when student learning leads the way, it changes far more than just test scores.

## Key Drivers from Implementation Rubric

- *Engaged students* know the end goal, how they did, and what actions to improve.
- *Implementation calendar:* begin school year with a detailed calendar that includes time for assessment creation/adaptation, interim assessment analysis, weekly data meetings, and re-teaching (flexible enough to accommodate district mandates/changes).
- *Introductory professional development:* introduce teachers and leaders to data-driven instruction—understand how assessments define rigor, how to analyze student work, and how to adapt instruction.

In the context of school management, a great many things are easier said than done. Action will never be easy, but by employing the strategies necessary for effective student, teacher and school leader action, data-driven schools can ensure that their plans become reality.

## DATA MEETINGS, PART II: LOCKING IN QUALITY ACTION

We saw the power of Data Meetings in Chapter 2 to do effective deep analysis. The second part of the data meeting is where the magic happens: turning quality analysis into action. Let's see how that happens.

### Plan

Let's return to Juliana Worrell's data meeting, of which we saw the first few segments in Chapter 2. After Juliana and her team have cooperated in analyzing data, watch how they transition to crafting a plan for action.

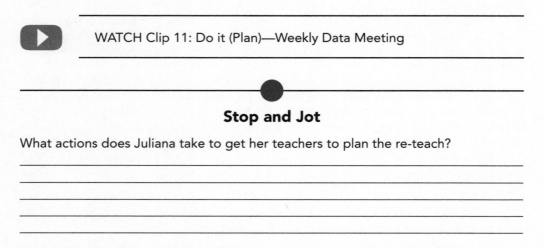

WATCH Clip 11: Do it (Plan)—Weekly Data Meeting

### Stop and Jot

What actions does Juliana take to get her teachers to plan the re-teach?

_____

_____

_____

_____

_____

_____

What Juliana leads her team to do—plan the re-teach—seems relatively straightforward. Yet most teams of teachers never get that far when analyzing student work. How Juliana goes about this is what makes her leadership so effective. Giving her teachers time first to plan independently actually saves time: they have already articulated their ideas before they speak! But the real magic is having them "spar" with another re-teach plan: that pushes them to excellence so much faster. You need to perfect a re-teach plan before you practice: if not, you'll just practice doing it wrong.

Juliana's teachers all have the opportunity to improve their re-teaching plan based on each other's. Bringing the focus to "what would you add?" to your plan ensures they focus on the most positive parts of the plan—the strongest elements of it. This way, they can combine their own strength as school leaders. Juliana uses some key prompts to get her teachers there that could be used in nearly any data meeting:

- Should we use modeling or guided discourse? Why?
- Take _____ minutes and write your script. I will do the same so we can spar.
- Let's compare our re-teach plans. What do you notice? What can we pull from each to make the strongest plan?

This doesn't just work for elementary school: watch how Denarius Frazier applies the same strategies to HS math:

WATCH Clip 12: Do it (Plan)—Weekly Data Meeting

## Practice

At this point, teachers are ready to put it all together. Watch how Mary Ann Stinson supports them to do so:

WATCH Clip 13: Do it (Practice)—Weekly Data Meeting

---

### Stop and Jot

What actions does Mary Ann take to facilitate effective practice? Jot down what you notice below.

_____

_____

_____

_____

_____

_____

_____

Note how natural practice is for Mary Ann and her teachers: as routine as any other part of the meeting. Rehearsing in this way may feel awkward at first, but develop it as an expectation with your teachers, and it will quickly become more comfortable for them (and for you!).

---

### Core Idea

Teachers will rise to the level of our expectations.
If we expect them to practice, they will.

---

Build a culture of practice, and practice will happen—and it will change your school. The "Do it" part of a meeting doesn't just work for literacy: it works for math as well. Watch as Laura Garza (See Success Story) leads a math weekly data meeting through plan and practice:

  WATCH Clip 14: Do It (Practice)—Weekly Data Meeting

In other situations, your teacher is working on balancing more effective re-teaching implementation while still mastering classroom management. Watch how Denarius coaches his teacher to focus on both:

  WATCH Clip 15: Do It (Practice)—Weekly Data Meeting

## Follow-Up

Once you've practiced, it's time to lock in the success you've just rehearsed. Watch how Mary Ann and Denarius make sure the re-teaching happens in the classroom once it's been practiced in the meeting.

 WATCH Clip 16: Do It (Follow-up)—Weekly Data Meeting

 WATCH Clip 17: Do It (Follow-up)—Weekly Data Meeting

Mary Ann and Denarius leave nothing to chance: they name how they'll follow up and the additional tasks that will help a teacher be ready to carry this out in their classroom.

Think of the power of what you just witnessed. In thirty minutes, these leaders' teaching teams deeply analyzed student work and came up with a concrete re-teach plan for a challenging standard. Now multiply that impact by the regular meetings that her teachers have at every grade level across the entire year. Not only do these meetings impact the assessment items that they directly tackle; they also build the habits of mind for teachers to repeat this process every day with student learning in their classrooms.

Juliana has truly shifted the focus from the teaching to the learning, and by doing so, she has raised expectations for everyone in school. Her results tell it all.

On the following pages, we've consolidated all the best practices of weekly data meetings into one precise, packed guide that you can use to lead data meetings yourself.

### Data Meetings

#### Leading Teacher Teams to Analyze Student Daily Work

| Prepare Before the Meeting | Prepare |
|---|---|
| | • **Materials ready:** student exemplar, teachers turn in student work, pull and categorize hi/med/lo student work (just a few of each), pull upcoming lesson plan(s) and pertinent prompting guides |

| | |
|---|---|
| | • **Prime the pump:** script the re-teach plan and the gap in student understanding; unpack the standard<br><br>• **Preview protocol with teachers:** assign roles, novice teachers speak first, veteran teachers add on and clarify, leader provides additional clarity at end, chart, preview the need for concision from more verbose team members, use of a timer, creation of note-taking template |
| **See It**<br>**13–18 min.** | **See Past Success, See the Exemplar,**<br>**and See and Analyze the Gap** |

**See Past Success (1 min.):**

• "Last week we planned to re-teach XX and we went from X% proficient to XX%. Nice job!"

• "What actions did you take to reach this goal?"

**See the Exemplar (8 min.):**
• Narrow the focus: "Today, I want to dive into [specific standard] and the following assessment item."

• Interpret the standard(s):
  ○ "Take 1 min.: in your own words, what should a student know or be able to do to show mastery?"

• Unpack the teacher's written exemplar:
  ○ "Take 1–2 min. to review the exemplar: What were the keys to an ideal answer?"
  ○ "How does this [part of the exemplar] align with the standard?"

• Analyze the student exemplar:
  ○ "Take 1 min.: How does your student exemplar compare to the teacher exemplar? Is there a gap?"
  ○ "Do students have different paths/evidence to demonstrate mastery of the standard?"
  ○ "Does the student exemplar offer something that your exemplar does not?"

**See the Gap (5 min.):**
• Move to the sample of un-mastered student work (look only at representative sample):
  ○ "Take 2 min.: What are the gaps between the rest of our student work and the exemplar?"
  ○ "Look back at our chart of the standard and exemplar: What are key misconceptions?"

| | |
|---|---|
| **Name It**<br>**2 min.** | **State the Error and Conceptual Misunderstanding** |
| | **Punch it—Stamp the Error and Conceptual Understanding:**<br><br>• "So our key area to re-teach is?":<br>  ○ Describe the conceptual understanding<br>  ○ (if needed) Describe the procedural gap (e.g., memorize multiplication tables) and/or missing habits (e.g. annotating text, showing work)<br><br>• Write down and/or chart the highest leverage action students will take to close the gap |
| **Do It**<br>**Rest of the**<br>**meeting** | **Plan the Re-teach, Practice, and Follow Up** |
| | **Plan the Re-teach (8–10 min.):**<br>• Select the re-teach structure:<br>  ○ "Should we use modeling or guided discourse?" "Why?"<br><br>• Select the task and identify exemplar response:<br>  ○ Select materials: task, text, student work to show-call, what to chart<br>  ○ "What is the ideal answer we want to see that will show we've closed the gap?"<br>  ○ (If needed—follow-up question): "What is the 'why' that students should be able to articulate?"<br><br>• Plan the re-teach:<br>  ○ "Take _____ minutes and write your script. I will do the same so we can spar."<br>    ▪ **If a model:** write the think aloud and questions<br>    ▪ **If guided discourse:** select student work for show-call, write prompts<br>  ○ "Let's compare our re-teach plans. What do you notice? What can we pull from each to make the strongest plan?" (Revise the plan)<br><br>• Plan the independent practice:<br>  ○ "What will you monitor to see if they are doing this correctly? What laps will you name?" |

| Do it (con't.) | **Practice the gap (remaining time):** |
|---|---|
| | "Let's practice." |
| |    ○ **If a model:** practice modeling the thinking, precision of language, and change in tone/cadence |
| |    ○ **If guided discourse:** practice show-call, prompting students, and stamping the understanding |
| |    ○ **If monitoring:** practice the laps, annotations, prompts when students are stuck, or stop the show |
| | • (If a struggle) "I'm going to model teach for you first. [Teach.] What do you notice?" |
| | • Repeat until the practice is successful. CFU: "What made this more effective?" |
| | • Lock it in: "How did our practice meet or enhance what we planned for the re-teach?" |
| | **Follow-up (last 2 min.):** |
| | • Set the follow-up plan: when to teach, when to re-assess, when to revisit this data |
| |    ○ Observe implementation within 24 hours; teacher sends re-assessment data to leader |
| | • Spiral: |
| |    ○ Identify multiple moments when teacher can continue to assess and track mastery: Do Now questions, homework, modified independent practice |
| | • Move to the lowest scoring work: |
| |    ○ "What students do we need to pull for tutoring? What do we need to remediate?" |
| |    ○ "How can we adjust our monitoring plan to meet the need of these students?" |

Data meetings create a fantastic, high-leverage opportunity to create and prepare to implement effective re-teaching action plans. The final step for a leader is to follow up to make sure the re-teaching happens effectively. Read on.

## ACCOUNTABILITY: FOLLOW UP ON ACTION PLANS

Every good plan is for naught if it isn't implemented. It's all too easy for even the most targeted action plans not to translate from the data meeting to the classroom. While data meetings can plan and practice re-teach lessons, effective school leaders don't leave the implementation to chance. They follow up and monitor to guarantee effective results.

Here are some of the most effective ways to make sure that action is happening.

## Follow-Up Systems for Instructional Leaders

### Posted Action Plans and Lesson Plans

When a leader typically observes a class, he/she can only see that moment in time. With one small shift—asking teachers to physically post their action plans in their classrooms—you can see far more. Keeping six-week plans publicly in the classroom allows you to see whether that lesson is aligned to the six-week plan. Having the lesson plans posted allows you to see what just happened in the minutes prior to your entry and what will happen when you leave, allowing you to see the trajectory of the lesson rather than a single point in time. You can also see how this lesson builds off of—or not—the previous day's lesson.

Laura Garza of Blanton Elementary School (see Success Story, Introduction) in Dallas, has mastered this strategy. When she prepared to observe a classroom, she would review the six-week action plan to see the area of focus. Then she would open up the original data spreadsheet to determine which students were struggling with particular standards. Then she would observe teacher questioning to see if those students were being given opportunities to practice that difficult standard. For example, in a third grade reading class, she noticed that during Read-Aloud the teacher predominantly asked basic comprehension questions, but that was a reading strategy the students had already mastered! Moreover, when she asked author's purpose questions, she unknowingly called on the students who had mastered that standard rather than on those who needed the extra help. Laura was able to jump in and prompt the teacher to use a different question and call on different students. The teacher was grateful to have another set of eyes looking for these issues, and she became more intentional in shaping and directing her questions.

Having the assessment analysis and action plans readily at hand when you observe is like putting on 3-D glasses! Leaders can observe both for implementation of those plans, and for whether the rigor of the classroom activities meets the rigor of the upcoming assessment. Such analysis for rigor is extremely difficult without a well-defined assessment as the guide.

> ## Core Idea
>
> Observing with action plans and lesson plans in hand is like putting on 3-D glasses: they enhance your vision to observe for rigor.

### Reflection Box with Lesson Plans

To make this ability to monitor re-teaching even easier, many schools have implemented a change to their lesson plan format to include a weekly "Reflection" box. Here is a sample from a ninth grade literacy class:

---

## Sample Lesson Plan Reflection Box

### Ninth Grade Literacy Lesson Plan

**Reflection**

Students continue to struggle with characterization. I think there's a twofold problem there. One issue is the level of vocabulary in the text and the prompts, and we're continually trying to close vocabulary deficits with direct vocabulary instruction, word parts, and vocabulary-in-context questions. The other problem is that we haven't addressed characterization as purposefully as necessary in the class novels. We're going to start that this week with a focus on characterization and draw on some inferencing skills when we begin *The Color Purple*. It seems authentic because Walker's work is so character-driven.

---

On a weekly basis, teachers can highlight any particular skills they are re-teaching based on their action plan.

Think of the power of this simple action. You build the habit of mind for your teachers to plan constantly with assessment analysis in mind, and you make it easy to spot-check when a teacher is not incorporating that habit into their planning!

### Observation Tracker

Many schools implement some sort of observation tracker: a tool where they track their observations of teachers. Often those are disconnected from the work of data-driven instruction. However, as we've seen in the above recommendations, observation can work hand-in-hand with data-driven instruction, and when doing so can drive even stronger results. One way to make the link intentional is to observe not only for teacher craft but also for learning. Leaders can make adjustments to their observation trackers to monitor re-teaching of key standards—and proficiency levels of the students on re-assessments—in addition to traditional monitoring of teaching techniques.

### Monthly Maps

To ensure action plans remain in motion, successful leaders incorporate them into their monthly maps—a calendar of key actions they need to take each month. We cover monthly maps in greater detail in Chapter 4 on Data-Driven Culture as well as in *Leverage Leadership 2.0*. This keeps each action on their radar as the time comes to take it.

## Building Follow-up into Teacher Meetings

Another way to manage the follow-up on action plans is to build it into every type of teacher meeting. Here are some examples:

- **Planning meetings:** If your teachers are meeting to build unit or lesson plans, you can super-charge that meeting simply by having the six-week re-teach plans in hand as a driving force of learning. By doing so, teachers will be planning with the end in mind and meet students where they are.

- **Weekly data meetings:** Earlier in this chapter we highlighted the role that follow-up can play in a weekly data meeting. You can take this one step further by starting each meeting reporting on the progress students made on the re-teach standard. This can and should be the foundation for the "See the Success" part of the meeting.

All of these follow up steps are captured in one place here:

| Accountability: Core Drivers | |
|---|---|
| **Locking in the Follow-up** | **INSTRUCTIONAL LEADER SYSTEMS:** |
| | **Posted Plans in Classrooms:** |
| | • Posted six-week re-teach action plans |
| | • Posted lesson plans |
| | **Lesson Plan Reflections:** |
| | • Reflection box on lesson plans to indicate where re-teaching is occurring |

| | |
|---|---|
| **Observation Tracker:**<br>• Place DDI actions in your observation tracker<br>**Monthly Maps:**<br>• Add actions to monthly map to monitor progress | |
| **MEETINGS:** | |
| **Lesson Plans:**<br>• Six-week plans and upcoming lesson plans at every teacher meeting<br>**Weekly Data Meetings:**<br>• Teacher shares classwork (tasks, quizzes, writing assessments, Do Nows and Exit Tickets) that address an action plan step | |

## IMPLEMENTATION: FIRST STEPS FOR TEACHERS AND LEADERS

A summary of the keys to effective action is listed here as part of the overall implementation rubric.

### Implementation Rubric

### Action

The rubric is intended to be used to assess the present state of data-driven action in your school. The rubric specifically targets interim assessments and the key drivers leading to increased student achievement.

4 = Exemplary implementation 3 = Proficient implementation 2 = Beginning implementation 1 = No implementation

| Action | |
|---|---|
| 1. **6-week action plans:** execute plans that include whole-class instruction, small groups, tutorials, and before/after-school supports | __/4 |
| 2. **Re-teach:** use guided discourse or modeling strategies to re-teach difficult standards | __/4 |

| Action | |
|---|---|
| 3. **Ongoing assessment:** check for understanding every day: aggressive monitoring of independent work, questioning, and in-class assessments to ensure student progress between interim assessments | __/4 |
| 4. **Engaged students:** know the end goal, how they did, and what actions to improve | __/4 |
| 5. **Follow-up/accountability:** instructional leaders review lesson and unit plans and give observation feedback driven by the action plan and student learning needs | __/4 |
| | TOTAL: __/20 |

What follows are the first steps that classroom teachers, school leaders, or multi-campus/district office leaders can take to put this into action.

## Level 1—Teachers

Three of the resources mentioned above are of the highest leverage for teachers:

- **Create your own six-week action plans:** Regardless of what systems your school has in place, you can develop your own 6-week action plans coming out of each major assessment. Use the templates in the Appendix in the DVD to replicate the actions described in this chapter: plan out the times for whole-class, small-group and individual re-teaching, including whatever time you can make work during other times of the day.

- **Action in the classroom—get better at re-teaching:** Work on improving the quality of your modeling, guided discourse, and monitoring. Watch the videos of effective practice in this book, and if you want to go deeper, use the Get Better Faster Scope & Sequence for rigor (located in the Appendix in the DVD). You can get a more complete coaching guide for these action steps in the book *Get Better Faster* (Bambrick-Santoyo, 2016), which breaks down how to improve teaching practice in the concrete ways that make the greatest difference for student achievement.

- **Student reflection template:** Implement the student reflection template from this chapter (also in the Appendix in the DVD) or create your own so that students are part of the data-driven process.

Each of those is available electronically on the DVD for your use. The most effective recommendation is to have these documents present while you lesson plan. Make sure you're addressing the standards in need of re-teaching, and enhance the quality of your teaching to match!

## Level 2—School-Based Leaders

Here is where all the previous chapters come together: effective assessments, analysis, and action plans are meaningless if they are not implemented. The most effective ways to ensure that teaching practice is changing to meet students' needs are:

- **Re-purpose PD to give teachers time to plan jointly:** Utilize professional development time to participate in data meetings and build effective action plans. It can take time to become comfortable with the protocol. To that end, we recommend that for your initial launch you have all results meetings run simultaneously with all faculty gathered together. That way you can identify best practices and nudge groups that need more guidance. Over time, the Data Meeting protocol can become a part of the fabric of team meetings looking at data.

- **Monitor the Lesson Plans and the Teaching for Action Plan implementation:** See above for details. The posted lesson plans and posted 6-week action plans are particularly powerful. Look for re-teaching in lesson plans, student notebooks, class materials, and the teaching itself. When you find best practices in one classroom, pass them on to other teachers.

- **Tighten re-teaching/support systems outside the classroom:** Are all staff members connected into the re-teaching process? Are there non-traditional staff members who could support individual students or small groups? Are Special Education teachers and ELL teachers following the same protocols as regular education teachers? Often schools overlook the natural connection between the work of these support staff members and the work around interim assessments.

## Level 3—District-Level or Multi-Campus Leaders

If districts have set up effective interim assessments and analysis structures, you have done what's most important to set up principals to lead the core elements of Action effectively. Your core work here is to "block and tackle:" keep everything else away from school leaders so they can focus on these elements. Some of the most important ways to do that are as follows:

- **Minimize requests to principals during interim assessment weeks:** Free up reporting requirements and off-site meetings during each interim assessment cycle so that principals can focus on their teachers during that time.

- **Join principals in doing building walkthroughs post-interim assessments to look for action plan implementation:** Join principals to analyze assessment data, observe analysis meetings, and walk around to see action plans being implemented in the classrooms.

- **Lead data meetings:** If data meetings are a new system in your district, lead by example by leading them yourself at the beginning of the year. LaKimbre Brown, an incredibly successful district leader in Lorraine, Ohio, recalls leading at least three data meetings at each of her schools when she first rolled out this system. That way, every school leader she worked with learned to lead data meetings that drove results.

- **Identify areas of strength to leverage best practices:** Often data-driven instruction focuses on areas of struggle. However, it's just as important to leverage your strengths. Look at the various schools and see which teachers/schools are performing most effectively. Ask those teachers and leaders to share their best practices and even lead professional development for others. Your role is to disseminate the practices that are working to reach a larger audience.

# Reflection and Planning

Take this opportunity to reflect upon Action at your own school or district. Answer the following questions:

- After reading this chapter, what are the key steps around Action that you are going to implement in your school (which can you realistically do)?

  _____

  _____

  _____

  _____

- Who are the key people in your school with whom you need to communicate this plan and have on board? How are you going to get them on board? What are you going to do when someone says no? (What's Plan B?)

  _____

  _____

  _____

  _____

- Set the key dates for each action step, write them here, and then put them in your personal agenda/calendar to hold yourself accountable for implementing these steps.

  _____

  _____

  _____

  _____

## Chapter 4

# A Data-Driven Culture: Clearing the Road for Rigor

Google "culture of high expectations," and you will find hundreds of articles devoted to the topic. More concretely, studies of high-achieving schools often talk about the influence of "culture" or "shared vision" in their success.[1] One such study is Jon Saphier's research on strong adult professional culture. In his 2015 article "Strong Adult Professional Culture—The Indispensable Ingredient for Sustainable School Improvement," he noted among the top factors for strong adult culture are:

- deep collaboration and deliberate design for interdependent work and joint responsibility for student results;

- non-defensive self-examination of teaching practice in relation to student results;

- constant use of data to re-focus teaching.

Clearly by simply creating the structures for weekly data meetings established in the previous chapters, you are laying the groundwork for a strong data-driven culture!

Yet the question remains: how does your entire staff become invested in this culture? If high-achieving schools have a strong culture of high expectations, what are the drivers that create that culture?

In traveling around the country, I have yet to meet a teacher or school leader who did not believe they had high expectations for student learning—but not all of those educators saw the same extraordinary results. The difference is not in what is said but what is practiced.

Just as standards are meaningless until you define how to assess them, working to build a data-driven culture is fruitless until you define the concrete drivers that guarantee it. Once you do so, however, you won't need to build buy-in for data-driven instruction: your implementation of these drivers will create it for you. This chapter will show how.

## Data-Driven Success Story

## Achievement First, New York City, New York

The Results

**Figure 4.1** New York State Exam: Achievement First Middle Schools, ELA Percentage at or Above Proficiency

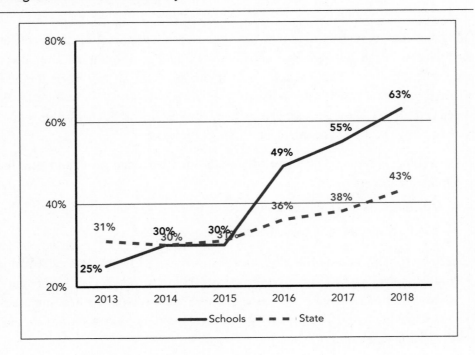

**Figure 4.2** New York State Exam: Achievement First Middle Schools, Math Percentage at or Above Proficiency

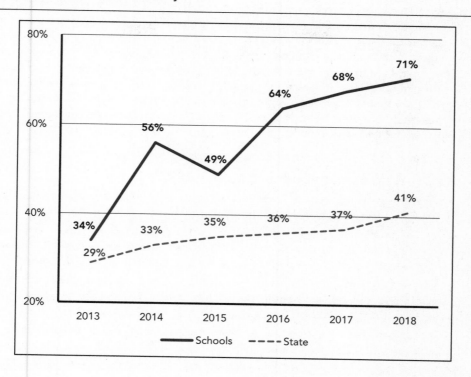

### The Story

When the state of New York raised the bar of their state tests in 2012, student achievement plummeted, especially at schools with high percentages of students who qualified for free/reduced lunches, like Achievement First East New York and Apollo middle schools. Like most schools across the state, they struggled to teach students to a higher bar. Chi Tschang, the regional superintendent, knew he had to make a change. "The more I immersed myself in the failure of our schools, the more I realized that the lessons we were offering to students simply weren't rigorous enough. We had to start over from scratch."

He started by giving a focus to each quarter of the year. The first quarter was devoted to student culture—laying the groundwork for learning to occur. The second quarter, with the results of the first interim assessment in hand, turned to the launch of weekly data meetings and a focus on aggressive monitoring (monitoring student work during class and coaching students during independent practice to improve). "I found that when we focused on one thing at a time," Chi recalled, "it brought a clarity to the work. With so much on a principal's plate, having a singular purpose made the daily life easier to manage." The third quarter shifted to leading discourse with students that responded to student learning needs, and the fourth quarter put it all together in what Chi calls "Crescendo." Having this yearly calendar set in place dramatically changed the quality of what principals were doing each day to drive student learning.

Particularly in the second quarter, the school leaders shifted from asking teachers to fill out data analysis plans and plan re-teaching on their own to diving into weekly data meetings. The school leadership teams met to plan the weekly data meetings for every grade, focused on the key standards that would unlock the learning for the week. Before the start of the 2nd and 3rd quarters Chi led a "Triathlon" where every instructional leader had to practice leading data meetings and observation and feedback meetings to perfect their skill.

The result: consistent, remarkable gains in achievement over a five-year period that made them the highest gaining schools and among the highest-achieving schools in all of New York. When praised about his success, Chi was quick to credit others. "I didn't figure this out on my own. I learned from others who had implemented *Driven by Data* and *Leverage Leadership*. I thank them for their impact on us."

---

## Key Drivers from Implementation Rubric

- *Active leadership team:* facilitate teacher-leader meetings looking at student work (interim assessment analysis and weekly data) and monitor the follow-up.
- *Implementation calendar:* begin school year with a detailed calendar that includes time for assessment creation/adaptation, interim assessment analysis, weekly data meetings, and re-teaching (flexible enough to accommodate district mandates/changes).
- *Ongoing professional development:* PD calendar is aligned with data-driven instructional plan: includes student work analysis, action planning and learning how to teach content.
- *Build by borrowing:* Identify and implement best practices from high-achieving teachers and schools: visit schools/classrooms, share and disseminate resources/strategies.

---

## Building Buy-in

Earlier in this book, we rejected the notion that initial faculty buy-in was required before starting to implement data-driven instruction. (One could potentially argue that any initiative that requires complete buy-in prior to implementation will likely fail.) The best initiatives in schools—and elsewhere—do not require buy-in; they create it. In fact, the Camden County, Georgia School District published a very persuasive article about the phases of data-driven instruction. It illustrated how teachers in their district moved from Stage 1 to Stage 5:

- **Phase 1 Confusion and overload:** "This is too much!"

- **Phase 2 Feeling inadequate and distrustful:** "How can two questions on a test possibly establish mastery of an objective? These questions are terrible!"

- **Phase 3 Challenging the test:** "That is a poor question. Answer 'b' is a trick answer."

- **Phase 4 Examining the results objectively and looking for causes:** Which students need extra help and in what topic? Which topics do I need to re-teach in different ways?

- **Phase 5 Accepting data as useful information, seeking solutions, and modifying instruction:** "Their inability to subtract negative integers affected their ability to solve the algebraic equation. I need to re-visit the concept of negative numbers and how to use them."[2]

Rather than hoping that teachers will enjoy the process from the very beginning, school leaders should anticipate that it will take various phases from everyone to see the value of data-driven instruction.

---

### Core Idea

Any initiative that requires buy-in from the beginning will fail.
When done well, data-driven instruction doesn't require buy-in: it creates it.

---

The article from Camden County, Georgia, is one of the few articles that discusses the hurdles and challenges that occur early on in the implementation of data-driven instruction. If you would like to look at an even more concrete example, read the case study included in the DVD about Douglass Street School. While the names were changed to allow for a candid sharing of the details, the case study is a true story and can give more insight into how schools make dramatic gains in achievement despite initial resistance.

Much of what builds an effective data-driven culture is embedded with the drivers of Assessment, Analysis, and Action. This chapter focuses on the remaining explicit structures that build buy-in and guarantee an effective data-driven culture. It is our experience that following the drivers identified in this book will lead directly to increased student achievement.

## CONDITIONS FOR SUCCESS

To get an idea of how rolling out a data-driven culture looks on the ground, here are the conditions for success.

### Active Leadership Team

At the heart of this work is the identification and development of the school leadership team.

## Identification—Bridges to Buy-in

School leaders should identify and cultivate relationships with key faculty leaders; ties which can be thought of as "bridges to buy-in." As long as structures exist to ensure the participation of key school leaders, improved results will be able to win over the rest of the faculty in time. In the article "Informal Networks: The Company Behind the Chart" (1993), David Krackhardt and Jeffrey Hanson[3] argue about the importance of making sure that the leadership team included members of two important networks with an organization: the *expert network* and the *trust network*. The expert network consists of those members with the greatest expertise: in the case of a school, your strongest teachers. These are the people teachers admire for the quality of their teaching. The trust network, by contrast, consists of teachers to whom others turn for personal support or guidance. While not necessarily the strongest teachers (in the case of the school), they are the ones with the greatest influence on their peers in the day-to-day working of the school. Most school leadership teams already consist of leaders of the expert network. Securing the input and involvement of leaders of the trust network as well will go a long way toward creating a solid culture of data-driven instruction.

Once these staff members are identified, every effort should be made to include them in the process of implementing data-driven instruction. Of course, not every school leader will initially embrace data-driven instruction, and some will initially dislike it. By keeping such faculty leaders involved in the process, however, the principal will be able to minimize resistance and at least ensure participation on the part of the most influential teachers. This is extremely significant, because as long as leaders are involved and willing to follow the plan, then buy-in will inevitably follow.

## Development—The "Monday Meeting"

Antonio Burt and Laura Garza had not met each other when they both made dramatic gains in achievement in their schools—Antonio in Memphis and Laura in Dallas (both are highlighted in *Leverage Leadership 2.0* and Laura is also mentioned in a success story in this book). Yet when I first met them, they both described a "Monday Meeting" as the key to their success. I highlighted one of those meetings in *Leverage Leadership 2.0*:

---

### *The Monday Meeting—A Vignette*

#### *Start of the Meeting*
*At Ford Road Elementary School, Principal Antonio Burt and his leadership team are sitting around a table with their notes from the week's classroom observations*

*in front of them. The notes are familiar to Antonio, since he has his leaders share them with him throughout the week. This meeting, however, is the team's chance to look over them together and reach a shared understanding about where they are as a school—and where they want to go next.*

*"Where are we this week?" Antonio asks, kicking things off. "What are the patterns that you saw?"*

*Assistant principal Laquita Tate peruses the notes from her observations and begins by praising the third grade teachers she observes for having students annotate the texts they're reading in class. Then she expresses concern that students seem to be reading more for summary than for well-backed analysis.*

*"I saw that as well in fourth and fifth grade," says coach Chavon VanHooks. "Students aren't backing up their arguments with the best evidence. I noticed that during discussion as well as with written assignments," Chavon adds.*

*Antonio nods. "I had the same impression when I observed this week," he says. "So if this is the pattern, what should we do to address this?"*

\* \* \* \*

### At the Close of the Meeting

*"Let's review your schedules for the upcoming week," says Antonio. Each leader pulls out their observation schedule. "Given the patterns we just identified, what changes would you make to it?"*

*Each leader quietly looks over the weekly schedule of observations that they had from the previous week. "Given that most of the problems are occurring during Guided Reading, I think we need to double down on our observations during the reading block."*

*"That sounds right," shares Leader 2. "I will change my observation block from Tuesday afternoon to Tuesday morning so I can observe an extra third grade Reading block and second grade as well."*

*"Sounds good," replies Antonio. "And I can observe _____ [the other third grade reading teacher] at 9:30 on Tuesday so that we can compare notes."*

---

The heart of a Monday meeting for the school leadership team—although it really could occur any day of the week—has one simple purpose:

- What are the obstacles that are getting in the way of student achievement?
- How do we remove those obstacles and take immediate action?

The team cannot leave the meeting without identifying the gaps or obstacles, presenting a plan to change it, and most importantly, *changing their schedules* to monitor and follow up on those changes.

> ## Core Idea
>
> An effective leadership team has a singular purpose:
> What is getting in the way of student achievement?
> And how can I remove those obstacles?

What is striking about Antonio's and Laura's experience is that they are not alone: this precise conclusion has been reached by some of the most successful businesses as well. In the (2016) book, *The Founder's Mentality*, Chris Zook and James Allen study companies who went through massive growth, and they look at what separates those companies that eventually fall off or fail (e.g., Toys 'R' Us, once the toy giant of the world) to those that keep rising. Among some of the key factors is a commitment to a "Monday meeting":

> The simple idea [of the Monday meeting] is for leaders of the company to meet once a week with a promise: no matter how long it takes, they will work to unblock any obstacle that is preventing key players from doing their jobs ... Team members can't leave the meeting until they solve problems, so they learn to deconstruct problems and to make big issues small enough to be fixable.[4]

There is no other agenda at these meetings, and leaders are not allowed to walk out of the meeting without a solution. And as you can see in the vignette from Antonio Burt, they cannot walk out of the meeting without changing their schedule for that week to meet the needs.

This type of action changes stagnant leadership teams to active, and it models a mentality that we can solve any problem—and we won't stop until we do. That mentality is infectious and can influence the culture of the entire staff.

## Train and Monitor Data Meetings

It is one thing to roll out data meeting with your instructional leadership time: it is another to monitor them and make those meetings stronger. Tildi Sharp, principal of

North Star Lincoln Park High School in Newark, uses the following protocol at her leadership team meetings to get every leader practicing their preparation and implementation of data meetings. In just 30–45 minutes, every leader has prepared and practiced the core parts of the data meeting that they plan on leading that week, and Tildi has had the chance to monitor their preparation and make them stronger.

## Instructional Leadership Team Meeting
### Managing Leaders to Weekly Data Meetings

| Prepare Before the Meeting | Prepare |
|---|---|
| | • **Materials ready for each instructional leader:** Unpacked standard, initial gap, initial re-teach plan for their upcoming Weekly Data Meeting<br><br>• **Chart paper posted:** Two pieces of chart paper (or whiteboard space) for every instructional leader |
| **See It/Name It**<br>**12 min.** | **See Past Success, See the Exemplar, and See and Analyze the Gap** |
| | **Name the Process:**<br>Thank them for their preparation for the meeting<br><br>• "There are three keys to an effective weekly data meeting: an unpacked standard plus exemplar, the key gap, and a detailed re-teach plan. We are going to work on these three elements today, because if you have these in place, everything else is just prompting."<br><br>• "Take out your student work and assessment for the teacher that you will guide through a weekly data meeting."<br><br>**See the Standard/Exemplar (5 min.):**<br><br>• "Take 5 min: Chart the key parts of the standard and exemplar that you need to identify the gap: what should students know and do to show mastery."<br><br>• "Remember: don't chart every part of the standard: just the key parts that the participants will need to reference when naming the gap." |

| | |
|---|---|
| **See It/Name It (con't.)** | **See the Gap (5 min.):**<br><br>• "Take 5 min.: Chart the key gap: what do students need to know or do to master this assessment item?"<br><br>• Monitor the leader's charts and check for aligned standards and gaps:<br>  o "I don't see the gap reflected in your unpacked standard."<br>  o "This gap is too broad: break it down to what students have to know or be able to do."<br><br>**Peer Feedback:**<br>Pair each leader up with someone with similar content and/or grade-level expertise<br><br>• "Pull out the representative student work that has the gap you've charted. You have 2 minutes to present your student work, unpacked standard and gap statement to your peer."<br><br>• "Now give your peer feedback:<br>  o "Does this gap match what you see as the error in the student work?"<br>  o "Is the gap clearly taken from the unpacked standard?"<br>  o "How could you make the link better the standard, gap and student work?"<br><br>• Repeat the process for second partner<br><br>• Offer batch feedback: any patterns you see across the instructional leaders |

| Do It<br>20–45 min. | Plan the Re-Teach, Practice, and Follow-Up |
|---|---|

**Chart the Re-Teach (5 min.):**

- "Now chart the key parts of your re-teach lesson:
  **If a model:** key part of the Think Aloud script
  - **If guided discourse:** key work to show-call and key prompts
  - **If monitoring:** key laps and prompts for each lap
  - "Select the part that will be most challenging for your teacher."

- Monitor the leader's charts and check for quality:
  **Model:** "Pause here and reveal your thinking. Don't just tell me what to do: tell me the thinking you did to get there."
  - **Guided discourse:** "Show-call just part of the task—don't review the entire task."
  - **Monitoring:** "Make sure your laps match the gap."

**Peer Feedback:**

- Go back to same partner

- "Read your partner's re-teach plan. Ask yourself: will the students be successful after this re-teach lesson?"

- "Now give your peer feedback:
  - "What do you need to emphasize to close the gap for the students?"
  - "What else do you need to do to make sure students get it?"

- Repeat the process for second partner

- Offer batch feedback: any patterns you see across the instructional leaders

**Script your Meeting:**

- "You now have 5 minutes to prep for your meeting."

**(If time) Practice the meeting:**

- 5 min. role play, feedback, re-do

**Follow-up (last 2 min.):**

- Set the follow-up plan: when to teach, when to re-assess, when to revisit this data

# Data-Driven Success Story

## Friends of Education, Minnesota

### The Results

**Figure 4.3** Minnesota Multiple Measurements Rating (MMR): Friends of Education Schools, MMR Average Score

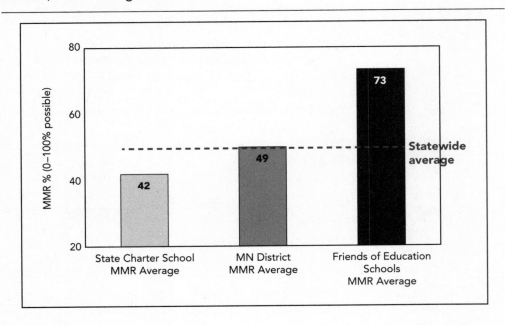

### The Story

The thirteen schools that are a part of Friends of Education in Minnesota don't fit a cookie-cutter model. You have schools that specialize in Classical Studies, Chinese immersion, the Arts, Sciences and everything in between. What is remarkable is despite the vast differences in their educational and pedagogical models, as a unit, they are achieving exceptional results. Four of the 13 schools are ranked in the top ten of all 440 districts in Minnesota based on achievement results, and three more are in the top 30. Collectively, their results vastly outpace every other district and organization in the state. So what makes the difference?

Jon Gutierrez, Executive Director of St. Croix Preparatory Academy says that the driver is data-driven instruction. "We all analyze data and expect high achievement. We have high expectations for our students, and Friends of Education has high expectations of us."

Beth Topoluk, Executive Director of Friends of Education, puts it this way. "You can be about classical education, bilingual education, Montessori or anything in between. It's not the pedagogical model that matters—it's driving your teaching to respond to student needs."

Topoluk made sure that each of the thirteen schools had the resources and training to launch effective data-driven instructional practices. They each built a calendar that locked in interim assessments, analysis, and re-teaching days. They trained their leadership teams and staff in the principles of data-driven instruction. They visited other high-achieving schools to replicate their best practices. And they constantly analyzed the results to make sure that their teaching was effective. In the end, the creation of a data-driven culture drove achievement to levels never before seen in Minnesota.

"We don't just read about data-driven instruction," states Beth, "we implement it. The state of our schools demands it."

---

### Key Drivers from Implementation Rubric

- *Implementation calendar:* begin school year with a detailed calendar that includes time for assessment creation/adaptation, interim assessment analysis, weekly data meetings, and re-teaching (<u>flexible</u> enough to accommodate district mandates/changes).
- *Common interim assessments:* 4–6 times/year.
- *Aligned* to state tests <u>and</u> college readiness.
- *Build by borrowing:* identify and implement best practices from high-achieving teachers and schools: visit schools/classrooms, share and disseminate resources/strategies.

---

## Implementation Calendar

A story that sticks (author unknown): during one lecture, an expert in time management walked into the lecture hall and approached his desk to begin class. On the desk, he had placed three large rocks, a dozen smaller rocks, a pile of sand, and a glass jar. He placed the big rocks in the jar first before asking the class if there was still room in the jar. When the class responded that there was still room, he put the small rocks in and repeated his question. Finally, the professor poured the sand, then the water into the jar, at which point the class declared that the jar had been exactly filled. Next, the professor turned to his students and asked them what lesson they had learned from the jar.

> "Well," responded one student, "the lesson is that there is always room for more."
>
> "No," the professor replied. "The lesson is that if you don't put the big rocks in first, they don't fit."

The lesson of the story is clear: if certain key fundamentals are not secured first, then nothing else will be possible. Although this principle applies to many facets of life, it is especially apparent in data-driven instruction when it comes to creating a culture in which assessment, analysis, and action can thrive. The "jar" in this arena is the school calendar. The "big rocks" are interim assessments, analysis, and action. Without the "big rocks" firmly in place within this calendar, it is almost impossible to create a truly excellent data-driven school.

Schools live and die by their calendars: whatever makes it first onto the schoolwide calendar trumps other activities that come later. Given that data-driven instruction is based upon timely and regular assessment, analysis, and action, placing these events first on the school calendar is essential for student achievement. Without being embedded in the structure of the calendar and school schedule, analysis and action will likely be ignored, overlooked, or delayed, causing the project to fail. There are too many moving pieces in a school year to expect effective data-driven instruction to "just happen"; schools must consciously craft a calendar that lays the foundation for genuine progress.

> ## Core Idea
>
> Look at a school's calendar, and you'll know its priorities.
> Put first on your calendar time for assessments, analysis, and action:
> everything else follows.

To do so, a calendar must do the following:

### Make Time for Data

The first critical feature of the calendar is that it blocks off time for interim assessments to be administered, scored, and analyzed. All too often, schools will make time to test but leave no time to grade exams, a situation which gives teachers and school leaders an excuse to postpone analysis until it is useless.

### Space Out Your Interim Assessments with the End in Mind

Beyond fixing the time for interim assessments, the school-wide calendar must also take into account the state and national tests taken by students during the year. Given that interim assessments are most effective in 6–8-week periods, plan the timing of the interim assessments working backwards from the summative state/national tests, and then working forwards for the rest of the school year after these assessments. (For example, if your state test is in February, plan for an interim assessment cycle that leads up to the February state test, and then, post-February, start working towards the standards of the following year, allowing you still to have a full-calendar year of interim assessments.)

## Mark Professional Development in Relation to Your Interims

As a further important feature, plan for professional development days before and after each round of interim assessments to allow for implementing each step of the data-driven process. This will also allow the school to provide content-focused professional development in response to the learning needs identified in the assessment.

## Leave Room for Re-teaching

Finally, and perhaps most importantly, an effective calendar is one that builds in time for the re-teaching necessitated by the assessment analysis. North Star Academy, for example, formally allots a week following assessments to re-teaching and reviewing earlier standards. Of course, this is not to say that this entire week is spent in review; in most cases, teachers integrate and spiral re-teaching while presenting new material. Nevertheless, the very existence of this re-teach week sends a powerful signal that assessment results will guide curriculum and that data results are to be taken seriously.

Here are three sample assessment and analysis calendars—for elementary, middle, and high school (Figure 4.4).

**Figure 4.4** Sample elementary/middle/high school assessment calendars

| Sample elementary school assessment calendar | | |
| --- | --- | --- |
| **Time frame** | **Unit/Assessment** | **Notes** |
| Math IA #1 Oct. 12–13 (8 weeks of instruction) | Interim Assessment for Math | |
| **10/17–10/19** | Scoring, Analysis, and Planning | |
| **10/20–21** | PD with Math Staff Developers Focus: priorities from the data | |
| **1 Week (10/24–10/28)** | RE-TEACH week | Re-teach based on test results analysis |

*(Continued)*

**Figure 4.4** (*Continued*)

| Sample elementary school assessment calendar | | |
|---|---|---|
| **Time frame** | **Unit/Assessment** | **Notes** |
| ELA IA #1<br>Math IA #2<br>**Dec. 7–8** | Interim Assessment for English and Math | |
| **1 Week**<br>**(12/5–12/7)** | Scoring, Analysis, and Planning | |
| **12/8–12/9** | PD with Literacy Staff Developers<br>Focus: priorities from the data | |
| **1 Week**<br>**(12/13–12/16)** | RE-TEACH week | Re-teach based on test results analysis |
| ELA IA #2<br>Math IA #3<br>**Feb. 6–7** | Interim Assessment for English and Math | |
| **1 Week**<br>**(2/8–2/10)** | Scoring, Analysis, and Planning | |
| **2/11–2/12** | PD with Literacy or Math Staff Developers<br>Focus: priorities from the data | |
| **1 Week**<br>**(2/13–2/15)** | RE-TEACH week | Re-teach based on test results analysis |
| ELA IA #3<br>**Mar. 20–21** | Interim Assessment for ELA | |
| **1 Week**<br>**(3/22–3/24)** | Scoring, Analysis, and Planning | |
| **1 Week**<br>**(3/27–3/29)** | RE-TEACH week | Re-teach based on test results analysis |
| **3/30–3/31** | PD with Literacy Staff Developers | |
| Math IA #4<br>**April 3–4** | Interim Assessment for Math | |
| **1 Week**<br>**(4/5–4/7)** | Scoring, Analysis, and Planning | |
| **2–3 Weeks**<br>**(4/10–4/28)** | Re-teach Key Gaps Across Units, and Test Preparation | |

**Figure 4.4** (Continued)

| Sample elementary school assessment calendar | | |
|---|---|---|
| **Time frame** | **Unit/Assessment** | **Notes** |
| **1 Week** (4/24–4/28) | PARCC ELA + Math for Grades 3–4 | |
| Final 5/10–5/18 | Final Interim Assessments for Grades K–2 | |

| Sample middle school assessment calendar | | |
|---|---|---|
| **Time frame** | **Unit/assessment** | **Notes** |
| **8 Weeks** (8/22–10/11) | Unit 1 | |
| IA #1 Oct. 12–14 | Interim Assessment #1 | |
| **1 Week** (10/17–10/21) | Scoring, Analysis, and Planning | |
| **1 Week** (10/24–10/28) | RE-TEACH week | Re-teach based on test results analysis |
| **5 Weeks** (10/31–11/29) | Unit 2 | |
| IA #2 Nov. 29–Dec. 1 | Interim Assessment #2 | |
| **1 Week** (12/5–12/9) | Scoring, Analysis, and Planning | |
| **1 Week** (12/12–12/16) | RE-TEACH week | Re-teach based on test results analysis |
| **5 Weeks** (1/3–2/2) | Unit 3 | |
| IA #3 Jan. 31–Feb. 2 | Interim Assessment #3 | Cumulative |
| **1 Week** (2/6–2/10) | Scoring, Analysis, and Planning | |
| **1 Week** (2/13–2/17) | RE-TEACH week | Re-teach based on test results analysis |
| **5 Weeks** (2/17–3/21) | Unit 4 | |

(Continued)

**Figure 4.4** *(Continued)*

| Sample middle school assessment calendar | | |
|---|---|---|
| **Time frame** | **Unit/assessment** | **Notes** |
| <u>IA #4</u><br>**March 22–24** | Interim Assessment #4 | |
| **1 Week**<br>**(4/3–4/7)** | Scoring, Analysis, and Planning | |
| **3–5 Weeks**<br>**(4/10–4/28)** | Re-teach of All Units and Test Preparation | |
| **1 Week**<br>**(5/1–5/5)** | PARCC ELA + Math for Grades 6 + 7 | |
| **1 Week**<br>**(5/8–5/12)** | PARCC ELA + Math for Grades 5 + 8 | |
| **4–6 Weeks**<br>**(5/5–6/17)** | Unit 5 | Objectives for new year |
| <u>IA #4</u><br>**6/6–6/7** | Final Exams | |

| Sample high school assessment calendar | | |
|---|---|---|
| **Time frame:** | **Unit/assessment:** | **Notes:** |
| <u>PSAT</u><br>**Oct. 19** | **PSAT—9th, 10th, 11th grade** | |
| <u>Assessment #1</u><br>**Oct 26–28**<br>(9 weeks of instruction) | 1st Semester Mid-term (Interim Asst #1) | |
| **1 Week**<br>**(10/31–11/4)** | Scoring, Analysis, and Planning | |
| **1 Week**<br>**(11/7–11/11)** | RE-TEACH Objectives from Mid-term | Re-teach based on test results analysis |
| <u>Assessment #2</u><br>**Jan 18–20**<br>(10 weeks of instruction) | 1st Semester Final (Interim Asst #2) | |
| **1 Week**<br>**(1/23–1/27)** | Scoring, Analysis, and Planning | |
| **1 Week**<br>**(1/30–2/3)** | RE-TEACH Objectives from Final | Re-teach based on test results analysis |

**Figure 4.4** (*Continued*)

| Sample high school assessment calendar | | |
|---|---|---|
| **Time frame:** | **Unit/assessment:** | **Notes:** |
| Assessment #3<br>**April 5–7**<br>(10 weeks of instruction) | 2nd Semester Mid-term<br>(Interim Asst #3) | |
| **1 Week**<br>**(4/10–4/14)** | Scoring, Analysis, and Planning | |
| **1 Week**<br>**(4/17–4/21)** | RE-TEACH Objectives from Mid-term | Re-teach based on test results analysis |
| SAT & AP Exams<br>**May 1–12** | May SAT Date for 11th graders<br>AP Exams for Various Subjects | |
| Assessment #4<br>**June 13–15**<br>(9 weeks of instruction) | Year-end Final Exam<br>(Interim Asst #4) | |

As can be seen from the example above, an effective calendar need not be overly complex or difficult to create, but it must include the basic elements outlined above if it is to be successful.

Here is a simple guide for creating such a calendar from scratch. You'll also find this in the Appendix on the DVD.

## Monthly Map—Create a Schedule for DDI

### Pre-Work

Pull out the Monthly Map template (see Appendix), which includes one line for each week of each month. Start by writing down the following:

1. Starting week of school.
2. Ending week of school.
3. Long vacations (take up all or most of a week): Spring Break, Winter Break, Thanksgiving.

# Start with Data-Driven Instruction

Place the following events on your calendar in this order:

1. State test dates (or year-end testing that matters most—AP, ACT, etc.).
2. If applicable, the district-mandated interim assessments or benchmarks.
3. Interim assessments (IAs)
   - Count total number of free weeks from start of school to state test.
   - Divide that number by 8 and by 6: this is the range of the number of assessments you should have in that span.
   - Start from second week of school, count 6–8 weeks, put the first IA, then put the next one.
   - If the date of the IA conflicts with the calendar (e.g., it happens right after a vacation period), adjust it forwards or backwards. You will just cover more or less content on that IA based on the new number of weeks.
   - If the state test comes early, add IAs every 6–8 weeks after the state test.
4. For each IA week, add the following events right around that date:*
   - 2 weeks prior: teachers predict performance on the IA.
   - 1 week prior: data report templates and analysis/action plan templates ready.
   - 1 week after: analysis meetings and re-teach.
   - 2 weeks after: teachers preview upcoming IA (add this to the second week of school as well).
5. Professional Development dates
   - Opening PD on DDI for all teachers (first year of implementation) or new-to-the-school teachers (every year thereafter)—put ideally in teacher orientation or at least right before the first IA cycle.
   - Ongoing PD: build time after each IA cycle to have targeted PD on the needs that arise from the assessment analysis: Results Meetings (see protocol), content-specific PD, etc.
6. Revise/acquire the interim assessments you will use.
   - Ideally this should occur in Spring or Summer; select dates when you will realistically be able to work on this or pay a team to do this for you.

*NOTE: Chapter 2 (Analysis) highlighted a one-week schedule of how to structure the week itself when assessments occur and then analysis meetings and re-teaching.

## Data-Driven Success Story

## Dan D. Rogers Elementary School, Dallas, Texas

The Results

**Figure 4.5**   Texas State Assessment (STAAR): Dan D. Rogers Elementary School, ELA Percentage at or Above Proficiency

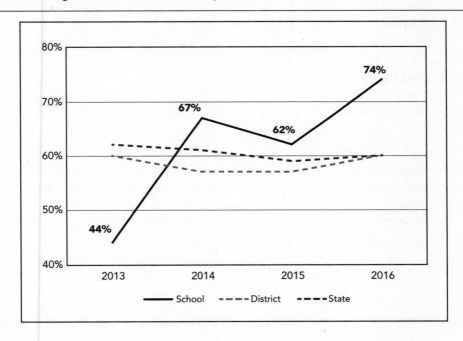

The Story

"I was shocked when I got to Dan D. Rogers," Lisa Lovato says of her earliest days at the elementary school she leads. "I had parents running up to me with transfer forms." Lisa describes the academic results at the time as "Okay, but only with a certain subset of kids." "We weren't doing as well with English language learners, who are about 50% of our student population," she says. To Lisa, positive outcomes for only half of her students weren't enough. So how did she transform Dan D. Rogers into a school that met *all* its students' needs?

To Lisa's own surprise, the key was her calendar. "I think of myself as a butterfly Gemini," Lisa laughs, "but without my calendar, I would be lost. I also have my schedule on a whiteboard in my office, so everyone can see what I prioritize. I wasn't born with that skill, but it's been instrumental."

Lisa relied on the implementation rubrics in *Driven by Data* to fill her calendar with the tasks that would make the biggest difference for student learning at Dan D. Rogers. One key was to give teachers time specifically allotted for data-driven planning. "Giving them discrete time for data changed their perception of how time was being used," Lisa observes. "It helped us all to make sense of what our priorities were. It also helped build buy-in, because teachers felt they had autonomy but also support."

All this work has paid off, earning Dan D. Rogers an A grade with the state of Texas. But Lisa knows her work isn't over. "To get an A is one thing, but to keep an A is another," Lisa remarks wisely. Fortunately, sticking to her calendar has nurtured a data-driven culture, which plays a major role in sustaining growth at the school. "I think the culture is probably what I'm most proud of," says Lisa. "We foster a growth mindset, and we can really depend on our instructional team to sustain our best practices. Now that we've closed the achievement gap, our potential is endless. And that's really exciting."

---

## Key Drivers from Implementation Rubric

- *Implementation calendar:* begin school year with a detailed calendar that includes time for assessment creation/adaptation, interim assessment analysis, weekly data meetings, and re-teaching (<u>flexible</u> enough to accommodate district mandates/changes).

- *Follow-up/accountability:* instructional leaders review lesson and unit plans and give observation feedback driven by the action plan and student learning needs.

- *Build by borrowing:* identify and implement best practices from high-achieving teachers and schools: visit schools/classrooms, share and disseminate resources/strategies.

---

## Introductory Professional Development

Once you have a leadership team and a calendar in place, the next key is to bring on board your staff. You cannot expect your teachers to be data-driven if you do not show them how. No matter how many years we've done data-driven instruction, we always make sure to train our new teachers at the beginning of each year so that they can join the same level of work of their peers. The Appendix offers all the materials that you need to turnkey a training for your staff:

- **Session plans:** minute-by-minute guides for how to lead an introductory PD on data-driven instruction.
- **PPT slides and handouts:** all the materials participants need to participate.
- **Videos:** all the videos you need to show to the staff (or where to find them if you need to gather them yourself).
- **Model to follow:** we've included of few videos of leading this PD in action. This way you can see how it looks and feels to deliver this PD.

In short, we have tried to make it as easy as possible for you to make this come alive with your own staff!

## Ongoing Professional Development

One-time PD is essential but it never works on its own. A school is only as good as its follow-up.

---

### Core Idea

A school is only as good as its follow-up.

---

As you can see from the sample calendars above, effective schools lock in professional development time right after interim assessments so that they have the chance to respond to their own data. Just as we said for students, teach teachers not what they already know but what they need.

Doug Lemov's *Teach like a Champion* and my previous books *Get Better Faster* and *Great Habits, Great Readers* all provide PD materials to develop teachers in what they need. Teacher investment in PD goes way up when it responds to the data rather than being a canned workshop that isn't what they are looking for!

## Data-Driven Success Story

## Eagle Ridge Academy, Minnetonka, Minnesota

The Results

**Figure 4.6** Minnesota Comprehensive Assessment (MCA): Eagle Ridge Academy, Math Percentage at or Above Proficiency

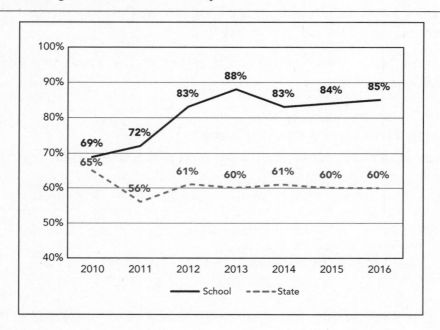

The Story

When Susan Bloomgren and Jason Ulbrich first implemented data-driven instruction at Eagle Ridge Academy in Minnetonka, Minnesota, they saw results right away: they jumped to the 99th percentile in state. "We thought we were awesome," Jason remembers, laughing. "But then we grew."

The challenge the school faced was a changing student population as they increased the number of students they served. They had begun practicing data-driven instruction in a school with a relatively privileged student population with low percentages of low-income or minority students. But as their enrollment grew, their school changed to being 58% students of color, with five times as many students eligible for a free or reduced-price lunch. "Focusing on our school's growth distracted us from what mattered most," shares Jason. "We stopped identifying what students need to learn and making sure they learned it."

Their solution? Reboot data-driven instruction, and this time build systems to sustain it. Susan and Jason's first priority was to go back to the most basic question: what standards do students need to learn? Then they led start-of-year professional development that brought all teachers up to speed on how to implement data-driven instruction. Susan remembers having to remind teachers to focus on the root learning challenges that caused students not to master material. Susan comments, "The teachers were very intentional about asking, 'Why didn't the students learn it?' but too often the answer would be 'We didn't have enough time' or 'The kids didn't memorize the vocabulary.'" To change that mindset, Susan asked teachers to focus on what standards students were struggling with, and why those topics were challenging.

As the year went on, school leadership found that common assessments enabled them to identify both the right standards for re-teaching and the right students for specialized additional instruction in either math or reading. "We're being proactive now, not reactive," Jason says. Monitoring learning allows staff to meet their students where they are—before they're drowning.

Now, the students are thriving across the board, and the systems around data-driven instruction allow instructors to focus explicitly on the needs of their most struggling students in particular. Today, Eagle Ridge Academy is a school where all students have an equal opportunity to succeed.

---

## Key Drivers from Implementation Rubric

- *Introductory professional development:* introduce teachers and leaders to data-driven instruction—understand how assessments define rigor, how to analyze student work, and how to adapt instruction.
- *Deep:* move beyond *what* students got wrong and answer *why*: identify key procedural and conceptual misunderstandings.
- *Six-week action plans:* execute plans that include whole-class instruction, small groups, tutorials, and before/after-school supports.

---

## Building by Borrowing

In building a data-driven culture, few skills are as vital as the ability to identify and adapt best practices from other successful schools: seeing what success looks like so that you can replicate it. All of the highest achieving schools highlighted in this book are masters of "building by borrowing." They visited schools that were achieving better results than their own and borrowed any and every tool that could increase their own results. With the sheer numbers of schools that have made dramatic gains in achievement, you don't have to re-invent the wheel! Rather, strive to create an ethos in which teachers and school leaders perpetually seek out the best ideas beyond their building.

During their initial roll-out of data-driven instruction, leaders should make an effort to visit effective schools and see data in action. Such visits will surely provide important insights into the mechanics of data-driven instruction, but they also provide something more important: hope. By seeing with their own eyes how data-driven instruction succeeds, school leaders and teachers will gain the confidence to articulate a compelling and coherent vision of what data-driven excellence looks like and what it will take to truly excel.

## Data-Driven Success Story

## Denver Green School, Denver, Colorado

The Results

**Figure 4.7**   School Performance Framework: Denver Green School, School Report Card Percentile Ranking

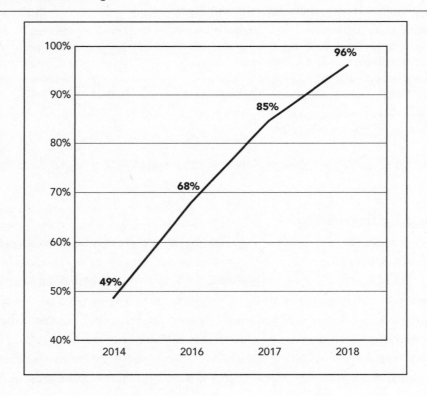

### The Story

Like any school leaders, Frank Coyne and Prudence Daniels have specific student needs to consider in their work at Denver Green School. They serve a highly diverse neighborhood with a large number of immigrant families. "We have a very transient population," says Prudence, "with 25% turnover each year. 30% of our students are English language learners. So our responsibility to provide targeted instruction to students is vital."

Frank and Prudence knew they needed to make the most of any time they had to teach any individual student, but determining how to do so was a challenge. "In the first years, we knew what data-driven instruction was, but we struggled to find time and space to implement it," Frank recalls. "Our competing priorities were overwhelming."

Things changed about five years into Frank and Prudence's tenure at Denver Green, when they began to strengthen systems for data-driven instruction after learning from other leaders who had implemented data-driven systems successfully. "Because we did collaborative work with colleagues, we were able to implement a data meeting structure that worked," says Frank.

Prudence describes in more detail what those data meetings look like. "They're an opportunity to discuss data every week," she says. "Between teacher leaders and ourselves, we've been able to make this part of our Friday afternoon release time. We use DDI analysis rooted in exemplars. We'd unpack what was necessary to be exemplary and then plan targeted instruction to address student gaps the very next week. Then students could succeed in that standard."

"Initially, we worked with student data, but we didn't have the systems to respond to it effectively," adds Frank. "Data meetings changed the game. After that, the proof was in the pudding. We started seeing growth among our students, especially marginalized student groups."

Prudence reflects that Denver Green has become a different place since data meetings were implemented. "At first, we needed to convince teachers this was a valuable use of their Friday afternoon," she says. "Now, there would be an uprising if we changed that schedule!"

---

## Key Drivers from Implementation Rubric

- *Ongoing professional development:* PD calendar is aligned with data-driven instructional plan: includes student work analysis, action planning and learning how to teach content.

- *Build by borrowing:* identify and implement best practices from high-achieving teachers and schools: visit schools/classrooms, share and disseminate resources/strategies.

- *Teacher-owned:* teacher analyzes own student work supported by instructional leaders.

---

Doug Lemov, author of *Teach like a Champion*, has taken this concept to another level. He has devoted the past ten years to finding the most accomplished urban school teachers in the country—"Master Teachers." He has videotaped them in action and identified the shared strategies that all of them use to be so successful. He compiled these experiences into a Taxonomy of Effective Teaching, which eventually became *Teach Like a Champion*, which includes a framework, actual video clips, and resources to be used in training teachers. Lemov is proving that teachers don't have to be born "great;" they can also be developed into high-achieving teachers. More importantly, you don't have to know all the answers yourself: you can borrow from exemplary practice from across the country. It is much easier to believe in success when a teacher can see examples of success. This happens naturally in the assessment cycle when a teacher sees his/her students improve on subsequent assessments. In these video clips, Lemov has also allowed you to "build by borrowing" without ever leaving your school!

## IMPLEMENTATION: FIRST STEPS FOR TEACHERS AND LEADERS

A summary of the keys to effective data-driven culture is listed here as part of the overall implementation rubric.

---

### Implementation Rubric

### Data-Driven Culture

The rubric is intended to be used to assess the present state of data-driven culture in your school. The rubric specifically targets interim assessments and the key drivers leading to increased student achievement.

4 = Exemplary implementation   3 = Proficient implementation   2 = Beginning implementation   1 = No implementation

| Data-Driven Culture | |
|---|---|
| **1. Active Leadership Team:** facilitate teacher-leader meetings looking at student work (interim assessment analysis and weekly data) and monitor the follow-up | __/4 |
| **2. Implementation Calendar:** begin school year with a detailed calendar that includes time for assessment creation/ adaptation, interim assessment analysis, weekly data meetings, and re-teaching (*flexible* enough to accommodate district mandates/changes) | __/4 |

---

| Data-Driven Culture | |
|---|---|
| 3. **Introductory Professional Development:** introduce teachers and leaders to data-driven instruction—understand how assessments define rigor, how to analyze student work, and how to adapt instruction | __/4 |
| 4. **Ongoing Professional Development:** PD calendar is aligned with data-driven instructional plan: includes student work analysis, action planning, and learning how to teach content | __/4 |
| 5. **Build by Borrowing:** Identify and implement best practices from high-achieving teachers and schools: visit schools/classrooms, share and disseminate resources/strategies | __/4 |
| <div align="right">TOTAL:</div> | __/20 |

What follows are the first steps that can be taken to build a data-driven culture for classroom teachers, school leaders, or multi-campus/district office leaders:

## Level 1—Teachers

As a teacher, you have the most influence over the data-driven culture in your own classroom. If your school doesn't have one, set up your own assessment calendar. Visit the classes of the highest achieving teachers you can find (within your school and in neighboring schools) to identify best practices that could increase your repertoire and make you a stronger teacher. But more than anything, focus on the key steps listed for assessment, analysis, and action (Chapters 1–3).

## Level 2—School-Based Leaders

The core drivers listed in this chapter are the basic roadmap for your work as school leader. Listed here are just some final tips during the implementation of each of these drivers.

- **Active leadership team:** Facilitate teacher-leader meetings looking at student work (interim assessment analysis and weekly data). Create "Monday Meetings" to constantly remove obstacles and adjust course in response to student learning needs and coach your leaders to get better at implementing effective data meetings.

- **Implementation calendar:** Begin the school year with a detailed calendar that includes time for assessment creation/adaptation, interim assessment analysis, weekly data meetings, and re-teaching (*flexible* enough to accommodate district mandates/changes).

- **Introductory professional development:** Introduce teachers and leaders to data-driven instruction—understand how assessments define rigor, how to analyze student work, and how to adapt instruction.

- **Ongoing professional development:** The best agenda for professional development after each round of interim assessments is the data meeting protocol (see Chapter 3 and the Appendix). After that, some of the most fruitful topics to address after each round of interim assessment implementation can be the action steps for rigor from the *Get Better Faster* Scope & Sequence: a sequence of proven action steps for how a teacher can effectively implement techniques that increase the learning throughout each part of the lesson. (You can find these in *Get Better Faster: A 90-day Plan for Coaching New Teachers.*)

- **Build by borrowing:** Identify and implement best practices from high-achieving teachers and schools: visit schools/classrooms, share and disseminate resources/strategies.

## Level 3—District-Level or Multi-Campus Leaders

If districts have set up effective interim assessments and analysis structures, you have done the most important things to set up principals to lead the core elements of Action effectively. Your core work here is to "block and tackle," keep everything else away from school leaders so they can focus on these elements. Some of the most important ways to do that are as follows:

- **Professional development for leaders:** Just as teachers need training, so do leaders. You will not make district-wide gains in achievement until you've trained every principal and school leadership team in the art and skill of data-driven instruction. Depending on the size of your district/organization, you can train all principals and then have them train their second-tier leaders (coaches, assistant principals, etc.), or you can set up district-wide training for all school leaders. Plan for a leadership retreat, or gather a few afternoons over the summer. Utilize the professional development activities listed in Part II, and the leadership protocol on page 143. *If a principal is not fully trained in data-driven instruction, the initiative will likely fail.*

- **Make a district-wide calendar that prioritizes interim assessments first, every-thing else second:** As the big rocks analogy suggests, make sure the interim assess-ment cycle drives the rest of the district calendar and meets the criteria established in each chapter. Keep all other events/requests away from leaders during those crit-ical times.

- **Use the data-driven instruction implementation rubric:** As mentioned in Level 2, the first document in Chapter 5 is the implementation rubric you can use to evalu-ate each school's overall progress in implementing data-driven instruction. After the first cycle of interim assessments and then mid-year, have school leaders evaluate their school using this rubric and develop a corresponding action plan for the leader-ship team. Collect the evaluations from all the schools and look for common trends across your district as well as differences. Are your assessments not seen as aligned by your principals (despite all your best efforts to do so at the district level)? Are schools struggling to lead analysis meetings? This evaluation can give you insight into the additional professional development school leaders need and help you cre-ate a roadmap for district-wide improvement.

# Reflection and Planning

Take this opportunity to reflect upon Culture at your own school or district. Answer the following questions:

• After reading this chapter, what are the key action steps around Culture that you are going to implement in your school (which can you realistically do)?

_____

_____

_____

_____

• Who are the key people in your school with whom you need to communicate this plan and have on board?

_____

_____

_____

_____

• How are you going to get them on board? What are you going to do when someone says no? (What's Plan B?)

_____

_____

_____

_____

• Set the key dates for each action step, write them here, and then put them in your personal agenda/calendar to hold yourself accountable for implementing these steps.

_____

_____

_____

_____

# PART TWO

# Where the Rubber Hits the Road

Chapter **5**

# Overcoming Obstacles: Answers to Frequently Asked Questions

## DDI IMPLEMENTATION RUBRIC

Assessment, analysis, action, and culture. We've now examined each of the core drivers of data-driven instruction. We've incorporated all of these key actions into one easy-to-use implementation rubric for data-driven instruction:

---

### Implementation Rubric

#### Data-Driven Instruction and Assessment

The rubric is intended to be used to assess the present state of data-driven instruction and assessment in a school. The rubric specifically targets interim assessments and the key drivers leading to increased student achievement.

---

4 = Exemplary implementation 3 = Proficient implementation 2 = Beginning
implementation 1 = No implementation

| Data-Driven Culture | | |
| --- | --- | --- |
| **1. Active Leadership Team:** facilitate teacher-leader meetings looking at student work (interim assessment analysis and weekly data) and monitor the follow-up | | ____/4 |
| **2. Implementation Calendar:** begin school year with a detailed calendar that includes time for assessment creation/adaptation, interim assessment analysis, weekly data meetings, and re-teaching (*flexible* enough to accommodate district mandates/changes) | | ____/4 |
| **3. Introductory Professional Development:** Introduce teachers and leaders to data-driven instruction—understand how assessments define rigor, how to analyze student work, and how to adapt instruction | | ____/4 |
| **4. Ongoing Professional Development:** PD calendar is aligned with data-driven instructional plan: includes student work analysis, action planning and learning how to teach content | | ____/4 |
| **5. Build by Borrowing:** Identify and implement best practices from high-achieving teachers and schools: visit schools/classrooms, share and disseminate resources/strategies | | ____/4 |

| Assessments | Lit. | Math |
| --- | --- | --- |
| **6. Common Interim Assessments:** 4–6 times/year | ____/4 | ____/4 |
| **7. Transparent Starting Point:** Teachers see the assessments at the beginning of each cycle; assessments define the roadmap for teaching | ____/4 | ____/4 |
| **8. Aligned:** To state tests and college readiness | ____/4 | ____/4 |
| **9. Aligned to Instructional Sequence** of clearly defined grade level and content expectations | ____/4 | ____/4 |
| **10. Re-Assess:** previously taught standards | ____/4 | ____/4 |

| Analysis | | |
| --- | --- | --- |
| **11. Immediate:** Aim for fast turnaround of assessment results (ideally 48 hrs) | | ____/4 |

| | |
|---|---|
| **12. Simple:** User-friendly, succinct data reports include: item-level analysis, standards-level analysis and bottom line results | ___/4 |
| **13. Teacher-owned:** Teacher analyzes own student work supported by instructional leaders | ___/4 |
| **14. Test and Student Work in Hand:** Start from the exemplar and identify the gaps | ___/4 |
| **15. Deep:** Move beyond *what* students got wrong and answer *why*: identify key procedural and conceptual misunderstandings | ___/4 |
| **Action** | |
| **16. Six-Week Action Plans:** Execute plans that include whole-class instruction, small groups, tutorials, and before/after-school supports | ___/4 |
| **17. Re-teach:** Use guided discourse or modeling strategies to re-teach difficult standards | ___/4 |
| **18. Ongoing Assessment:** Check for understanding every day: aggressive monitoring of independent work, questioning, and in-class assessments to ensure student progress between interim assessments | ___/4 |
| **19. Engaged Students:** They know the end goal, how they did, and what actions to improve | ___/4 |
| **20. Follow-up/Accountability:** Instructional leaders review lesson and unit plans and give observation feedback driven by the action plan and student learning needs | ___/4 |
| TOTAL: | ___/100 |

Take a moment before reading and score your school on the rubric. Don't spend a lot of time on the scoring: a quick judgment will likely give you the accuracy you need to start doing what is most important: taking action. In fact, in the workshops I lead, I encourage leadership teams to spend no more than 2 minutes filling out the rubric—and many more minutes figuring out how to respond.

**Stop and Jot**

Fill out the implementation rubric. What is the score of your school right now? What are the key areas that you want to address first in order to improve the achievement in your school?

_____

_____

_____

_____

_____

_____

The remainder of this chapter is to help you close the gaps on your rubric.

## WHAT TO DO WHEN THERE'S A "2"

All of us will have some gaps to close on the DDI implementation rubric—you are not alone! What we've tried to do is gather the actions and resources that schools across the country have used to close those gaps—thus our guide "What to Do When There's a '2'."

In the following guide, you can see:

- what partial/beginning implementation looks like in every part of the rubric;
- the key actions you can take to close each implementation gap in your school;
- the resources we have provided to help you close those gaps.

In the remainder of the chapter, we'll address some other frequently asked questions that come up when implementing each of the four core components of data-driven instruction. First, let's start with our What to Do guide (Table 5.1).

**Table 5.1** What To Do When There's a "2": Recommended Action Steps to Increase Proficiency on the DDI Rubric

| | I Data-Driven Culture | | |
|---|---|---|---|
| | Beginning Implementation | Action Steps for Principals and Coaches | Resources |
| 1. Active Leadership Team | **Partial Implementation**<br>• Some leadership team members have received training in leading analysis meetings and supervising teachers for implementing action plans<br>• Responsibilities for leadership team members for data-driven instruction are partially outlined<br>• Leadership team members are attempting to implement effective analysis meetings, but they are not proficient | • Set up times to train the leadership team in leading data analysis meetings (interim assessments, weekly data):<br>  ○ Full-day training<br>  ○ Leadership Team Meetings over time<br>  ○ 1-on-1<br>• Plan and execute the training of the leadership team, including but not limited to the following critical components:<br>  ○ Leading interim assessment analysis meetings<br>  ○ Leading weekly data meetings<br>  ○ Holding teachers accountable to implementing action plans<br>• Create clear responsibilities for each member of the team:<br>  ○ Identify which teachers each leader will manage in terms of analysis/data meetings and observation of implementation<br>  ○ Create schedule of data meetings/professional learning communities to look at student work | ***Driven by Data 2.0***<br>• One-Pager: Leading Weekly Data Meetings (DVD)<br>• PD agendas and training materials for data-driven instruction (DVD)<br>• One-Pager: Instructional Leadership Teams Managing Leaders to Effective Data Meetings (DVD)<br>• Video of Data Meetings (DVD)<br><br>***Leverage Leadership 2.0***<br>• Videos of Data Meetings (DVD, Clips 1–14)<br><br>***Get Better Faster***<br>• Videos of Weekly Data Meetings (DVD, Clips 20–22) |

*(Continued)*

Table 5.1 (Continued)

| | | I Data-Driven Culture | |
|---|---|---|---|
| | Beginning Implementation | Action Steps for Principals and Coaches | Resources |
| | | • Monitor implementation of data-driven at leadership team meetings<br>  ○ Set up a "Monday Meeting" to remove obstacles and close gaps<br>  ○ Follow the protocol: Managing Leaders to Weekly Data Meetings (DVD)<br>  ○ Film data meetings to review together<br>  ○ Look at student work together to identify the gaps | |
| 2. Introductory Professional Development | **Partial Implementation**<br>• Opening PD addresses the topic of data-driven instruction, but teachers leave without the opportunity to fully understand and apply the tenets of assessment, analysis and action | • Review PD agenda for introducing DDI<br>• Role play the delivery of the PD and get feedback<br>• Execute DDI PD for teachers | ***Driven by Data 2.0***<br>• PD Session plan, videos, and materials (DVD)<br>***Leverage Leadership 2.0***<br>• Videos of Data Meetings (DVD, Clips 1–14)<br>***Get Better Faster***<br>• Videos of Weekly Data Meetings (DVD, Clips 20–22) |
| 3. Calendar | **Partial Implementation**<br>• Calendar includes some but not all of the items needed for proficient analysis and action | • Build more complete data-driven instruction calendar following the samples in the book<br>• Generate strategies (if needed) to find extra paid-time for scoring and analysis | ***Driven by Data 2.0***<br>• Sample Assessment Calendars (DVD) |

| | | | |
|---|---|---|---|
| | • Calendar is partially in place from the start of the year.<br>• Calendar is not very explicit within the culture of the school | • Make a plan to disseminate the assessment calendar among all the staff in the school | ***Driven by Data 2.0***<br>• PD Session plans, videos, and materials (DVD)<br>***Get Better Faster***<br>• Videos and coaching materials for action steps for increasing rigor (DVD, Clips 2, 5, 10, 16–20, 23–35)<br>• *Get Better Faster* Scope and Sequence of Action Steps<br>**Other Resources**<br>• *Great Habits, Great Readers:* PD agenda and videos for training around K–4 Reading (40+ clips)<br>• *Teach Like a Champion 2.0* (Lemov, 2016): PD agendas and 75 video clips for a large set of elements of effective teaching |
| **4. Ongoing Professional Development** | **Partial Implementation**<br>• A couple of PD sessions are offered throughout the year that are aligned with the data-driven cycle<br>• PD is delivered with quality, but some participants may not have skills needed post-PD<br>• PD may lack sufficient modeling and application so that teachers have the skills needed to do analysis and action | • Evaluate the core need areas of students and teachers after each round of interim assessments<br>• Design PD agendas to meet those needs<br>• Observe leader facilitating the PD session | |

(Continued)

**Table 5.1** (Continued)

| | Beginning Implementation | Action Steps for Principals and Coaches | Resources |
|---|---|---|---|
| **I Data-Driven Culture** | | | |
| **5. Build by Borrowing** | **Partial Implementation**<br>• Some leaders and teachers are borrowing ideas from their peers and from other schools, but that does not translate to schoolwide action<br>• Many teachers work in complete isolation | • Identify high-achieving schools with the city and outside the city that would merit a visit<br>  ○ Schedule a visit to one of these schools<br>  ○ Debrief the visit with team: what could you apply to your school?<br>• Identify ways to increase collaboration and sharing between high-achieving teachers within the school and the rest of their peers<br>  ○ Generate team meeting protocols to share best practices<br>  ○ Create formal mentoring roles | ***Driven by Data 2.0***<br>• Success Stories (embedded throughout the book)<br>***Leverage Leadership 2.0***<br>• Chapter 1—Data-driven instruction<br>• Success Stories (start of every chapter)<br>***Get Better Faster***<br>• 50 tips/testimonials from school leaders across the country (embedded in text) |

| | Beginning Implementation | Action Steps for Coaches | Resources |
|---|---|---|---|
| **II Assessments** | | | |
| **1. Common Interim** | **Partial Implementation**<br>• Administered two or three times per year<br>• Common for grade and content area<br>• Only given in math and literacy at every grade level 3–11 | • Insert an additional interim assessment into the gap between two assessments that are too far apart<br>• MS/HS: Acquire Science/Social Studies interim assessments for implementation<br>• ES: Acquire K–2 math and early literacy assessments<br>• Common for grade and content area<br>• Given in math and literacy at every grade level 3–11 | ***Driven by Data 2.0***<br>n/a<br>**Other Resources**<br>• STEP Assessments: K–2 literacy Assessments (University of Chicago)<br>• Assessments from other schools<br>• PARCC and SBAC website<br>• www.engageny.org |

| | | | Driven by Data 2.0 |
|---|---|---|---|
| **2. Transparent Starting Point** | **Partial Implementation**<br>• Teachers see assessments weeks before the administration or at a minimum, teachers are able to see the assessment before it is administered | • Where transparency is not an option:<br>  ○ Find the best proxy for the interim assessment and have teachers review that proxy at the beginning of each IA cycle<br>• Work to build in time for teachers to review upcoming interim assessments | **Driven by Data 2.0**<br>n/a<br>**Other Resources**<br>• STEP Assessments: K–2 Literacy Assessments (University of Chicago)<br>• Assessments from other schools<br>• PARCC and SBAC website<br>• www.engageny.org |
| **3. Alignment with State and College** | **Partial Implementation**<br>• Assessment items and tests match the state test level of rigor at least 50% of the time<br>• Alignment to college readiness is understood by leaders, but little action has occurred to make this alignment happen in the assessments | • Where this is possible, build a long-term plan to enhance the alignment and college readiness of the interim assessments<br>  ○ Identify the resources within your city: which schools have quality assessments/assessment supplements<br>  ○ Build a Spring/Summer design plan<br>  ○ Identify the resources to support the revision of the interim assessments<br><br>Note: This is <u>not</u> a quick hit. Only prioritize this when other areas are strongly in place. | **Driven by Data 2.0**<br>• Assessment Alignment Spreadsheet (DVD)<br>**Other Resources**<br>• Other schools in your state who have quality interim assessments<br>• PARCC and SBAC website<br>• www.engageny.org |

*(Continued)*

Table 5.1 (Continued)

| | | II Assessments | | |
|---|---|---|---|---|
| | Beginning Implementation | Action Steps for Coaches | | Resources |
| **4. Aligned to Instructional Sequence** | **Partial Implementation**<br>• Grade level or content area has a clearly defined scope and sequence of standards, but assessments only partially match the scope and sequence. What is taught is assessed | • Build a long-term plan to improve the alignment between the teaching scope and sequence the interim assessments<br>  o Identify the resources within your city: which schools have quality alignment<br>  o Build a Spring/Summer design plan<br>  o Identify the resources to support the revision of the scope and sequence<br>*Note: This is not a quick hit. Only prioritize this when other areas are strongly in place.* | | ***Driven by Data 2.0***<br>n/a<br>**Other Resources**<br>• Same as above |
| **5. Reassess** | **Partial Implementation**<br>• Assessments sporadically reassess standards throughout the year | • See above: same next steps | | ***Driven by Data 2.0***<br>• Assessment Alignment Spreadsheet (DVD)<br>**Other Resources**<br>• Same as above |
| | | III Analysis | | |
| | Beginning Implementation | Action Steps for Coaches | | Resources |
| **1. Immediate Turnaround** | **Partial Implementation**<br>• Results available within a week<br>• Teachers not involved, or minimally involved in scoring | • Evaluate the process of scoring turnaround: where can the scoring be accomplished more quickly?<br>• ID necessary supports/resources to quicken the scoring | | ***Driven by Data 2.0***<br>• Sample Interim Assessment Schedule (Chapter 2, Analysis) |

| | Partial Implementation | | Resources |
|---|---|---|---|
| **2. Simple Data Reports** | • Reports either have too little or too much information<br>• Reports might not include item analysis or overall results<br>• Reports are understandable for leaders but require some interpretation for teachers | • Utilize an existing template in your city to design a more concise analysis report/spreadsheet for teacher analysis<br>• Create a calendar for implementation of the better data report | **Driven by Data 2.0**<br>• Sample Data Report/Analysis Spreadsheet (DVD)<br>**Other Resources**<br>• Illuminate software<br>• Other data reporting software that meet the criteria |
| **3. Teacher-Owned** | **Partial Implementation**<br>• Teachers do too little of the analysis; analysis mostly done by principal, instructional leader or a "data team"<br>• Teachers may lack knowledge and skill to effectively and efficiently analyze results<br>• Teachers analyze, but may blame test or students for poor results | • Watch video of effective leader facilitation of assessment analysis meetings that get teacher to own the analysis. Debrief and discuss techniques to improve implementation<br>• Execute weekly data meetings | **Driven by Data 2.0**<br>• One-Pager: Leading Effective Weekly Data Meetings (DVD)<br>• PD Agendas for "Analysis" (Chapter 9)<br>• Conceptual Understanding of "Analysis" (Chapter 2)<br>**Leverage Leadership 2.0**<br>• Videos of Data Meetings (DVD, Clips 1–14)<br>**Get Better Faster**<br>• Videos of Weekly Data Meetings (DVD, Clips 20–22) |

(Continued)

**Table 5.1** (Continued)

| | | III Analysis | |
| --- | --- | --- | --- |
| | Beginning Implementation | Action Steps for Coaches | Resources |
| **4. Test in Hand** | **Partial Implementation**<br>• Teachers or leaders have the assessments in hand during analysis, but not both<br>• Teachers look mostly at the assessment questions, and do not focus strongly on the student responses | • Set up plan to lead assessment analysis meetings: ensure that the test will be used during the analysis meeting<br>• Observe assessment analysis meetings<br>• Execute weekly data meetings | ***Driven by Data 2.0***<br>n/a<br>***Leverage Leadership 2.0***<br>• Videos of Data Meetings (DVD, Clips 1–14)<br>***Get Better Faster***<br>• Videos of Weekly Data Meetings (DVD, Clips 20–22) |
| **5. Deep Analysis** | **Partial Implementation**<br>• Teachers reach actionable conclusions with analysis, but often conclusions are general and not fully based on a deep understanding of results<br>• Analysis includes some generalizations like "students need to read more" or "students need to practice problem-solving" | • Watch video of effective leader facilitation of assessment analysis meetings that get teacher to own the analysis. Debrief and discuss techniques to improve implementation<br>• Execute weekly data meetings | ***Driven by Data 2.0***<br>• One-Pager: Leading Effective Weekly Data Meetings (DVD)<br>• Conceptual Understanding of "Analysis" (Chapter 2)<br>***Leverage Leadership 2.0***<br>• Videos of Data Meetings (DVD, Clips 1–14)<br>***Get Better Faster***<br>• Videos of Weekly Data Meetings (DVD, Clips 20–22) |

| | Beginning Implementation | IV Action – Action Steps for Coaches | Resources |
|---|---|---|---|
| **1. Re-teach** | **Partial Implementation**<br>• Teacher teams problem-solve and plan together based on data, but often not focused on specific student needs or don't have specific lesson plans as a result<br>• Planning conversations often focus on teaching it again, and less on how to teach it differently | • Do a review of teacher lesson plans with leadership team: is there evidence of re-teaching or targeted teaching of key standards on the interim assessments?<br>• Plan with leadership team the support for teachers who are struggling to implement new teaching strategies for re-teaching difficult standards<br>• Deliver PD for teachers on core re-teaching techniques:<br>  ○ Modeling<br>  ○ Guided Discourse<br>  ○ Monitoring | ***Driven by Data 2.0***<br>• Video clips of Monitoring, Modeling and Discourse (DVD)<br>***Leverage Leadership 2.0***<br>• Video clips of Monitoring, Modeling and Discourse (DVD, Clips 3–5)<br>***Get Better Faster***<br>• Video clips of Monitoring, Modeling and Discourse (DVD, Clips 28, 29, 31–33)<br>• *Get Better Faster* Scope and Sequence of Action Steps |
| **2. Six-week Action Plans** | **Partial Implementation**<br>• Teachers plan for re-teaching, but often planning is not specific regarding goals, time, and strategy<br>• Differentiation is present in planning, but often only superficial | • Analyze exemplar six-week action plans in the book and do a gap analysis with school's current teacher action plans with leadership team: where are they lacking?<br>• Plan out the work with each teacher to improve their action plans | ***Driven by Data 2.0***<br>• Teacher Action Plan Template (DVD)<br>• Exemplar Six-week Teacher Action Plans (DVD) |

(Continued)

**Table 5.1** (Continued)

| | | IV Action | |
|---|---|---|---|
| | Beginning Implementation | Action Steps for Coaches | Resources |
| **3. Ongoing Assessment** | **Partial Implementation**<br>• Teachers assess at least weekly based on previous data and standards currently being taught<br>• Teachers link weekly assessment to re-teaching, but often fail to act based on reassessment results<br>• Ongoing assessment efforts rarely take into account the different levels of proficiency present in the class | • Lead PD for teachers on aggressively monitoring independent practice and/or check for understanding techniques<br>• Schedule periodic building walk-through with leadership team:<br>  ○ Are they monitoring independent practice effectively?<br>  ○ Is there evidence of checking for understanding in the classes (questioning, Do Now review, exit tickets, etc.)?<br>  ○ Do a spot check of teacher quizzes/tests: are they aligned to or exceed the rigor of the interim assessments?<br>• Plan out the work of the leadership team with the teachers who need the most support in this area | ***Driven by Data 2.0***<br>• Videos of Effective Reteaching (DVD)<br>***Get Better Faster***<br>• Video clips of aggressively monitoring student work (DVD, Clips 17–18)<br>• Video clips of check for understanding (DVD, Clips 26, 27, 31)<br>• *Get Better Faster* Scope and Sequence of Action Steps |
| **4. Follow-up/ Accountability** | **Partial Implementation**<br>• Leaders are aware of action plans but don't have much personal knowledge of their content<br>• Leader is only periodically observing for re-teaching and rarely focused on specific re-teaching efforts | Create simple, effective systems for monitoring follow-up:<br>• Post six-week action plans in the classrooms<br>  ○ Put DDI action plans on a clipboard hanging on the wall in the back of each classroom so leaders can review them while observing | ***Driven by Data 2.0***<br>• Accountability Measures one-pager (DVD)<br>***Leverage Leadership 2.0***<br>• Observation tracker<br>• Observation schedule |

| | |
|---|---|
| • Leaders follow up with teachers after observing, but often this follow-up is not specifically linked to the data and instructional practice<br>• Follow-up by leader often lacks clear, actionable changes sought to classroom instruction | • Post lesson plans in the classroom:<br>  o Post lesson plans on a clipboard in the back of each classroom so leaders can review them while observing<br>  o When observing, check with the lesson plan to see if the overall objective is being taught and assessed, and if challenging standards are being re-taught<br>  o Add a "reflection" box to the lesson plan template where teachers identify which action step from their data analysis they're working on each day/week<br>• Bring student work to teacher-leader check-ins:<br>  o Monitor the progress of students<br>• Schedule periodic building walk-through with leadership team:<br>  o Is there evidence of checking for understanding in the classes (questioning, Do Now review, exit tickets, etc.)?<br>  o Do a spot check of teacher quizzes/tests: are they aligned to or exceed the rigor of the interim assessments? |

(Continued)

**Table 5.1** (Continued)

| | | IV Action | |
| | Beginning Implementation | Action Steps for Coaches | Resources |
|---|---|---|---|
| | | • Create an observation tracker for leaders to track follow-up observations; review the tracker at your regular check-ins | |
| **5. Engaged Students** | **Partial Implementation**<br>• Students are aware of their performance on the assessments<br>• Students can articulate why the interim assessments are important<br>• Students know they are working during class time to develop mastery toward standards | • Generate a calendar of action steps that will get students more involved in their analysis<br>• Acquire a student engagement reflection sheet and adjust to his/her needs<br>• Do a spot check with students during school visits: whether they know/don't know about their assessment results | ***Driven by Data 2.0***<br>• Student Engagement Reflection Template (DVD)<br>**Other Resources**<br>• Student Engagement templates from other leaders in your city |

# FREQUENTLY ASKED QUESTIONS

Even with this guide in hand, you might have some key questions. We've tried to answer the questions we have received over the years with the responses from schools like yours. Here are the top questions and a corresponding answer.

## Assessment Questions

### Are interim assessments and formative assessments the same thing?

Kim Marshall has established himself as one of the definitive authors on this topic. We recommend four to six interim assessments which follow the key drivers outlined in Chapter 2. This definition of interim assessment coincides with Marshall's. Still, teachers assess every day. As Kim Marshall defines them, formative assessments are "in-the-moment" checks for understanding: dipsticking, Do Nows, exit tickets, quizzes, etc. There is no end to the times when teachers can use such assessments.

The difference between interim assessments and formative, in-the-moment assessments, is their scope. Interim assessments cover all material taught up to that point, whereas formative assessments can look at any subset of what has been taught. Therefore, a unit test that only assesses standards from Unit 2 and not Unit 1 cannot be an adequate interim assessment. In the end, both interim assessments *and* in-the-moment assessments are necessary and important. In this book, we consider in-the-moment assessments a part of the action steps teachers take pre- and post-interim assessment. Thus, look in Chapter 4 (Action) for more details on in-the-moment assessments.

### Aren't formative assessments enough to drive learning?

Kim Marshall's work is useful here as well. *By not assessing all standards taught up to that point, formative assessments run the risk of not gauging student retention of their learning.* Most learning is not like riding a bike: if you stop practicing, you forget what you've learned. (Poll the room at your next workshop: of all the people who took calculus in HS/college and do not currently use it, how many actually are still proficient at it?) I cannot tell you how many times I have seen a teacher check for understanding in the classroom and see that the students have mastered the material, only to find out that a month later they no longer are able to show the same mastery. Interim assessments make sure not to leave this to chance: you effectively track student progress on all standards.

**We have so many state/district-mandated assessments being thrown at us, far more than the 4–6 per year per subject recommended in the assessment section. Don't we reach a point of "over-assessing?" How should we cope with this?**

You definitely can reach a saturation point, and unfortunately many districts have. We recommend having a strong school focus on just 4–6 assessment cycles per year, and giving little emphasis to any other assessments you are required to implement. By "strong," we mean full scoring, deep analysis, and effective action as outlined by the data-driven model presented here. For the other assessments, don't build in analysis/action focus. More than that can be overwhelming, especially for a staff who has not engaged in this work before. Additionally, by limiting this to 4–6 times per year, you keep it manageable from a leadership perspective . . . and you will be able to dedicate the time to leading the analysis and action components.

Schools have used many strategies to deal with over-assessing mandated by districts:

- Actively lobbying districts to change their assessment policy to meeting the principles shown here (show them this book!).
- Creating a "normal" class tone for mandated assessments that won't be the focus of the school year: treating them as simply an in-class assignment, not giving it importance for students or teachers, simply complying with the mandate.
- (If permitted) even assigning the district assessment as a homework assignment!

**My district only has 2–3 assessments, and they aren't cumulative. How can we cope with this most effectively?**

It is much easier to deal with too few assessments than too many. In this case, simply build an additional assessment that you can put in the largest time gap between district assessments, and make sure it covers all standards up to that point.

**My district assessments are poor. They don't follow the key principles: they're not aligned to our sequence, or they're not aligned to the state tests, or they're not cumulative. How do we deal with each of these situations?**

Poorly designed mandated interim assessments are one of the most common failures of school districts. Until the districts design better assessments, use the following strategies:

- For non-cumulative assessments, build a supplemental assessment to give alongside the district assessment that fills in the gaps of all the standards not covered. Give it to the students at the same time as the district assessment so it still feels like only one test administration. Do the analysis of both assessments combined.

- De-emphasize the district assessments completely (see strategies above) and use an alternative set of interim assessments.

**Our district has secretive interim assessments: they don't let leaders or teachers see what is being assessed as a roadmap for instruction. We've tried to talk to them about the importance of transparency, but they're not changing. What can we do?**

A lack of transparency around interim assessments continues to be one of the biggest errors of many districts. Rather than seeing the interim assessments as teaching tools, they see them as evaluative, which defeats the whole purpose! I have personally met many school leaders who have been able to use the guidance of this book to "manage up" and convince their districts about the importance of transparency and they have been successful. If, however, you are unable to succeed, here is the best alternative:

- Build a "proxy" interim assessment: something that is as close as possible to the real thing. Share that with teachers so that they can plan backwards in their teaching. A proxy assessment won't be perfect but at least it will give your teachers something to shoot towards.

- Borrow interim assessments from another organization/district that has the <u>same</u> end-goal test as you have. They will likely be aligned to the end goal and will help prepare you for that test (they might be even better than your district's own interim assessments!).

- Borrow interim assessments from another organization/district that has a more rigorous, challenging end-goal assessment than you have. If you don't have clear guidance, shooting higher will often land you in a good place.

**We don't have interim assessments. Creating our own seems like a monumental task. Should we just purchase a commercial set of assessments?**

Creating your own interim assessments is indeed a monumental task. If you have the time and personnel to do so, it can be a very valuable experience that increases teacher buy-in. However, it is not essential. The best strategy is to *consult the highest-achieving urban schools in your state* that use interim assessments, and follow their lead ("Build by Borrowing" at its best!). If you choose to look at commercially made assessments, beware that most of these companies are national and design almost identical assessments for every state, despite the differences in state assessments. Don't take my word for it (or theirs). Evaluate any product according to the assessment principles presented in Chapter 2. Ask them to give you an actual interim assessment and compare it to your state test. We've included a template in Chapter 1 to assist you in doing a question-by-question analysis: "Assessment Evaluation Template." If the assessment doesn't meet your specifications, *push the assessment company to improve their product.*

Ideally, you want a product that gives you flexibility to match your school's specific scope and sequence. I see no reason why each school should not make their own decision about the order in which they will teach their standards. As long as the final interim assessment is the same (and aligned to state tests and college-ready expectations), the first interim assessments can follow any particular sequence.

**What do you do when the students have done poorly on every aspect of an interim assessment? You cannot really re-teach all of it.**

An excellent question. When students fail on almost all of the questions of an assessment, there are obviously major problems. The reasons behind this performance probably include one or more of the following:

- The test was well above what the students were able to master in the prescribed time period.
- The test doesn't assess what the teacher taught during that time period.
- The students arrived years below grade level, so a grade-level assessment is beyond their reach at the moment.
- Teaching was inadequate.

One of the core premises of assessment is that you must start at the students' learning level. However, if our goal is for all students to be proficient, and in many urban settings students arrive well below grade level, how do we address the need to cover more than a year's worth of learning in one year? *You need to map out an interim assessment cycle that takes students on an accelerated path to grade-level proficiency.* Here are some examples of how the highest-achieving urban schools have accomplished this:

- **Middle Schools:** The initial grade levels have assessments that start with pre-grade-level material and progressively advance to grade-level material, reaching proficiency by the end of the first year/beginning of the second. For example, the first sixth grade interim assessment included all pre-sixth grade content (e.g., fourth and fifth grade math standards), the second sixth grade interim assessment included 25% sixth grade material, and the last sixth grade interim assessment covered 75% of grade-level year-end standards. By the middle of seventh standard, every interim assessment was at or above grade level in terms of its materials.

- **High Schools:** Here, where the gap is even greater, high-achieving high schools have created pre-Algebra classes that cover all necessary building blocks to prepare for Algebra. They often double up math classes—having students take Pre-Algebra before school and then a standard Algebra class during the school day—in order for students to still complete a standard math sequence.

- **Elementary Schools (K–5):** At this grade level, the highest achieving urban schools have been able to close the achievement gap almost immediately by using the existing plethora of early literacy assessments effectively.

**What about K–2 assessments? Why is there no clear-cut consensus on assessing at this age?**

There are a lot of reasons for difficulties here. On one side, people argue that children are too young to be assessed at this age. Ironically, there are more early literacy assessments than any other age. In fact, when you think about the time it takes to administer individual reading assessments, there is more time spent assessing in K–2 than any other grade span. Often, these teachers have more data than anyone else and yet don't know how to piece it all together in a coherent package that can drive instruction. Here are some recommendations for K–2 assessment:

- Beware of using an early literacy assessment that does not assess for critical reading comprehension along with more standard fluency and decoding. (Re-visit Chapter 1, Assessment, for more details.)

- Young children do not have to know they're being assessed. They're excited to "read to their teacher!" The key is that we know how they're doing, and that what we assess for is the most effective.

- Kindergarteners absolutely can master K–1 math standards, conceptually and procedurally. Design a rigorous assessment of the foundational math skills (counting principles, basic number sense, addition/subtraction, etc.) and give students multiple opportunities to experience the mathematics and practice it. Uncommon Schools (see Alexander Street case study as one example) has developed K–1 math assessments that have led to dramatic achievement results. The assessments are only four times a year, only 20–30 questions.

- The curriculum chosen isn't what determines student achievement results; it's the data-driven drivers listed in this book. Case in point: both Saxon Math and Investigations, two math programs that are often considered at two opposite ends of the spectrum of math pedagogy, have led to strong achievement results. By driving yourself via results, you add rigor to whatever curriculum you choose (often by supplementing from other sources!).

- Below grade 2, it is almost always necessary to administer the assessment one-on-one or in small groups to ensure you get valid information. Remember, a student's reading difficulties should not impede your ability to understand their math skills . . . therefore, reading the math test to them is likely a good idea.

**Is it OK to postpone content on an interim assessment because teachers simply aren't getting enough covered?**

Yes. For the moment, let us assume you have control over the content of the interim assessment. *The key is that the content is not eliminated, but simply postponed until the next interim assessment.* Some might argue that this is lowering the standard. But consider the alternative: you decide not to be flexible and leave the content that the teacher hasn't covered on the interim assessment. The interim assessments results come in, and the teacher's students do very poorly on these questions. Immediately the teacher will fixate on this and protest that the interim assessment wasn't fair. While you can argue with that teacher, you have already set up a resistant analysis conversation. If the students are going to do poorly on the questions anyway, then postponing the questions validates the teacher's concern and forces him/her to focus on those standards that they covered that students still didn't master. Postponed content will still appear on the next assessments, and the teacher will still be held accountable to mastery of those standards. Most districts have eliminated the possibility of making adjustments to the interim assessments. The above principles can still apply. If there are a series of questions that measure content that hasn't yet been taught, while you cannot postpone that content, you can focus your analysis with the teachers on the rest of the standards. That's the most important content to analyze.

## Analysis Questions

**There's so much data: what should we focus on?**

One of the number one errors in this world of data is too much information. *As a general rule of thumb, each teacher should have only one piece of paper for each classroom of students or subject that they lead.* This flies in direct contrast to most state and commercial data analysis companies. They think that more is better. This is far from the truth. In this framework, the single-most important driver of student achievement is teacher analysis of specific assessment questions (called item analysis by many). Standards-level and summative analysis won't drive change without looking at individual questions.

These are the three levels of analysis that matter, in this order:

- question-level analysis;
- standards-level analysis (particularly, how students performed differently on questions measuring the same standard, and on related standards);
- overall analysis: how students did in one class compared to another, or one school compared to the district.

Teachers can do very effective analysis with the first two levels of analysis; leaders benefit the most from adding the third level.

**But isn't it important to do a thorough analysis of last year's test data, which normally doesn't include question-level analysis?**

Richard DuFuor provided an excellent analogy that addresses this question. He mentioned that when someone is sick, you normally see a doctor or go to the hospital. You don't wait until someone dies to figure out what is wrong! *Analyzing year-end test data is just that: you are doing an autopsy on last year's data.* The performance of the students is gone: the data is "dead." The students are older, they're in a new grade level, and they have new standards to learn. It is far better to analyze data from the current year—to go to the hospital right away—rather than wait until the end of the year. Thus, I argue it's far better to focus efforts on analyzing interim assessment data—or a pre-test at the beginning of the year. This is the analysis that will drive change while there's still something we can do about it. (The one notable exception to this rule is K–5 leveled reading assessments. It is essential to know what reading level a child had in first grade to determine their reading instruction at the start of second grade.)

**What is the best way to begin data analysis when I'm just starting at a school?**

Give a quick look at the available test data from the previous year to see if you can identify any best practices within your school. Then focus on the implementation of your first interim assessment. The best possible thing you can do is give an interim assessment that matches the concepts/skills (standards) that the teachers have been teaching (or were supposed to be teaching) during the first 8–9 weeks. This will provide you with instant information on how the students are doing on material they were taught.

**Many districts promote teacher "data teams" that lead analysis for the entire school. Does that meet the "teacher-owned" criteria?**

Not by itself. "Teacher-owned" analysis refers to teachers owning the data *for their own students*. Another teacher is *not* a replacement for teachers doing their own analysis. If a school data team is in charge of setting up effective analysis spreadsheets and getting them into the hands of teachers, then the data team is on the right track. If they are trained in facilitating effective analysis meetings (as the Follow-up Workshop provides), then they can be even more effective agents of change! However, a data team that tries to analyze data for the other teachers will fail at making the largest impact it can.

## Action Questions

**What are the most effective strategies for action that are not content-specific? Does one strategy fit all teachers?**

Clearly not. As Jon Saphier has stated so precisely, teaching is all about matching: choosing the right strategy for the right circumstance. Therefore, the keys to creating more effective teachers in their action plans are two-fold:

- Develop a larger repertoire of strategies from which to choose.
- Build the capacity to understand when is most effective to use each of these strategies.

To help teachers develop more targeted action strategies, we observed the highest-achieving teachers in the country (teachers who have achieved either 30+ point gains in student achievement and/or have reached 90%+ proficiency) and generated a list of the most effective techniques to add rigor to any lesson. That was the origination of the Get Better Faster Scope & Sequence of teacher action steps. Half of the action steps relate to classroom management, but the other half are about rigor, and they center on more effective data-driven practices at all levels. That document is available on the DVD that accompanies this book, and the book *Get Better Faster* walks through the process of coaching teachers on each item on the Scope & Sequence in detail.

**So does that mean that all teachers should be allowed to have their own style and not have to plan together?**

Style and effectiveness are two separate things. The power of data-driven instruction is that every decision can be based on the impact on student achievement. What normally happens in a school that implements interim assessments effectively is that best practices rise to the top and are adopted by others in the school (the Culture principle "Build by Borrowing"). Every teacher can have their own "style," but that style cannot interfere with student learning. Therefore, collective planning—especially when using a tight format like the Results Meeting protocol—is very important.

**How do we guide teachers when they choose different strategies?**

Simple: Let the results do the talking. At the beginning, allow (even encourage) teachers to choose different strategies. After each round of interim assessments, see which strategies were most effective based on the results on the assessments. Over time, clear best practices will emerge. In the case where they don't (i.e., no teachers in the school have had success with a particular standard), look to best practices in neighboring schools that have achieved stronger results with the same students.

## Culture Questions

**You say that data-driven instruction creates buy-in rather than requires it. So what are effective strategies to deal with initial resistance, especially given how many bad experiences teachers have had with data-driven instruction done poorly?**

The number one tool you have is quality professional development and formation, which is why that has been the core content of this book. Second, you need to create the ideal conditions for data-driven instruction to succeed, thus using the drivers listed in the summative data-driven rubric here. Third, you need to allow teachers to progress naturally in their acceptance of the power of this model. As highlighted in the follow-up workshop, Camden County, Georgia School District, wrote an excellent article describing the phases of acceptance that teachers/leaders go through before embracing this approach to teaching and learning. What makes the model presented here so effective is that you already start to get results even before staff really believes in its power. In fact, once data-driven instruction is implemented effectively, it often becomes such a part of the fabric of the school that staff members don't even identify it as one of the drivers of student achievement—it just becomes inherent to the school's DNA!

One final important piece is for everyone to experience little successes. All it takes is identifying how students did better on certain standards on the second interim assessments based on teacher re-teaching, and you create the awareness that this works. Always note what went well even when focusing on standards that need major improvement. (For other ideas, read the answer to the next question as well.)

**Why is there no mention of S.M.A.R.T. goals in your list of most important drivers of data-driven instruction?**

S.M.A.R.T. goals have reached almost universal acceptance as a driver of change in education. Yet when looking only at the highest-achieving urban school in the country, there is not consensus on its importance. While some schools have found them useful to drive achievement, other highest-achieving schools have not. Once a culture has been established of driving instructional change via interim assessments, S.M.A.R.T. goals become less important or no longer useful. Thus, the drivers listed for data-driven culture do not include S.M.A.R.T. goals.

**Our school doesn't need to be convinced of the importance of being data-driven, but they're only doing some of the core drivers listed in this book. Our results are good, but they're not excellent. The good results, however, create a sense of complacency. How can we build urgency about moving from good to great?**

The "Build by Borrowing" driver is essential here. You need to get the school staff to look outside their building at schools that are getting even better results. Use the case studies in this book to identify these schools. Read your state's annual report cards and see which schools have similar student populations and are achieving even more strongly. But the single-best creator of urgency is to take as many of your leaders and teachers to visit a data-driven high-achieving school. Most of the schools in the case studies in this book describe their visits to higher-achieving schools than they were at the time as one of the pivotal urgency-creators for the school community. Seeing success in action creates belief that you, too, can succeed at a higher level. Reading case studies are never as powerful as seeing them!

# Chapter 6

# Leading PD for Adults

Now you've learned it all: you've read up on assessment, analysis, action, culture, and the tools for overcoming obstacles in implementing them all. But unless you pass that knowledge along to other instructors, it won't have an impact on more than a few students. How will you train the teachers and leaders in your school or district in the principles of data-driven instructors?

That's where adult professional development (PD) comes in. At this point, if you're remembering a sequence of PD sessions you've attended that failed to transform your instruction, you're not alone: all too often, PD sessions are a weak driver of school improvement, with the lessons learned falling by the wayside as participants make the trek back from the conference room to the classroom. The good news is that the path to breaking that pattern, replacing lackluster PD with transformative PD, leads us straight back to data.

The qualities of an effective PD are, in fact, remarkably straightforward:

1. Effective PD responds to a real need revealed by data.

2. Effective PD gives participants time to *practice* the skills they'll need to succeed.

In this chapter, we'll show you how to determine both the content and the structure of your PD. This will give you the ability both to lead the PDs on data-driven instruction provided on the DVD that accompanies this book, and to create powerful PD of your own.

First, though, let's examine some common errors in PD presentation, and the reasons they hold PD back from changing the game.

## FIVE FREQUENT ERRORS ASSOCIATED WITH ADULT PD

The most critical errors in leadership training stem from an incomplete understanding of core principles involved in adult learning.

1. **Teaching by Talking:** Even though research consistently shows that adults rarely retain what they hear (retaining far more when they have to use it), adult leadership training consistently errs on the side of lecture. PowerPoint can simply be a modernized form of an outdated approach. This may seem counterintuitive; after all, when presenters are chosen to run workshops, surely people expect them to do the talking, right? Not exactly. Think about how few details you can remember even from the most engaging lectures. If we want leaders to walk away with concrete tools to build systems in their schools, trainers need to reduce their own talking to a minimum.

2. **Treating Adults Primarily by "I do-We do-You do" (Guided Practice):** While some leaders err on the side of lecture, others err on the side of leading adult PD in the same way they would in a traditional K–12 classroom: "I do-We do-You do." The leader presents information, models using it, and then asks to adults to use it. While this framework significantly increases learning when compared to a standard lecture, it does not address a core tenet of adult education: adults need to generate the content they are learning to be invested in it and to retain it longer. "I do-We do-You do" also sends an implicit message that the participants don't

have much to offer on the topic and the presenter is the knowledge-generator. Yet adults learn the most when they reach conclusions mostly on their own. Few workshop leaders think about creating the learning experiences that allow for this sort of adult investment.

3. **Not Specifically Targeting Leaders:** When presenting data-driven instruction to school leaders, many educators focus primarily on the perspective of classroom teachers. Although this is an intuitive inclination, it is a poor strategy because it ignores the specific role that school leaders must play in implementing any data-based strategy. Rather than focus on the classroom, effective leadership training must emphasize the specific, concrete skills needed by school leaders. If the concerns unique to school leaders are neglected, then not only will they lose focus, but when they return to their schools they will be unable to implement data-driven instruction effectively. As such, it is imperative that every single activity on every day of training is aimed at building effective data-driven *school leaders*.

4. **Struggling to Structure Large Group Sharing:** A core element of many workshops is large group dialogue: question and answer session with the presenter, small group presentations to each other, conversation around a topic presented, etc. Allowing for large group sharing makes sure that participants have a chance to verbalize their learning and share their knowledge with each other, a critical learning component. However, this is also one of the most difficult components to manage, as group participation can vary significantly from one group to the next. Presenters often struggle to know when to let a conversation continue and when to cut it off. Also, when looking for the group to reach a certain conclusion and hearing an incorrect answer, presenters will often state the conclusions themselves rather than allowing more time for participants to unearth these conclusions. Invariably, some participants will make an off-topic observation or ask an off-task but fascinating question. Without proper management, participants risk going off-track, or if the presenter cuts them off too abruptly, they can decide to shut down.

5. **Poorly Planning Transitions and Time Management**: When presenting a workshop to a group of 15 people or less, leaders do not have to worry as much about the quality of their instructions or the transitions between activities. If a small group didn't understand what they were supposed to do, you can simply walk

over to that group and re-explain the instructions without pause. If there is any uncertainty about the task at hand in a workshop with 100 people, however, it will take too long to communicate this message to all the small groups, resulting in significant wasted time. In addition, getting a group of 100 to "form groups of four" requires far more planning and potentially more structure. Without attention to instructions and transitions between activities, significant learning time can be lost.

## FOLLOW THE DATA . . . AND JUST DO IT

So what's the alternative to all these ineffective approaches to PD? The answer is the same sequence we applied to data meetings: See It, Name It, and Do It. First, get your participants to see what the ideal action you want them to learn looks like; next, get them to name the characteristics of that ideal action; and most importantly by scores, get them to do it. The Do It is the portion of your PD that participants will practice. It will make or break the session, because it will equip them to use their new skills on the ground.

---

### Core Idea

Your PD is only as powerful as what you practice.

---

As a result, the first step to crafting powerful PD is identifying the content your participants will practice. Your data will tell you what that content is.

### Follow the Data

Depending on what your school is working to improve, data about your school's PD needs could come from teacher observations, culture walkthroughs, or any number of other sources. When it comes to PD that directly addresses student learning, however, look no further than assessment data and student work. Assessments will point you to school-wide areas for curricular or instructional improvement. Analyzing interim assessment data or even daily exit tickets reveals larger patterns that cut across classes and grade levels. Recall an example of exemplary analysis from Chapter 2:

## ELA IA #7–1—Network Analysis

### Most Significant Trend of Errors in Seventh Grade

Uncommon Schools | Change History.

INTERIM ASSESSMENT #7–1 TEACHER DATA ANALYSIS

| What? | Deep Drive Analysis—Why? |
|---|---|
| **Standard/Questions not Mastered** | **Which incorrect answer did students choose? Why did students not master this standard?** |
| **Central Idea & Evidence:** Determine a theme or central idea of a text and analyze its development over the course of the text; provide an objective summary of the text.<br><br>**Multiple Choice:** Question #7 (evidence)—17% correct Question #18 (claim)—42% Question #19 (evidence)—20%<br><br>**Open-Ended:** Essay: Claim—71% Essay: Evidence—52% | **What misunderstandings are revealed in the responses compared with the exemplar?** Across the IA, students struggled to identify the best claim and matching evidence to establish the claim of the text, both in their writing and on the multiple choice section of the test:<br><br>• **Questions 7 & 19** – Most students could find the main idea (questions #6 and 18) but that number dropped when needing to find evidence to support the claim. They often chose the answer that was general evidence but not the best answer that was more narrowly connected to the claim.<br><br>• **Writing**<br><br>   o **Essay – Claim (71%)** – Students often gave the approximate claim in response to the prompt and addressed the viewpoints in a general sense–but struggled to articulate the distinct techniques (the how) that the author's use to establish their viewpoints. This also led to an even lower evidence score. |

| What? | Deep Drive Analysis—Why? |
|---|---|
| Standard/Questions not Mastered | Which incorrect answer did students choose? Why did students not master this standard? |
| | o **Essay – Evidence (52%)** – Students chose evidence that was not completely without merit, but evidence chosen often was not the strongest possible to support the prompt–then students did not explain the "so what" behind their evidence, just restating the quote or simply explaining it without using it to build on the central idea. Students also struggled to limit their evidence ("chunk it") to the most critical part. |

**What gaps in the instruction contributed to these misunderstandings?**

As I compared student work to the exemplar response, I noticed that my students did not annotate the text in any way. I realized that I had focused so much of my instruction on getting the general gist of the passage but I had not taught them to focus on key evidence and to annotate while reading. I also did not teach the students how to pre-write for the essay. Thesis statements, in some cases, were unclear or vague–they didn't provide a clear, underlying argument for the essay.

**What will you do to help students achieve mastery? How will it be measured?**

- We'll conduct a lesson in week 10 on creating "just right" claim sentences–ones that aren't too broad or too narrowly tailored. In the lesson, students will evaluate a series of claims/arguments based on recent class prompts, labeling them as "just right," "too general," or "too specific." They will then develop their own topic sentences/arguments, using a graphic organizer, and complete peer revision to evaluate each other's work.

| What? | Deep Drive Analysis—Why? |
|---|---|
| Standard/Questions not Mastered | Which incorrect answer did students choose? Why did students not master this standard? |
| | • We'll also conduct a lesson where I will model how to annotate for claim: how to select evidence that supports my claim and how to take simple margin notes while reading. That will set up a 2nd model lesson later in the unit on how to pre-write for an essay: organizing evidence to support each sub-claim to make a stronger essay.<br><br>• We'll spiral this expectation into the grading of student writing by adding "best evidence" to the writing rubric.<br><br>○ Re-teach Lesson Objective: 70% of SWBAT earn a "3" or higher on the writing rubric for argumentation by writing a "just right" claim supported by the best evidence. |

With the tools for assessment and analysis already provided in this book, you already know how to determine what content will make for the highest-leverage PD objective for your staff (in this case, a focus on claim and evidence). Now the question becomes: what do you do with that information?

## Narrow the Focus

Designing a PD that tries to do too much leads to only one outcome: you end up talking too much. Teresa Khirallah, Program Officer for the Teaching Trust (and highlighted in *The Principal Manager's Guide to Leverage Leadership 2.0* for her outstanding work at scale in Dallas), has experienced this firsthand over the course of her career. "In the beginning of being a principal, I would talk most of the time and end up with only twelve minutes at the end for practice," Teresa remembers. "That meant when my teachers left the room, I still didn't really know if they could do the skill or not."

How, then, can you narrow the focus of your PD to what matters most? Once again, the heart of the matter is the Do It: what do you want them to practice? When it comes to great PD, practice and objective are one and the same.

---

### Core Idea

Narrow the focus of your PD with one simple question:
What do you want them to practice?

---

What participants practice is what they learn, and what you want them to learn is your objective. Successful leaders use the process of narrowing their objective to ensure the practice portion of the PD will also be effective. They do so by developing objectives that are highest leverage, measurable, and bite-sized:

---

### Practice What Matters: Keys to PD Objectives

Great PD objectives are:

1. **Highest-leverage.** The objective must be the most important skill teachers currently cannot do that will increase student learning and teacher proficiency.
2. **Measurable.** Can anyone practice this objective? Can a leader easily measure if teachers have met the objective (via observation, rubric, data, etc.)?
3. **Bite-sized.** Can you accomplish this objective in the time allotted for this PD?

---

What it means to make your PD bite-sized depends on the time you have for PD—an hour, a half-day, or several days. What you can accomplish will grow with the amount of time that you have.

Once you know what you're going to practice, you're ready to design and lead your workshop! Let's walk through the components of PD that stick.

## LIVE THE LEARNING

Most of us can remember a speaker who captivated us: someone who was inspiring, who punched their points with clever jokes, and who left us thinking about our work in a new way. And many of us are intimidated when we take on the task of emulating inspiring speakers, feeling we may lack the charisma or "presenter personality" to make an impact on our fellow educators.

The good news, though, is that making an impact as a presenter isn't about charisma or personality. Instead, the key to leading PD that makes an impact is meticulous preparation and using the See It-Name It-Do It framework—both of which are replicable steps for anyone. Let's see how.

## See It

Leading PD can be incredibly complex, especially when focusing on teaching content. The solution to this complexity is the same as in feedback and data meetings: let participants see it. Take a look at this clip of a PD I led recently in Dallas, Texas:

▶ WATCH Clip 18: See it, Name it—Leading PD

● 

### Stop and Jot

What does Paul do to launch his PD? Jot down what you notice below.

_____

_____

_____

_____

_____

Watching how the audience responds to the model reveals something crucial about leading PD: seeing is believing. If I'd simply told the instructors at this PD what constituted an effective model, they'd have had no reason to believe it, but when they see it for themselves, they buy in right away. Seeing the exemplar sets teachers up to be able to put it into action.

┌─────────────────────────────────────────────────┐
│                   **Core Idea**                   │
│   If you want a teacher to get it, get them to see it.   │
└─────────────────────────────────────────────────┘

These are the key actions that make the See It portion of a PD effective:

- **Choose the best model.** In this case, what teachers most needed to see first was how to prepare to observe students' reading—thus the teacher's plans were the best model. Later, they will need to see the teaching itself, and video clips of exemplary teaching are one of the most powerful ways for teachers to see the model. If you don't have one from your school, you can use one from another campus! Even more, there are many effective teaching clips that you can find in the books *Teach Like a Champion*, *Get Better Faster*, and *Great Habits, Great Readers*. If an exemplary video of an action is not available, an equally strong option is to model it yourself, or ask one of your teachers to do so. You can immediately earn your staff's respect when you are willing to model what you'd like them to do as well: you show that you are "walking the walk."

- **Keep it short.** A long See It won't hold the participants' attention—and will take valuable time away from practicing. Accordingly, keep it short: no longer than five minutes.

- **Target the focus.** The goal of the See It is to codify what makes the exemplar great, not to get caught up in its flaws. That's why I kicked off the activity with a targeted question *before* showing the model. Those questions focused participants' attention on what the master teacher in the exemplar was doing right, not what they were doing wrong. I also kept these questions visible (on a PowerPoint screen or handout) while the exemplar was being observed. This keeps participants' thoughts on what you want them to notice—and it will ensure they remember the questions even as they devote their full attention to the exemplar!

## Name It

Once teachers have had time to review the model, the next step is to lead them into a discussion as to why each part of the exemplar was important. Once they've mentioned the key concepts, stamp their understanding—Name It—by showing a "Core Idea" slide and summarizing the key components that the group mentioned.

Those few minutes are highly valuable. By sharing a key idea with them, you give the participants a common language with which to remember what they've just discovered. You also make it memorable and pause long enough to let it sink in. Put words to what you see, and you see it more clearly.

Here are the actions that make a Name It effective:

- **Prompt the group to focus on the key actions.** Ask a series of prompts that point teachers to key takeaways from the See It without giving those ideas away. Starting with a Turn & Talk allows every person in the room to share and crystallize their thoughts. When they then share out in a large group, universal prompts like "What is the purpose?" or "Why is that important?" become especially effective. By using prompts that don't reveal the answer you're looking for, you quickly get PD participants to do the thinking, and they learn on their own.

- **Punch it.** Once the participants have generated all of the most essential cognitive work, punch the core idea with formal language. Even at this point, keep language succinct and precise—a two-sentence summary, not a lengthy explanation. By following these steps, you put the famous advice of Bill Graham into action: you make the complicated simple, and the simple powerful.

> **Core Idea**
>
> Make the complicated simple and the simple powerful.
>
> —Bill Graham

## Do It

The See It and Name It of a PD are both designed with a very specific goal in mind: setting teachers up to practice effectively during the Do It. Let's see how that looked at the PD in Dallas:

 WATCH Clip 19: Do it (Plan)—Leading PD

## Stop and Jot

What actions does Paul take to make the Do It effective? Jot down what you notice below.

_____

_____

_____

_____

_____

_____

_____

Anyone who's ever stood up to rehearse a set of actions can testify that if you haven't thought ahead, you freeze up. To get out ahead of this challenge, give participants the opportunity to plan before they practice. That sets everyone up to practice perfectly.

---

### Core Idea

The precision of your plan determines the quality of your practice.
Perfect the plan before you practice.

---

Three key actions will lock in the success of this planning time:

- **Script it.** Have participants script what they will do and say before the actual practice. That way when teachers stand up to practice, they'll already have their first moves down.

- **Use your tools.** Utilize resources to make the plan as specific as possible. I prompted teachers to use the resources they already had to optimize their plan's precision and effectiveness on the first go.

- **Tighten it.** Have participants give feedback on each other's plans before they transition to practice. Getting this feedback from their peers gives participants' practice an additional layer of relevance and precision before they dive into practice.

When the plan is in place, it's time for participants to take that plan live! Here's how it looked in Dallas when I led the practice itself:

▶ WATCH Clip 20: Do it (Practice)—Leading PD

## Stop and Jot

What does Paul do before and during the practice to maximize its effectiveness? Jot down what you notice below.

_____

_____

_____

_____

_____

_____

_____

_____

Here, the participants have arrived at the heart of the PD. Let's unpack what had to happen to make their practice powerful.

> ## Core Idea
> Your PD is only as powerful as what you practice.

- **Deliver clear instructions.** When the time comes to begin practicing, deliver clear directions for the practice and post this protocol for the duration of the Do It. PD practice directions should include, at a minimum, the following information: what the main participant who is practicing will be doing, and what the other participants in the group will be doing during that time.

- **Practice the gap.** I chose an activity for participants to do during practice that focused on the part of the skill participants were learning that would be most difficult for them to master. When you lead this part of a PD, initially keep the practice simple and straightforward, with layers of complexity (such as role-playing student confusion) being added in subsequent rounds of practice.

- **Target the feedback.** A "feedback cheat sheet" to point participants to the highest-leverage areas you anticipate they'd need to receive feedback on is a simple tool that goes a long way. It increases the likelihood that teachers will receive the quality of feedback you'd be able to give them even if you don't happen to be monitoring their practice in that moment—effectively letting you be in multiple places at once! Other ways to optimize feedback include monitoring practice and responding to what you hear participants struggling with.

- **Do it again.** The goal of the PD is not simply to experience practice: it is to practice perfectly! As such, make sure each participant has a chance to do it again, incorporating the feedback and getting even better.

## Reflect

Learning a new skill is just like weightlifting: the real magic of long-term gains is not just in the practice but in the rest that occurs after the work. A weightlifter needs sleep—physical rest—for the body to actually build stronger muscles. Without sleep, it does not matter how much the weightlifter trains—he or she will not make progress. For the learner, that time to rest translates to time to think.

For years, PD deliverers have made it their goal to pack as much content into one session as possible, to the detriment of time to practice or even simply reflect. New research highlights the need for targeted time for reflection. Giada Di Stefano and Francesca Gino from HEC Paris and the Harvard Business School have looked at models for organizational learning in their recent Working Paper, "Making Experience Count: The Role of Reflection in Individual Learning."[1] One of their core findings is that once an individual has practiced or built experience in doing something, reflecting on their experience adds far more value than additional practice without reflection. This helps not only in the cognitive mastery of a skill, but also in increasing the participant's belief in their ability to master the skill.[2] And this takes remarkably little time to add to our PD!

To see how that plays out in PD, watch what happens in this video:

WATCH Clip 21: Do it (Reflect)—Leading PD

To lock in learning, I had participants reflect on what they'd learned about the skill they were working on before diving into practice. It took a few steps to set up effective reflection time:

- **Keep reflections brief.** Most individuals only require 1–3 minutes to reflect on a given topic.

- **Provide a single place for participants to write reflections down.** Provide participants with a single colorful sheet of paper where they can record all reflections. They'll walk away after the workshop with a single, easy-to-find sheet of key takeaways.

- **Share out at key moments.** Finally, participants shared their reflections aloud so the whole group could hear key takeaways.

Reflection only takes a few moments, but it dramatically improves the internalization of the PD. It gives time to cement the learning and to clear space in the brain to learn what's next.

---

## Core Idea

Lock in learning by writing down your reflections.

---

## FOLLOW-UP

However excellent a PD is, it has to be remembered to be powerful. How many times have you learned something only to forget it a few days later? What keeps that from happening is follow-up: someone who helps us make those actions a habit.

For the most successful school leaders, that means seeing it in action. A PD without practice won't lead to learning, but practice without follow-up won't make it stick.

---

## Core Idea

A PD without practice won't lead to learning,
but practice without follow-up won't make it stick.

---

Luckily you've already addressed follow-up in Chapters 3 and 4: from monitoring lesson plans and six-week action plans to having effective leadership team meetings that respond to student and teacher needs.

## Living the Learning PD

### An Effective Approach to Leading Professional Development

| Objective = Do It | You real objective is determined by what they will practice: |
|---|---|
| | **Highest Leverage.** *Practice the gap:* do the most important skills to increase proficiency<br>**Clear and Measurable.** You can easily evaluate if they have accomplished the objective<br>**Bite-sized.** You can accomplish the objective in the time you have allotted |
| **See It** | **See It: a model of what the Do It will look like** |
| | **See the Model:** let them see the Do It in action (keep it short! <5 min.):<br>• Video clip of teaching/leading<br>• Written exemplar or case study<br>• Live model<br><br>**Target Their Focus:** ask questions *before* the activity to target what they should see:<br>• Focus on the positive: focus the question on observing the exemplary actions<br>  o What does [teacher/leader] do and say during _____?<br>• Always visible: keep questions visible during the See It activity |

| Name It | Name It: formal language to describe the Do It |
|---|---|
| | **Think-Pair-Share:** |
| | • Give time to reflect (individual), share with partner (Turn & Talk) and share large group |
| | **Prompt—focus on the key elements of the Name It:** |
| | • "What happened in [certain part of the teaching video]?" |
| | • "Why is that important?" "What's the purpose of that action?" "What's the value?" |
| | • "What would have happened if we didn't do that?" |
| | **Punch It:** |
| | • Wait until the end: let participants do the cognitive work first; then name it with formal language: "So we've come to a core idea. . ." |
| | • Say the key line, pause, then say, "Think about the significance of this." Then restate |
| | • Limit the words: keep framework succinct and precise (3–5 bullets, one-pager) |
| **Do It** | **Do It: Put it into practice** |
| | **Plan before Practice:** |
| | • Give participants time to script prompts/actions/activities before diving into practice |
| | • Leverage the Name It: encourage them to use their tools provided during the workshop |

| Do It (cont.) | Do It: Put it into practice |
|---|---|
| | **Clear What-to-Do:**<br>• What main participant will do: review protocol timing, where they will practice, and what tools they will use<br>• What the audience will do: cue cards, pre-prepared student work samples<br>• (If group is large) What small group facilitators will do: feedback tips, what to look for<br><br>**Practice:**<br>• Practice the gap: practice what participants will struggle to master on their own<br>• Monitor the room with exemplar in hand: ID common errors in implementation<br><br>**Give Feedback and Do It Again:**<br>• Give large group feedback on common errors; model again if necessary<br>• Peer-to-peer: use feedback cheatsheet to target feedback<br>• Do it again: each person implements their feedback before moving on<br>• Add complexity (e.g., student noncompliance) in subsequent practice rounds |
| **Reflect** | **Reflect: Lock in the learning by writing it down** |
| | **Brief and written in one place:** one or two minutes at a time, embedded throughout the PD |
| | **Repeat the cycle as needed** |

## Chapter 7

# All PD Workshop Materials and Key Documents

All key supporting documents can be found on the DVD: rubrics, one-page guides, PD materials, and videos of leaders in action.

## HOW TO USE THE RUBRICS AND ONE-PAGERS

Every one-pager, rubric, and exemplar mentioned in the text can be found on the DVD in printer-friendly format.

The power of the one-pagers that you've seen presented in each chapter is that they can easily be printed for daily use. Here are some of the highlights:

- Weekly-Daily Data Meetings One-Pager
- Cheat Sheet: Giving Feedback to Weekly Data Meetings
- Re-teaching One-Pager
- Action & Follow-Up: Key Accountability Measures
- Implementation Rubric for Data-Driven Instruction

- What to Do When There's a "2": Recommended Action Steps to Increase Proficiency on the Implementation Rubric
- How to Create Monthly Map One-Pager
- Results Meeting Protocol
- Instructional Leadership Team Meeting—Developing Leaders to Lead Weekly Data Meetings

## HOW TO USE THE WORKSHOP MATERIALS

On the DVD, we also include all the materials you need to lead workshops on the key leadership levers. This allows you to train your leadership teams and to bring these chapters alive with lots of practice.

### DDI Workshops Included in This Book
- Assessment (Chapter 1)
- Analysis (Chapter 2)
- Action (Chapter 3)
- Data-Driven Culture (Chapter 4)

### What Workshop Materials Will You Find on the DVD?
- A cover page that highlights the workshop's goals and intended audience
- A workshop preparation sheet that shows what materials you need for the workshop, how long the workshop runs, and how to assess the workshop's success
- A workshop overview that outlines the subtopics covered in the workshop
- The full-length presenter's notes to be used while presenting the workshop
- The PowerPoint presentation that accompanies each workshop
- The handouts you'll need to provide for each workshop

Read on for a quick preview of what the workshop materials look like!

# PREVIEW: DATA-DRIVEN INSTRUCTION

## An Excerpt from the Full-Length Presenter's Notes

To give you a taste of what it's like to lead this workshop, here's a small excerpt from the full-length Presenter's Notes you'll find on the DVD.

| Objectives: |
| --- |
| 1. Implement data-driven instruction effectively to increase student achievement in schools |
| **Document(s):** |
| ***See Separate Guide*** |

| ABBREVIATION KEY | |
| --- | --- |
| S | See It |
| N | Name It |
| D | Do It |

| | INDIVIDUAL TEACHER ANALYSIS MEETINGS: SEE IT |
| --- | --- |
| 5 | **Introduction:**<br><br>• "So we have talked about how to re-teach effectively. Now we have to ask the question: how can I coach my teachers to do so effectively?"<br><br>• "We are going to watch videos of a group of school leaders all leading weekly data meetings. Let's see what they do to support and develop their teachers." |
| 15 | **See the Exemplar—Interpret the Standard (S, N):**<br><br>• "We will start by watching a video of a weekly data meeting led by Mary Ann Stinson, principal of Truesdell Education Campus in Washington, DC. Mary Ann has used data-driven instruction to drive dramatic gains in achievement in her turnaround school."<br><br>• "In this clip, Mary Ann is working with her 3rd grade teacher on her ELA results on the last assessment."<br><br>• As you watch this clip, consider these two questions: What does Mary Ann say and do to launch her meeting? What did she have to prior to the start of the meeting to make sure it was effective? You can take notes in your handout. |

- Show Clip 2—Driven by Data 2.0

- "Turn and talk to your partner: What does Mary Ann say and do to launch her meeting? What did she have to prior to the start of the meeting to make sure it was effective? Take a minute to share your thoughts." Give participants one minute to share in small groups.

- (3 min.) Say: "Let's come back together. What did Mary Ann do prior to the start of this meeting to make sure it ran effectively? What does Mary Ann say and do at the beginning of the meeting to guide her teachers? Let's hear what you and your partners said." Spend three minutes on the large group share.
  - Listen for these responses:
    - "Mary Ann started by looking at the standard."
    - "Each member of the group had a clearly defined role."
      - Norming opportunity, making it visible
    - "The task the group worked on directly addressed the standard that they had identified as the key area where students were struggling."
    - "Mary Ann commented on the data last, which gave the rest of her team a chance to do their own thinking as they analyzed the data."
  - If you don't hear those responses, try following up with one or more of these probing questions:
    - "Why start with the standard and not with the task?" *Answer: Because the standard tells us what students need to understand.*

- (1 min.) Show Slide 13. Then say: "This brings us to our next Core Idea: You don't know where to go if you haven't determined the destination. Start with the end in mind, because you won't get there without proper preparation."

- (2 min.) Say: "Let's break down the actions it takes to prepare for a weekly data meeting like the one Mary Ann just kicked off." Then show Slide 14. Then say:
  - "Have your materials ready and assembled, including: copies of teacher exemplars, top student exemplars, other student work, and the standard, upcoming lesson plans, chart paper, a whiteboard, and a timer. You'll save time during the meeting by having teachers pre-sort student work."

| | |
|---|---|
| | o "Eventually, your teachers will get to the point where they can prepare to analyze their students' work on their own; but initially, Mary Ann would prime the pump by conducting her own pre-analysis before the meeting. Mary Ann had reviewed the standard, written her own interpretation of it, and identified critical takeaways before the meeting. She also sorted out high, medium, and low student work and pre-selected work that reflected typical errors for students at each achievement level—beginning by reading through top student work to determine the bar for excellence."<br><br>• Say: "Once Mary Ann has set the stage for success by preparing for her meeting in this way, her next step is to guide her teachers to see the exemplar." Then show Slide 15. Then say:<br><br>    o "Start by interpreting the standard. Use these questions to guide you: What does a student have to know or be able to do to show mastery of this standard? Push for deep understanding by prompting teachers to paraphrase the standard in their own words." |
| | o "Mary Ann and her teachers aren't using a teacher exemplar in this meeting, but if you had one lined up, that's where you'd go next. In any case, look to the best exemplar you have at this conjecture, and work as a group to determine the following: What are the keys to an ideal answer? What does an exemplar need to include? How does this align to the standard?"<br><br>o "Finally, Mary Ann leveraged a few key protocols to set her meeting up for success. She stuck to a leader-shares-last protocol, and she used timers to create urgency and instill purpose." |
| 10 | **See the Exemplar—Student Exemplar (S, N):**<br><br>• Let's watch what happens next in a weekly data meeting. This time we will watch principal Najee Carter from Alexandar St School in Newark, NJ. As you watch, consider: What are the next steps in the data meeting? What does Najee do to guide his teachers?<br><br>• Show Clip 3—Driven by Data 2.0<br><br>• (1 min.) Say: "Turn back to your partner! What were the next steps in the data meeting? What did Najee do to guide his teachers? Take a minute to share your thoughts." Give participants one minute to share in small groups. While they share, circulate the room to listen to their responses and gauge the extent to which they articulate the core ideas that derive from this clip. |

- (3 min.) Say: "What were the next steps in the data meeting? What did Najee do to guide his teachers?" Spend three minutes on the large group share.
  - Listen for these responses:
    - "Najee had pre-selected work that showed mastery, building out an exemplary vision."
    - "Najee picked a rigorous question and student work that solved it in multiple ways, which led to deep analysis."
    - "The group pushed for specificity around demonstration of mastery."
    - "Najee selected the work of students who may not always have been successful, which shows what's possible in terms of student growth."
    - "Najee leveraged the opportunity to build teacher content knowledge during the meeting."

- (1 min.) Say: "What we're seeing in Najee's meeting is that when you start with the exemplar, your analysis becomes exemplary." Then show Slide 17. Then repeat the Core Idea aloud: "When you start with the exemplar, your analysis becomes exemplary. Working with an exemplar is the fastest way to develop content knowledge."

- Say: "Let's name the actions that Najee took to leverage the exemplar successfully." Then show Slide 18. Then say:
  - "What we saw wasn't just analysis—it was analysis on speed! Najee and his team only spent two minutes analyzing the exemplar. To help keep things quick, Najee managed time and content so his teachers could focus on the analysis fully. He typed notes for teachers and synthesized action steps."
  - "Then, Najee and his teachers brought their focus to the student exemplar and work that reflected a high level of achievement. Their core goal here: to name what it means to be successful. These probing questions helped them set the stage for a deep level of analysis:
    - "What did students have to *do* to show mastery of this standard?"
    - "How does the student exemplar compare to the teacher exemplar? What is the gap?"
    - "Do students have different paths or evidence to demonstrate mastery of the standard?"
    - "Does the student exemplar offer something that teacher exemplar does not?" *Note: this happens often!*

| 10 | **See It—See the Gap (S, N):** |
|---|---|
| | • Now that you've unpacked the standard and the exemplar, what do you do next? We are going to watch a data meeting of Juliana Worrell. Her 4th grade math teachers have already charted the breakdown of the standard and the exemplar: they are about to look at the work of students who were not proficient on the assessment. |
| | • Have participants turn to Handout. Then say: "As we watch the next clip, you may use this page to take notes on the question: What makes the teachers' analysis maximally effective? Let's take a look." |
| | • (2 min. and 19 sec.) Show Clip 4—Driven by Data 2.0 |
| | • (1 min.) Say: "What makes the teachers' analysis maximally effective? Turn to your partner and share your thoughts." Give participants one minute to share in small groups. While they share, circulate the room to listen to their responses and gauge the extent to which they articulate the core ideas that derive from this clip. |
| | • (3 min.) Say: "Bring it back together! What makes the teachers' analysis maximally effective?" Spend three minutes on the large group share. |
| | • (2 min.) Say: "Let's name what Juliana and her team did to see the gaps in student achievement." Then show Slide 20. Then say: <br> ○ "Juliana and her team start with the medium-achieving student work—the samples from students who have almost mastered the standard. They call these the 2s. They zeroed in on what was most important about the 2s with these guiding questions: <br> ▪ "What are the gaps that we see between the 2s and our student exemplar?" <br> ▪ "What do we see students doing that led to this error?" <br> ○ "After this, Juliana was able to name the error and the conceptual misunderstanding, leading with the question: What is the conceptual misunderstanding that is evident from the student error? To make sure this would be successful, Juliana established norms for analysis: the teachers knew to state both the error and the misunderstanding. When this isn't an established practice yet, you may have a lead teacher model how to do this!" |

# Notes

## Introduction

1. See https://nces.ed.gov/nationsreportcard/pdf/studies/2009495.pdf, https://nces.ed.gov/nationsreportcard/pdf/studies/2011485.pdf

2. "History of PLC." All Things PLC. This article summarizes how Judith Warren Little and Milbrey McLaughlin originally coined the term "professional learning communities"; and how Richard DuFour later developed a modified definition of the same term that emphasized how essential data-driven instruction is to the success of PLCs. See http://www.allthingsplc.info/mobile/history-of-plc

## Chapter 1

1. CollegeBoard AP Results for North Star Academy, 2007–2012.

2. Mike Schmoker advocates for the same in *Results Now: How We Can Achieve Unprecedented Improvements in Teaching and Learning*, published in July 2006 by the Association for Supervision and Curriculum Development (ASCD).

3. There are multiple sources that provide extensive discussion of interim assessments and their effectiveness. For a further in-depth look at the research, consult the following titles:

   Richard DuFour. "What Is a 'Professional Learning Community'?" *Educational Leadership* (Marshall Memo 38, #1, 2004).

   Richard DuFour, et al. *Learning by Doing: A Handbook for Professional Learning Communities at Work* (Solution Tree, 2006).

David Foster and Pendred Noyce. "The Mathematics Assessment Collaborative: Performance Testing to Improve Instruction." *Phi Delta Kappan*, January 2004 (Marshall Memo 20, #1).

Nancy Love. "Using Data/Getting Results: A Practical Guide for School Improvement in Mathematics." *Harvard Educational Review*, Spring 2004 (Marshall Memo 30, #3).

Kim Marshall. "In Praise of Assessment (Done Right)." *Phi Delta Kappan*, March 2018.

Jay McTighe and Marcella Emberger. "Teamwork on Assessments Creates Powerful Professional Development." *Journal of Staff Development*, Winter 2006 (Marshall Memo 117, #4).

Jay McTighe and Ken O'Connor. "Seven Practices for Effective Learning." *Educational Leadership*, November 2005 (Marshall Memo 110, #1).

Douglas Reeves. *Accountability in Action* (Advanced Learning Press, 2000), pp. 67–68, 189–195.

Mike Schmoker. *The Results Fieldbook* (Alexandria, VA: ASCD, 2001), pp. 8–25, 101–119, 120–132.

4.  Marilyn Jager Adams "Advancing Our Students' Language and Literacy: The Challenge of Complex Texts", pp. 3–11 American Educator, Winter 2010–2011.

5.  See the following:

Paul Black, Christine Harrison, Clare Lee, Bethan Marshall, and Dylan Wiliam. "Working Inside the Black Box: Assessment for Learning in the Classroom." *Phi Delta Kappan*, September 2004.

Paul Black and Dylan Wiliam. "Inside the Black Box: Raising Standards Through Classroom Assessment." *Phi Delta Kappan*, October 1998. https://www.rdc.udel.edu/wp-content/uploads/2015/04/InsideBlackBox.pdf

Siobhan Leahy, Christine Lyon, Marnie Thompson, and Dylan Wiliam. "Classroom Assessment Minute by Minute, Day by Day." *Educational Leadership*, November 2005.

Robert Marzano. *The Art and Science of Teaching* (Alexandria, VA: ASCD, 2007).

Robert Marzano, Debra Pickering, and Jane Pollock. *Classroom Assessment That Works* (Alexandria, VA: ASCD, 2001), pp. 96–102.

Rick Stiggins. "From Formative Assessment to Assessment FOR Learning: A Path to Success in Standards-Based Schools." *Phi Delta Kappan*, December 2005.

Judith Warren Little, Maryl Gearhart, Marnie Curry, and Judith Kafka. "Looking at Student Work for Teacher Learning, Teacher Community, and School Reform." *Phi Delta Kappan*, November 2003.

Grant Wiggins. *Educative Assessment* (San Francisco: Jossey-Bass, 1998), pp. 43–69.

6.  Read more about the ways incorrect answer choices set rigor in:

    Mark Gierl, Okan Bulut, Qi Guo, and XinXin Zhang. "Developing, Analyzing, and Using Distractors for Multiple-Choice Tests in Education: A Comprehensive Review." *Review of Educational Research*, 87(6) (2017), 1082–1116.

7.  Read more in Chapter 2, Planning, from *Leverage Leadership 2.0* (San Francisco: Jossey-Bass, 2018), pp. 89–126.

## Chapter 2

1.  See https://www.darden.virginia.edu/uploadedFiles/Darden_Web/Content/Faculty_Research/Research_Centers_and_Initiatives/Darden_Curry_PLE/School_Turnaround/UVA_PLE_Farm_NE.pdf

2.  See https://www.daily-times.com/story/news/education/2016/12/13/northeast-named-title-distinguished-school/95378838/

## Chapter 3

1.  Doug Lemov, *Teach like a Champion 2.0* (San Francisco: Jossey-Bass, 2015), "Show Call," pp. 290–299.

2.  In 2013 on the third grade New York State Exam, Fromson's students were 80% proficient in math and 62% proficient in ELA. The following year (2014), they were 100% proficient in math and 80% proficient in ELA, ranking #1 in the state of New York. Fromson then proceeded to move to Boston and teach fifth grade math, where her Student Growth Percentile was 92, one of the highest in the state of Massachusetts.

3. Rick Stiggins and Jan Chappuis have done extensive research on the importance of student involvement in the assessment process. Two of those articles are:

Rick Stiggins. "Assessment Through the Student's Eyes." *Educational Leadership*, 64(8) (2007), 22–26.

Rick Stiggins and Jan Chappuis. "Using Student-Involved Classroom Assessment to Close Achievement Gaps." *Theory Into Practice*, 44(1) (2005), 11–18.

## Chapter 4

1. Some excellent articles on this topic are:

Kathy Christie. "Virginia's Excellent Adventure." *Phi Delta Kappan*, 85(8) (2004), 565–567.

Catherine Gewertz. "One Subject at a Time." *Education Week*, 24(21) (2005), 34–37.

Patricia Kannapel and Stephen Clements. *Inside the Black Box of High-Performing Schools* (Lexington, KY: Prichard Committee for Academic Excellence, 2005).

Jon Saphier. "Strong Adult Professional Culture—The Indispensable Ingredient for Sustainable School Improvement." In *Future Directions for Educational Change* (New York: Routledge, 2015).

David Strahan. "Promoting a Collaborative Professional Culture in Three Elementary Schools That Have Beaten the Odds." *Elementary School Journal*, 104(2) (2003), 127–146.

2. Susan Trimble, Anne Gay, and Jan Matthews. "Using Test Score Data to Focus Instruction." *Middle School Journal*, 36(4) (2005), 26–32.

3. David Krackhardt and Jeffrey Hanson. "Informal Networks: The Company Behind the Chart." *Harvard Business Review*, 71(4) (1993), 104–111.

4. Chris Zook and James Allen. *The Founder's Mentality* (Boston, MA: Harvard Business Review Press, 2016), p. 91.

## Chapter 6

1. Giada Di Stefano, Francesca Gino, Gary P. Pisano, and Bradley Staats. "Making Experience Count: The Role of Reflection in Individual Learning." Harvard Business School Working Paper, No. 14-093, March 2014 (revised June 2016).

2. Ibid. "Once an individual has accumulated experience with a task, the benefit of accumulating additional experience is inferior to the benefit of deliberately articulating and codifying the previously accumulated experience."

# Bibliography

The following books and articles give extensive background to the field of interim assessments and data-driven instruction. This book builds on the learnings from these sources.

## Interim/Benchmark Assessments

"Data in the Driver's Seat" by Paul Bambrick-Santoyo, *Educational Leadership*, December 2007/January 2008, 43–46.

"What is a 'Professional Learning Community'?" by Richard DuFour, *Educational Leadership*, May 2004.

*Learning by Doing: A Handbook for Professional Learning Communities at Work* by Richard DuFour, et al., Solution Tree, 2006.

"The Mathematics Assessment Collaborative: Performance Testing to Improve Instruction" by David Foster and Pendred Noyce, *Phi Delta Kappan*, January 2004.

"Using Data/Getting Results: A Practical Guide for School Improvement in Mathematics" by Nancy Love, *Harvard Educational Review*, Spring, 2004.

"Teamwork on Assessments Creates Powerful Professional Development" by Jay McTighe and Marcella Emberger, *Journal of Staff Development*, Winter, 2006.

"Seven Practices for Effective Learning" by Jay McTighe and Ken O'Connor, *Educational Leadership*, November 2005.

*Accountability in Action* by Douglas Reeves, Denver, CO: Advanced Learning Press, 2000, pp. 67–68, 189–195.

*The Results Fieldbook* by Mike Schmoker, Alexandria, VA: ASCD, 2001, pp. 8–25, 101–119, 120–132.

## Dipstick/Formative Assessments

"Working Inside the Black Box: Assessment for Learning in the Classroom" by Paul Black, Christine Harrison, Clare Lee, Bethan Marshall, and Dylan Wiliam, *Phi Delta Kappan*, September 2004.

"Inside the Black Box: Raising Standards Through Classroom Assessment" by Paul Black and Dylan Wiliam, *Phi Delta Kappan*, October 1998.

"You Will Be Tested On This" by David Glenn, *The Chronicle of Higher Education*, June 8, 2007.

"Classroom Assessment Minute by Minute, Day by Day" by Siobhan Leahy, Christine Lyon, Marnie Thompson, and Dylan Wiliam, *Educational Leadership*, November, 2005.

*The Art and Science of Teaching* by Robert Marzano, Alexandria, VA: ASCD, 2007.

*Classroom Assessment That Works* by Robert Marzano, Debra Pickering, and Jane Pollock, Alexandria, VA: ASCD, 2001, pp. 96–102.

"From Formative Assessment to Assessment FOR Learning: A Path to Success in Standards-Based Schools" by Rick Stiggins, *Phi Delta Kappan*, December, 2005.

"Looking at Student Work for Teacher Learning, Teacher Community, and School Reform" by Judith Warren Little, Maryl Gearhart, Marnie Curry, and Judith Kafka, *Phi Delta Kappan*, November, 2003.

*Educative Assessment* by Grant Wiggins, San Francisco: Jossey-Bass, 1998, pp. 43–69.

## Getting Students Involved in Their Own Improvement

"Helping Students Understand Assessment" by Jan Chappuis, *Educational Leadership*, November 2005.

"Assessment Through the Student's Eyes" by Rick Stiggins, *Educational Leadership*, 64(8) (2007), 22–26.

"Using Student-Involved Classroom Assessments to Close Achievement Gaps" by Rick Stiggins and Stephen Chappuis, *Theory Into Practice*, Winter 2005.

## Mastery Learning

"A Historical Perspective on Closing the Achievement Gap" by Thomas Guskey, *NASSP Bulletin*, September, 2005.

"Synthesis of Research on the Effects of Mastery Learning in Elementary and Secondary Classrooms" by Thomas Guskey and Sally Gates, *Educational Leadership*, May 1986.

## Effective Schools

"Effective Schools for the Urban Poor" by Ronald Edmonds, *Educational Leadership*, October 1979.

"Effective Schools" by Lynn Olson, a special section of *Education Week*, January 15, 1986.

## Total Quality Management

"Transforming Schools Through Total Quality Management" by Mike Schmoker and Richard Wilson, *Phi Delta Kappan*, January, 2003.

## Building Culture and Overcoming Resistance (Georgia Article)

"Using Test Score Data to Focus Instruction" by Susan Trimble, Anne Gay, and Jan Matthews, *Middle School Journal*, 36(4) (2005), 26–32.

## Making Analysis and Action Stick

"Classroom Assessment Minute by Minute, Day by Day" by Siobhan Leahy, Christine Lyon, Marnie Thompson, and Dylan Wiliam, *Educational Leadership*, 63(3) (2005), 18–24.

"High-Stakes Testing: Can Rapid Assessment Reduce the Pressure?" by Stuart Yeh, *Teachers College Record*, 108(4) (2006), 621–661.

## Building Effective Data-Driven Culture

"The Relation Between Professional Climate and Student Learning Depends on the Way a School Treats Teachers" by Janet Angelis, *Middle School Journal*, 35(5) (2004), 52–56.

"Virginia's Excellent Adventure" by Kathy Christie, *Phi Delta Kappan*, 85(8) (2004), 565–567.

"No Choice But Success" by Dick Corbett, Bruce Wilson, and Belinda Williams, *Educational Leadership*, 62(6) (2005), 8–12.

"One Subject at a Time" by Catherine Gewertz, *Education Week*, 24(21) (2005), 34–37.

*Inside the Black Box of High-Performing Schools* by Patricia Kannapel and Stephen Clements, Lexington, KY: Prichard Committee for Academic Excellence, 2005.

"Promoting a Collaborative Professional Culture in Three Elementary Schools That Have Beaten the Odds" by David Strahan, *Elementary School Journal*, 104(2) (2003), 127–146.

## Leading Professional Development for Adults

"Brain-Friendly Learning for Teachers" by David Sousa, *Educational Leadership*, 66(9) (2009).

# Index

Page references followed by *fig* indicate an illustrated figure; followed by *t* indicate a table.

content to strengthen retention, 99; teachers rise to the level of expectations, 122

Core ideas (analysis): analysis is meaningless without the assessment to guide us, 67; data analysis meetings shift focus from observing to learning, 73; less is more, 58; lock in learning by stamping it, 83; start from exemplar for exemplary analysis, 82; test-in-hand analysis, 60, 62, 70; to transform your school get the view from the pool, 52; use the exemplar, 81

Core ideas (assessment): assessments are the starting point for instruction, 22; keep re-assessing to increase student learning, 25, 26; on multiple-choice and open-ended questions, 39; standards are meaningless until you define how to assess them, 21, 67

Core ideas (culture): active leadership team's promoting student achievement purpose, 142; identify priorities for your school's calendar, 148

Core ideas (DDI): assessment of effective instruction and student learning, 19; key questions driving data-based instruction, 4

Coyne, Frank, 161

Culture: Google's "culture of high expectations," 135; Jon Saphier's research findings on adult professional, 135; key drivers in implementation rubric for transforming, 138

Culture drivers: active leadership team, 138, 139–147, 162; building by borrowing, 138, 159–162, 163; implementation calendar, 136fig–138, 147–156, 162; introductory professional development, 138, 156–159, 163; ongoing professional development, 161, 163

Culture implementation calendar: begin school year with the, 164; "big rocks" approach to, 147–148; district-wide, 165; leave room for re-teaching, 149; make time for assessment and data analysis, 148; mark PD in relation to your interims, 149; monthly map for scheduling DDI, 153–154; sample elementary/middle/high school assessment calendars, 149fig–153fig; space out interim assessments with the end in mind, 148–149

Culture implementation rubric: Level 1–teachers, 163; Level 2–school-based leaders, 163–164; Level 3–district-level or multi-campus leaders, 164–165; summary of the, 162–163

Cumulative assessment, 25

Curriculum sequence-aligned assessment, 25

**D**

Dan D. Rogers Elementary (Dallas, Texas), 155fig–156

Daniels, Prudence, 161

Data analysis: beware the false driver of over-reporting for, 60; commercial products used for, 60; fast turnaround example of, 55–56; implementation for teachers and leaders, 85–88; reflection and planning for, 89; sixth grade math results–a sample, 51–52. See also Data Meetings (data analysis); Data reports

Data analysis core drivers: deep, 62, 70, 71–85, 86; immediate, 54–56, 70, 86; simple, 58, 70, 86; teacher-owned, 57, 60, 62, 70, 86; test-in-hand, 60, 62, 70, 86

Data analysis implementation rubric: Level 1–teachers, 86–87; Level 2–school-based leaders, 87; Level 3–district-level or multi-campus leaders, 87–88; summary of the, 86

Data analysis process: example of Kenyatta's student-by-student analysis sample, 63–64; identify the gap, 65–67; look for the patterns technique, 63, 64–65; North Star Interim Assessment Results Analysis Template to use for, 58–60, 63, 64; scan by students technique, 63–64; search for

Team Meeting and charting the, 145; leaving room in your calendar for, 149; is a marathon, not a sprint, 111; modeling (teacher-driven) type of, 105–107; monitoring and give immediate feedback, 112, 113–115; six-week re-teach plans for, 129; strategies for effective classroom, 102–111; tightening support systems outside the classroom for, 132

Re-teaching guided discourse (teacher-facilitated): Alexander Street Elementary School's success with, 108*fig*–109; comparing modeling and, 105–106; description of, 105; Instructional Leadership Team Meeting monitoring of, 145

Re-teaching modeling (teacher-driven): comparing guided discourse and, 105–106; description of, 105; Instructional Leadership Team Meeting monitoring of, 145; key strategies to use for, 107; Stop and Jot on, 107; video clip 7 (Worrell–Re-Teach Modeling. Set the Task), 107; video clip 8 (Worrell–Re-Teach Modeling, Model the Thinking), 107

Re-teaching Stop and Jot: re-teach guided discourse, 110; re-teach modeling, 107

Re-teaching strategies: The Color Purple (Reading Response Journal), 105; designing academic calendar with time for, 100–102; guided discourse (teacher-facilitated), 105–106, 108*fig*–111; modeling (teacher-driven), 105–107; ongoing assessment, 111–115; re-write lesson plans with assessment analysis in mind, 104–105; student engagement, 115–119

Re-teaching videos: clip 7 (Worrell–Re-Teach Modeling. Set the Task), 107; clip 8 (Worrell–Re-Teach Modeling, Model the Thinking), 107; clip 9 (Shaefer–Re-Teach Guided Discourse), 110

Reading/literacy: action plan follow-up systems for instructional leaders for, 127; assessment myth on test outcomes and continued proficiency in, 41; college-ready example: rigor in HS multiple choice test, 36–37; college-ready example: rigor in MS reading, 30–31; The Color Purple (Reading Response Journal), 105; DIBELS (Dynamic Indicators of Basic Early Literacy Skills) test of, 41; Sample Action Plan, Part 1–Overall Analysis (Seventh Grade Literacy), 94–95; Sample Lesson Plan Reflection Box (Ninth Grade Literacy Lesson Plan), 128; strategies for implementing college-ready rigor in, 29

Reflection and planning: on action at your own school or district, 134; on assessment at your own school or district, 49; on data analysis at your own school or district, 89; on data-driven instruction in your own school or district, 13

Rigor: assessment aligned to state-test level of, 24–25, 26; creating the roadmap for meaningful, 19–22; HS math teacher on SAT, 40; of multiple choice questions and open-ended response questions, 35–39; observing action plans/lesson plans like using 3-D glasses to observe, 128; setting success stories as a part of, 4–5

Rigor strategies: for college-ready example: rigor in MS reading, 30–41; for college-ready example–algebra in fifth grade math, 29–30; for implementing college-rigor for every grade span, 29–32; for middle school reading–push for deeper reader, 30

"Ripple effect" (in-the-moment assessment), 32–33*fig*

Rolfert, Michele, 70

Running records: assessment myth on, 41; two samples of a, 42

It), 82; clip 6 (Stinson–See It, Name It), 82; clip 7 (Worrell–Re-Teach Modeling. Set the Task), 107; clip 8 (Worrell–Re-Teach Modeling. Model the Thinking), 107; clip 9 (Shaefer–Re-Teach Guided Discourse), 110; clip 10 (Fromson–Aggressive Monitoring), 113; clip 11 (Worrell–Do It [Plan]), 120; clip 12 (Frazier–Do It [Plan]), 121; clip 13 (Stinson–Do It [Practice]), 121; clip 14 (Worrell–Do It [Practice]), 122; clip 15 (Frazier–Do It [Practice]), 122; clip 16 (Stinson–Do It [Follow-up]), 123; clip 17 (Frazier–Do It [Follow-up]), 123; "Master Teachers," 161–162

"View from the pool" data analysis: analysis is meaningless without the assessment to guide us, 67; Question-level Analysis of Student Performance–Six Grade Math Sample, 66; Related Standards Analysis–Sixth Grade Math Sample, 67; Standard-level Analysis of Student Performance–Sixth Grade Math Sample, 65; as teacher-owner and test-in-hand analysis, 60, 62, 70; to transform your school get the, 52

## W

Weekly data meetings: accountability for action plans through, 130; data meeting (action), 120–126; data meeting (data analysis), 71–85; Instructional Leadership Team Meeting–Managing Leaders to Weekly Data Meetings (culture), 143–145

Whitewater Middle School (Charlotte, North Carolina), 92*fig*–93

Whittier Education Campus (Washington, DC), 43–44

Williamsburg Collegiate Charter School's Student Reflection Template, 116–117

Wondewossen, Rahel, 103–104

Worrell, Art: clip 7 Worrell (Re-Teach Modeling. Set the Task), 107; modeling re-teaching strategy used by, 106–107; video clip 11 (Worrell–Do It [Plan]), 120; video clip 14 (Worrell–Do It [Practice]), 122

Worrell, Juliana: on Alexander Street Elementary School's turnaround, 108*fig*–109; Prime the Pump–Sample Prep for Data Meeting by, 78–79; video clip 4 (Worrell–See It, Name It), 82

## Y

Year-end assessment analysis, 10

Yinghua Academy (Minneapolis, Minnesota): implementation rubric key drivers used at, 23; Minnesota Comprehensive Assessment (MCA) scores (2016–2018), 22*fig*; success with assessment, 23

## Z

Zook, Chris, 142